THE BOTTOM LINE

By
Tobie Carter

Copyright © 2024 by Tobie Carter

All rights reserved.

No part of this publication may be reproduced, distributed, or transmitted in any form or by any means, including photocopying, recording, or other electronic or mechanical methods, without the prior written permission of the publisher, except as permitted by U.S. copyright law. For permission requests, contact [include publisher/author contact info].

The story, all names, characters, and incidents portrayed in this production are fictitious. No identification with actual persons (living or deceased), places, buildings, and products is intended or should be inferred.

Praise for The Bottom Line

"With a clear tenderness for her imperfect characters, Tobie Carter tells a story of seeing the darkest parts of each other—and ourselves—and still finding each other worthy of redemption, happiness, and the soul-deep love and acceptance we all dream of." -Ingrid Pierce, author of NOT YOU AGAIN

"Tobie Carter brings a deft touch to deeper themes of redemption, striving, and imperfect people finding their perfect love. Sweeping drama, big emotion, and characters with unbreakable spirits - this book vibrates with the best kind of heartbreak and passion!" -Maggie North, author of RULES FOR SECOND CHANCES

THE BOTTOM LINE

"*THE BOTTOM LINE* IS MORE THAN WHAT YOU WANT IN A ROMANCE— A DRIVEN, BUT OPEN-HEARTED HEROINE, COMPLEX FAMILY DYNAMICS AND A SEXY, FLAWED HERO WHOSE STRUGGLES ARE MARKED IN HIS SKIN. TOBIE CARTER CRAFTS A STEAMY LOVE STORY WHILE HELPING THE READER BETTER UNDERSTAND MEN'S MENTAL HEALTH. TBL BELONGS AT THE TOP OF YOUR TBR!" –GIA DE CADENET, AUTHOR OF NOT THE PLAN

"AS SEXY AS IT IS VULNERABLE, TOBIE CARTER'S WORKPLACE ENEMIES TO LOVERS ROMANCE MANAGES TO SIZZLE WHILE PRESENTING AN ACHINGLY RAW DEPICTION OF MENTAL HEALTH. READERS IN SEARCH OF A RED HOT ROMANCE WITH AN EMOTIONAL CORE SHOULD LOOK NO FURTHER THAN *THE BOTTOM LINE* BY TOBIE CARTER." -ELLIE PALMER, AUTHOR OF FOUR WEEKENDS AND A FUNERAL

"A STEAMY, HEARTFELT STORY THAT TACKLES THE STRUGGLES OF MENTAL HEALTH WITH REALITY AND COMPASSION." -MARIAH ANKENMAN, AUTHOR OF PERFECT IMPERFECTIONS

TOBIE CARTER

"A PERFECT RIVALS-TO-LOVERS FULL OF STEAM, HEART, AND HEALING." -ETTA EASTON, AUTHOR OF
THE KISS COUNTDOWN

Content Warning

The Bottom Line is an adult romance that features mature themes and content that may not be suitable for all audiences. Reader discretion is advised. For all content warnings, check the author's website.

Tobiecarter.com

Contents

Dedication	XIII
1. Stella	1
2. Jameson	11
3. Stella	18
4. Jameson	27
5. Stella	35
6. Stella	45
7. Jameson	51
8. Stella	56
9. Stella	65
10. Jameson	74
11. Stella	81
12. Jameson	88
13. Stella	98
14. Jameson	104
15. Stella	111
16. Stella	122
17. Jameson	128

18.	Jameson	138
19.	Stella	147
20.	Stella	154
21.	Jameson	160
22.	Stella	165
23.	Jameson	175
24.	Stella	187
25.	Jameson	194
26.	Stella	199
27.	Stella	209
28.	Jameson	216
29.	Stella	221
30.	Jameson	229
31.	Stella	241
32.	Jameson	248
33.	Stella	259
34.	Stella	267
35.	Jameson	276
36.	Jameson	282
37.	Stella	290
38.	Stella	294
39.	Jameson	303
40.	Stella	309

41. Jameson	315
42. Stella	321
Bonus Scene	325
Thank You	327
Acknowledgements	329
About the Author	333

This book is for those fighting a silent battle when all they want to do is scream.

Find your passion

Light the fire

Burn everything that tells you that you can't do it.

You can, and you will.

Survive.

Chapter One
Stella

When you're hungover, there's no better place to nap than a casket.

I've spent the last twenty-five minutes encased in darkness, lying on a bed of luscious cream-colored satin. Having the lid closed would make most people claustrophobic, but instead, the silence brings relaxation. Something I desperately need, since I'm about to deal with the man who's been hassling my grandfather on every detail of his mother's cremation for the last week.

Normally, I'd be on my way to work, but no one—and I mean no one— yells at my Pop-Pop.

Faint vibrations rumble against the pillow beneath my head. I pry an eye open and my phone's light blinds me. *Oh shit.* I've been napping for nearly an hour—thirty-five minutes past what I planned.

I swipe my finger across the screen.

"Hey, Rosay," I sigh into the stale air.

"What happened last night? I tried to call you like twenty times." Her voice pitches up an octave, clanging around my head like a cymbal and making me wince.

Complete silence is the only way I'll survive this morning and the work meeting later.

She clears her throat. "Don't leave me hanging, Stella."

"We broke up." My stomach rolls.

I thought saying it out loud would remove the heaviness on my chest, but it doesn't.

She gasps, and I hold the phone away from my ear, preparing for the exclamations of jubilee I know my best friend is bound to let rip.

But she only asks, "How did he take it?" in a surprisingly nonchalant voice, like this isn't what she's been praying for.

I swallow past the throbbing in my throat. "Not great."

"That's no surprise, but he wasn't right for you anyway."

"I know."

She continues, oblivious to my quiet sigh. "He was immature and shit in the sack."

Thank God for this casket, otherwise everyone would see the heat of her statement stain my cheeks.

"Whoa, Rosay. That's my..." I pause, almost letting the word boyfriend fall into the slot. "My ex you're talking about."

She sighs. "I know, I'm sorry. It just made me so mad to see you settling."

"I wasn't settling. CJ is a great guy," I huff. "I just thought he needed more time."

"Stella." Her voice is stern and chiding. "It's been four years. How much more time did he need?"

Her accusation bangs like a gong, vibrating through my pounding head, searching for a place to sink in. I thought CJ and I would have a love that—like my grandparents—transcends even death. But was I hanging on because we'd been together so long it felt like a natural progression, because he was familiar and convenient?

No, that can't be it.

We loved each other.

My wine-scrambled mind doesn't appreciate all this deep reflection.

"You never liked him anyway," I say.

She laughs. "That's because I have good taste in men. But that's beside the point. We need to find you a rebound. A man who can appreciate a smart, black woman with long legs and a round ass."

I choke out a laugh. "No."

"No?" Rosay asks. "Why not?"

"Because I just got out of a relationship, and I have more important things to worry about, like making sure Mr. Weston doesn't fire me because I broke up with his son."

"Oh, I'm sure you'll be fine. You're one of the best advisors. He'd be stupid to let you go, and I'm pretty sure that's against the law."

"I *used* to be the best advisor. Now, I'm lucky if I get two new clients a year."

"Well, if you didn't spend so much time with dead people you'd probably get more," she says. "You know I love Pop-Pop, but you've gotta think about yourself too."

I chew on my fingernails and inhale the humid casket air, contemplating her suggestion. Taking over at the funeral home after Nunny passed wasn't a burden, but it wasn't helpful to my social life or career either. Seeking a promotion meant less time with CJ, and now that we're over, it's time to get serious about my career again.

Before I can respond, she says, "I'll make you a deal: if you land a big client by the end of the year, you can come with me to the Witte's Summer Gala. Canapes and Cocktails, bitch."

"Deal." The word speeds from my mouth before my mind has a chance to stop it.

The Witte Gallery's Gala is attended by the city's most prominent movers and shakers, but the ticket price is astronomical. With new funeral homes popping up in town and a loan payment looming over my head, my focus has been on helping Pop-Pop save the business, not pinching pennies for an event I can't afford.

A thump rattles the top of the coffin.

"Stella?" Pop-Pop's voice booms through the mahogany. "Get the hell out of Ms. Anderson's coffin."

I whisper to Rosay I'll call her back then push against the lid. The dim lights of the viewing room hang from the ceiling as Pop-Pop stands over me. His hair is whiter today against his dark skin, and his wrinkled dress shirt should be crisp, but I forgot to iron it this morning. Another failure on my part.

"He's here," Pop-Pop says.

"The asshole?"

He chuckles. "Stella. You can't call someone who's grieving an asshole."

"The hell I can't. He yelled at you, Pop-Pop. Anyone who does that, grieving or not, is an asshole." I hop out of the casket. "I'm going to the bathroom, and I'll be right there."

On my way to the bathroom to freshen up, I touch the picture in the hallway of my grandparents in front of their funeral home, vowing to not let this guy railroad my pops.

Tired brown eyes stare back at me from the mirror, and the normal glow to my golden brown skin is washed out from lack of sleep. I knew I shouldn't have had a fourth glass of wine last night, but despair is a lonely bitch.

Splashing water on my face, I run a hand through my tangled brown curls and push them behind my ears. Once I'm satisfied I don't look like one of the corpses magically reanimated, I head down the hallway and peer into the conference room.

Pop-Pop's at the table and the asshole leans against the wall, a phone pressed to his ear. This infuriating man called the other day and told my grandfather in no uncertain terms that he wanted his mother cremated by the end of the week. When Pop-Pop told him our cremation schedule was booked, he said that if we didn't do it, he'd find someplace else and pay them double.

Pop-Pop, being the sweet eighty-year-old man that he is and not wanting to turn down the much-needed business, didn't have it in his heart to tell the man no, so he asked me to help him.

My eyes journey up long legs covered in dark chino pants. He looks nothing like the short, weaselly man I imagined. He's tall, at least 6'2. His biceps strain against a green Henley. Dark hair shaved close on the sides but longer on top, and a closely trimmed beard striking against his light brown skin.

Despite being an asshole, he's an extremely good-looking man, so he probably has a small dick.

What a shame.

I step inside, and a deep English accent cuts through the silence of the room.

"I couldn't care less what you've got going on," he says, hand clenched around his phone. "If you couldn't do the job without help, you shouldn't have offered to do it." His other hand is tense at his side.

His annoyed tone makes me pause before I reach the table. He doesn't notice my presence and continues his conversation while Pop-Pop shifts in his seat.

I clear my throat once.

Twice.

The asshole doesn't even spare me a look.

Anger seeps into my chest, threatening the morsel of sympathy I have for this guy.

"Sir?" Pop-Pop rasps.

When he doesn't look up, I erupt. "I'm gonna die of old age waiting for you to finish your conversation."

His head snaps up, and his blazing charcoal eyes land on me. He clicks his tongue, and I catch the slight smirk before he says, "I guess it's a good thing you're already in a funeral home."

My heart slingshots inside my chest.

Swallowing would be a good idea right about now, but the intensity of this man's gaze is a chokehold that forces the rest of my body into a pile of goo.

Without another word, he hangs up and deposits the phone into his pocket. I school my face and calm my flipping stomach as he stalks toward me with broad shoulders, his jaw tense. *Focus, Stella. He's Satan beneath that God-like exterior.*

I exhale and give a weak smile to Pop-Pop. My grandfather extends his hand to the dark-haired Adonis, and to my surprise, the man takes it and greets him with a more cordial tone. "Thank you for being patient."

I don't miss the way his disapproving eyes flit to me.

I sit and gather the cremation paperwork along with the pictures of available urns, struggling to focus on anything but my pounding heart.

"And you are?" The deep timbre of his voice sends a zing of electricity down my spine.

"Stella." I look up at him, lips spread into a fine line. "Funeral Manager."

The warmth of his palm radiates up my arm. "Jameson."

He pulls out a seat across from me, pushing up the sleeves of his Henley, showcasing strong forearms lined with dark ink.

I clamp my teeth over my bottom lip and stare down at the papers. *Focus.*

Last night I was drowning my sorrows in wine, upset CJ hadn't proposed after four years of being together, and now I'm here imagining if this man's large hands are a precursor to what's beneath his clothes. I shake the thought away and push a pen and paper across the table.

"I need you to fill out this paperwork. If you'd like a lock of hair, I can get you that before we start the process. I'll also need an address to send the death certificate and the paintings."

His brows furrow. "What paintings?"

"The ones her caretaker sent over."

A perplexed look overtakes his relaxed features. "She wasn't an artist."

I freeze mid-showcasing, surprised by his conviction. His mother's paintings are dark and beautiful, but perhaps she didn't feel she could share them with him. This happens a lot after a loved one dies. You spend your whole life assuming you know everything about the people you love, and that the bond you have means no secrets. But each of us keeps something hidden away. Something we're scared we'd lose if the world ever knew how much we cared.

The world knew my mom was that thing for me, and it stole her before I ever had a chance to save her.

"I'm sorry." I look through the notes my grandfather scribbled on the intake form. "Her caretaker asked for her artwork to be displayed."

Jameson's fingers curl into his palms and he exhales harshly. "She wasn't an artist."

His annoyed tone is like a parent scolding their child for repeating an action they forbade.

I clench my jaw and roll my shoulders, ignoring his statement. "Do you require any assistance with the paper?" I tack on the word asshole under my breath, low enough he can't hear it.

"Stella," Pop-Pop cautions.

I know I'm being an asshole too. There's a special place in hell for being rude to someone who's grieving, but something about this guy rubs me all the wrong ways.

A few of the right ones, too.

Jameson sets the pen on top of the folder and turns to me. His gaze draws me in like a black hole, and I find my mouth dry as he stands. "Can we get this over with now?"

I stand and usher him toward the viewing room. My spine tingles as if he's reaching out to pull me back toward him. Pop-Pop clears his throat, and I turn, managing to catch Jameson looking at my ass. He doesn't look away in embarrassment. His eyes flick up to mine like a challenge.

I don't blink.

"She's in here." I open the door.

The casket sits at the front of the dim room. Her paintings cover the walls: some bright abstracts, some dark surrealism. One painting depicts an eye with a teardrop forming, but inside the tear is the silhouette of a child hunched over, lonely and afraid. Somehow, she managed to capture exactly how I felt as a kid.

Jameson stills the moment we enter the room, but he doesn't bother looking at the beautiful paintings off to the side. He marches to the casket and leans down, whispering into her ear. I'd like to imagine he's saying something poetic or reciting a prayer like some tend to do, but that spell is broken when he straightens abruptly and walks back toward us.

"Okay. I'm finished here. Where can I pay?"

Finished? Already? My mind blanks as if it stops working. In all the years I've helped at the funeral home, I've never seen someone treat a goodbye so…callously. My stomach knots, but I force myself to stay quiet as I go to the desk.

Pop-Pop stays in the room but Jameson follows closely behind me. A strangled sound escapes him as I lean over and grab the electronic cube we use for credit card transactions. He quickly recovers his composure and leaves the credit card loose between his fingers as he stares down at his phone.

My stubbornness waits for him to give it to me, palm up and challenging. I'm fully aware of the depths of my pettiness, but after searching my soul for all of two seconds, I can't find any reason to concede. He realizes I'm not taking the card from him and lays it in my palm. At the window, he pinches the bridge of his nose and stares into the parking lot.

I take his distraction as a chance to assess him. He strikes me as pensive and arrogant, but mysterious. Like getting inside his head would be more difficult than breaking into Area 51. CJ was an over-sharer. Always needing to fill the silence with something that would lead our conversations back to what he wanted to talk about.

The ripping sound of the receipt brings Jameson's attention back to me. I give him his card. Politely. Our fingers touch and electricity pings up my arm, raising goosebumps to my skin. He shakes his head, a ghost of a smile pulling at his lips before he takes it and leaves.

I follow, struggling to match his quick stride. Without my heels, he's got a good seven inches on me. He arrives at a sleek black motorcycle and picks up the helmet.

Sexy *and* dangerous.

If my body wasn't stupidly attracted to him before, it definitely is now.

"Where do you want me to send the paintings?" I rest my hands on my hips, a vain attempt at appearing more authoritative, but he ignores me and puts on the helmet. "Hello? I'm talking to you."

He flips up the face shield and lifts his leg over the seat, settling into the padded cushion and kickstarting the engine. His gaze slowly feasts on my body as he bites his lip and seemingly shakes away a thought.

"I don't care what you do with them. They're shit anyway." He revs the engine, leaving me stunned as he speeds away.

A soft clicking noise sounds behind me. I look over my shoulder to find Pop-Pop leaning on his cane, his normally hunched back and shoulders straight like he's proud. He pushes his glasses up his wide nose before he waves at Jameson's retreating form.

With a slight chuckle, he says, "I take it back. He *is* an asshole."

Chapter Two
Jameson

The memory of the tenacious woman with whiskey-colored eyes and disobedient curls chases me as I speed from the funeral home. The further I get, the more tension melts from my body and my stomach unwinds.

It's been years since someone has spoken to me with such candor, and I can't deny I've missed the exhilarating thrill of easy banter, but the smart attitude flowing out of her pouty lips and her hourglass figure are both things that would distract me from the reason I'm in America.

A shrill ring forces me to slow. I'd hoped I could avoid this conversation at least until I had some caffeine, but my dad will have a fit if I don't answer. He doesn't call to chit-chat but to dole out expectations.

I park in front of the coffee shop and kill the engine before removing my helmet to answer. "Hello, Dad."

"Did you finish whatever errand you had this morning?" His normal southern twang is tinged with annoyance. "You need to be in the office by noon so I can introduce you to everyone before the meeting."

I almost remind him of what I had to do but think better of it. He may not care that my mum—his mistress—is gone, but it would make her happy in death to know she was on his mind in some way.

"I'll be there shortly." I hop off the bike and head into the coffee shop, queuing behind a woman with a baby in a pram.

"Don't fuck up your chance to prove I made the right decision," Dad says. "It's important you make a good impression and keep our familial ties a secret. Colleen is already upset I've brought you on."

I straighten my posture as if he can see, absentmindedly scratching my thigh. Even though he runs the place, hiring his bastard child to work at his in-law's company has been a point of contention between him and his wife. If I want any chance at running the business over my half-brother when my father retires, I'll have to prove to everyone I deserve it.

"I'll show you no one's better for the job."

He huffs. "Come to my office when you get here."

The line goes dead, and a spell of nerves seeps into my stomach. Recalling the anxiety countdown my therapist back home taught me, I silently name off things I can see, touch, feel, smell, and taste to help me relax before I spiral.

"Jim," the male barista yells. "Your espresso with squirty cream." He snickers.

I take the espresso and leave, ignoring the Yank's juvenile jest. Getting used to the difference between English and American vernacular is still a struggle, but I doubt I'll ever manage to call it whipped cream if it squirts from a can.

I grab the thermos from my bag and pour my espresso into it for the ride to work. My phone buzzes, and relief fills my chest when it's Mike's name scrolling across the screen.

"Hey, mate. What's happening?"

"Ready for your first day?" Mike asks, a cacophony of children's voices in the background.

"It's normal to feel nauseous, right?"

I wouldn't admit that to anyone but Mike. He's my best friend, the only person I kept in contact with when my dad sent me back to the UK for boarding school after a few run-ins with the police.

Mike laughs and stops a moment to yell at his children for being too loud. "It's normal for your first day in a new job."

"It's not that. Dad already called this morning to ensure I make a good impression on my colleagues."

"And that's a problem for you, why?" Mike asks, surprise evident in his chipper voice. "You could charm the pants off anyone."

"Charming my coworkers shouldn't be an issue, but Cameron makes life difficult."

Mike grunts. "Is that douche still mad your dad let you transfer from the UK office?"

"Of course he is." I glance at my watch, spinning the bezel counter-clockwise a few times. "But I've got to get going. We're still meeting at the pub for a pint later, right?"

"Yeah," Mike says. "Have a good first day, and don't worry, your co-workers will love you as long as you're not an asshole."

I laugh and hop onto my bike. "I am an arsehole, though."

***

No one is more hated than the guy coming into an established company with new ideas. I know this, but I'm not here to be liked. I'm here to turn Thompson back into the top-ranked investment company in the South, and to finally prove to my dad I'm worthy of his full attention.

In the waiting area, I throw my bag onto the seat. "Can you tell him I'm here?"

Patty's snippy voice grates on my already depleting patience. "Good morning to you too, Jim."

Patty is a meticulous bulldog: short-statured, puffy white hair, and eyes that could kill you where you stand if she determined. She's been working for Thompson for over forty years, so she doesn't take crap from anyone, least of all, me. I adore her, though. She's a family friend and never treats me like a bastard even though my brother and his mother do, even sneaking me extra treats when I was here for the summer as a kid.

"Thank you, Patty." I open my mouth, ready to mention the encounter I had at the funeral home she suggested when my phone rings.

"Hello, baby brother," Cameron sneers when I answer. He could've walked upstairs from the accounting department to talk to me, but I'm sure it would create questions he wouldn't want. "How's your first day going? I've already acquired two new clients, and it's not even lunch."

The fact that I'm three inches taller, fitter, and ten times as smart does nothing to deter my slimeball half-brother from trying to one-up me. "What do you want?"

"Are you bringing anyone to the dinner at Dad's?"

My mind floats back to the woman from the funeral home.

Stella.

I let her see she got under my skin, but she's an itch I can't scratch. Unless I decide to kill my half-brother, which I consider daily, I have no reason to return to the funeral home to see her or ask for her number.

But why the hell did I tell her to get rid of the paintings? I could call and ask if she still has them and set up a time to retrieve them from her, maybe invite her out while I'm there.

"Hello?" Cameron sighs like he's exasperated. "You there, dickwad?"

"Yes, I'm here." I stroll to the window, looking out over the Riverwalk.

"So, are you?"

"Am I what?"

"Bringing someone to dinner, dumbass."

Dinner parties are amongst my least favorite activities in the world. My dad invites his business friends over at the end of the summer to talk about the upcoming year and shore up any loose deals. After he shipped me back to Manchester for boarding school, I thankfully never had to attend these events.

"I hadn't planned on it, but don't worry. I'm sure plenty of women will want to get to know the new CFO of Thompson by the end of the night."

He grunts. "You're not the new CFO."

"Yet." I hang up.

Taunting him will create trouble for me, but I don't have it in me to care. He always treats me like the scum beneath his shoes, and I don't expect that to change any time soon.

"Jameson," my father snaps through the wooden door.

I slip my phone into my pocket and salute Patty on my way inside.

"Shut the door," he grunts. "Let's make this quick so I can start the meeting."

I unbutton my suit jacket and take a seat.

"Most of our financial advisors are doing well, increasing the number of investors and capital, but some are coasting." His hands tense on the desk, and his Southern drawl lingers a moment before he clears his throat and his voice morphs into business mode. "Stagnant. I'll be clearing some of them out today to make room."

Taking note of the words he didn't say, *for you,* I hum an assent.

"There's a whale client I want you to handle, but I don't wanna deal with a mutiny by giving an outsider his portfolio. You'll have to compete against my top advisors to gain it, so it doesn't look like I brought you here for that specific reason."

Competing isn't foreign to me. I've competed with my half-brother for my father's attention for years, but doing it in a professional setting makes my stomach clench. I'm good at what I do, and I want to make my dad proud, but recently it's harder to cope with his expectations on top of everything else.

"Who's the client?" I ask.

He waves a hand. "It doesn't matter. I'll introduce you to the team and let them know about the project manager position opening up. I'm sure you'll impress everyone."

A sharp knock on the door steals my attention. A man with a maroon polo tucked into his trousers peeks inside. His hair is blond, medium length, and his beard needs a trim.

"The team's all here except Ella."

My dad rolls his eyes and leans back. "Thanks, Alex. Get everyone into the conference room."

I rise to shake Alex's hand.

"Alex Reyes, group one Advising Manager." He steps forward and passes my dad a blue binder. "I've brought the progress charts Patty asked me to draw up. They've got our highest—and lowest-ranking Wealth, Real Estate, and Corporate Investment Managers listed, and their strengths and weaknesses."

"I'm not worried about their strengths," my dad says, flipping through the material. "Their weaknesses are what they need to overcome if they want a shot at this promotion."

His eyes land on me, and uneasiness swells in my core. I cue up the breathing techniques my therapist taught me, but with my mum's death and leaving my clients and life back in the UK, the weight of my dad's potential disappointment is like an elephant on my chest.

"Let's go." Dad ushers me toward the conference room.

Chapter Three
Stella

"Come on, come on." I curse the slow elevator and the people stopping at every floor. I was supposed to be here twenty minutes ago, but the cremation took forever and mistakenly, I thought walking up four flights of steps would take me longer.

Joke's on me.

The doors finally open. I step out and a sobbing woman carrying a cardboard box bumps into me. I recognize her from our real estate department but don't know her well enough to stop and ask what's wrong. I'm already late enough.

"Stupid, freaking asshole," she murmurs, clearing away tears as the doors close.

I exhale, and dread floods my chest as I head to my desk. The once light and cheery air in the office has grown heavy since yesterday. Gone is the chatter, the laughter, the gathering in the break room.

Mindy, the office gossip, pops into my office, her eyes wide and full of mischief. She should be inside the conference room for the meeting I'm about to be late to. "Have you met the new guy? Mr. Weston brought him by my office earlier."

"No," I say, emailing one of my clients before the meeting. "I've been focused on work. Like you should be."

It's a lie.

I haven't been able to focus since Alex called and told me about the last-minute meeting CJ's dad called. I used vacation time to help Pop-Pop this morning but couldn't take the entire day off, and now I'm behind.

I wanted to write some talking points about my goals and aspirations with the company, but after breaking it off with CJ last night, I decided downing a bottle of wine was a better idea.

"He's gorgeous," Mindy says, waggling her eyebrows. "Think he's single?"

I shrug. "Why don't you ask him?"

"Maybe I will." She twirls a tendril of hair around her finger. "Are you heading to the meeting? I heard a promotion is up for grabs."

My ears tick up. "A promotion?"

She shrugs like it isn't important. I wish I had that luxury, but my parents died and left me with nothing. Mindy's father owns the most lucrative construction business in San Antonio, but she still works hard and is one of the top wealth advisors.

I, on the other hand, am hovering near the bottom lately.

With Pop-Pop's declining health and the loan payments due, I've focused more on helping at the family business than normal. I haven't had time to dedicate to acquiring more clients when I've barely been able to manage the ones I have now, but with a promotion comes more money. More money means getting the funeral home back into the black and saving Pop-Pop's dreams.

"Is it just me, or do British accents make things ten times sexier," Mindy says, waving a hand over her face as if the temperature has risen.

"British?" I squeak.

"Yeah, he's—"

"Stella?" CJ enters my office, halting Mindy's explanation. His eyes aren't red and puffy like mine, but he's tired; his brown hair is disheveled, and stubble peppers his ivory skin. Is it because he stayed up thinking about all I said last night?

"Hi, CJ." I stay seated as Mindy leaves, and he closes the door. When we first started dating, CJ would sneak up to visit during his lunch break and lock the door so we could fool around, but those stolen moments of happiness are long gone. He made sure of that last night when he didn't fight to keep me. "What are you doing up on this floor?"

"Uh." He rubs his cleft chin, eyes flitting to the pictures of us on the wall. I remind myself to take them down once he leaves. "I wanted to make sure you're okay."

Though my stomach tumbles around like a load of laundry, I shrug and give him a smile. "Of course, I'm okay."

"I know I messed up and took you for granted, and I know you said you needed space and time away, but I don't wanna lose you. Even if all I can have is your friendship."

I meet his imploring gaze and nod. "We'll always be friends, CJ."

"Okay, good." One corner of his mouth rises, and he backs toward the door, knocking his knuckles on the jamb like he has something else to say. "Have you seen my dad yet?"

"No." My stomach contracts at his question. "Why?"

He scuffs his foot along the carpet, eyes not meeting mine. "I haven't told him yet."

The rest of his sentence hangs in the air. *Can you tell him?* CJ hates confrontation with his dad, but now that we aren't together anymore, I don't need to buffer. "Okay."

"Okay?" he asks, clearly confused by my curt response. When I don't add more, his shoulders drop, and he nods. "Guess I'll let you go, but can I text you later?"

I know I should tell him no, but the longer he stares with those puppy dog eyes, the later I am for the meeting. "Sure, that's fine. I've gotta get ready for a meeting though, so we'll chat later."

The other half of his mouth ticks up into a full smile as he exits filled with false hope. I rise, still curious about what Mindy said. It must be a coincidence the new employee is British. Right?

I force my feet toward the conference room, and nausea swirls the closer I get to the door.

"Are you doing okay, dear?" Patty asks, peering through her bejeweled glasses. "You look a little pale."

I lean forward and reply through stiff lips. "Patty, didn't you say you were referring someone to my Pop-Pop's funeral home?"

Her eyes brighten. "Oh yeah, it was—"

"Stella." Mr. Weston steps out of the conference room with a frown. He checks his watch and motions for me to hurry, Mindy sliding in behind him without being noticed. "Stop chit-chatting and get in here."

The air thickens, and the coolness of the door handle does nothing to reduce the heat coursing through my veins.

"Come in, Ella." Alex greets me at the door with the disgusting pet name he tries to make stick. Normally it would've been Rosay with me, but since she's on vacation, I'm stuck with the guy who flirts with everyone.

The large oak table is filled with my coworkers, and Mr. Weston sits at the head in front of the projection screen. My stomach unwinds, and I send a small thank you to the Lord when I don't see anyone new at the table. I relax into my seat and unpack my materials for the meeting.

Movement by the window steals my attention.

"Fuck."

The room freezes.

Our eyes are locked in a paso doble, him the Matador, and me the bull. I'm not sure if it was me or him who uttered the curse, but as Mr. Weston's voice cuts through the haze, I'm relieved Jameson seems as shaken as I am.

"Is everything okay?" Mr. Weston asks.

Jameson breaks eye contact first. A win in my book. "Yes."

Mr. Weston's attention swivels between Jameson and me, unsure of what's transpired. His eyes narrow, but he continues as if my world didn't tilt on its axis. "Let's get started. As you can see, we have a new employee. Jim comes to us highly praised from our sister company in the U.K. He'll be working alongside you, and I expect each of you to show him how we do things here."

Jim? Vomit blasts up my throat, and I shift in my seat, inhaling as much air as possible. I never put stock into bad luck, but after today, I'm buying all the lucky rabbit ears I can find.

"Each employee will go through a performance review, and goals will be set for the next six months. We need to focus on increasing the growth of this company. I'm talking McCombs-level clientele." Silence descends over the room, and my heart pounds in my ears. "Since only three of you are eligible for a promotion, the board is making this a competition. Whoever secures the largest portfolio by the end of the year will be promoted to Project Manager with a significant pay raise."

A competition? I'm barely keeping my head above water now, splitting time between the funeral home and my current clients. How will I find time to schmooze a client like McCombs?

The side of my face is warm, almost as if Jameson's gaze could raise the temperature of my body with one look. I don't dare check and see if he's staring at me. I can tell he's agitated by the hands flexing in my peripheral vision.

"Stella," Mr. Weston's voice draws my attention. "I'd like you to help Jim get acclimated."

My heart stills, and cotton forms in my mouth.

"I can handle that, Mr. Weston," Mindy says.

"Stella has it covered, but thank you."

Swallowing the dryness, I focus on Mr. Weston. Inner Stella stomps her feet, throwing dishes on the ground in a fit, but my face betrays no hint of my inner turmoil. "Yes, sir."

Working with Jameson will stress me even further, but if this promotion allows me to repay a fraction of what Pop-Pop has done for me, then I'll swallow my pride and make it work.

Mr. Weston ends the meeting and calls me over. My feet are like cement weights as I walk to where he sits with Jameson, a smug look on the newcomer's face. He's so beautiful I want to punch him.

"You were late," Mr. Weston says. "Again."

I suck in a sharp breath. "I put in for time off. I had to help with a cremation this morning."

"Stella, we've talked about this." Mr. Weston approaches me at the door and lowers his voice. "This must be your priority. I've kept you on because you're a great advisor, and I promised your parents I'd take care of you if anything ever happened to them, but you've got to prioritize your commitments."

A lump takes up residence in my throat. Mr. Weston has always been a father figure to me. He and my dad were business partners years ago, and when my parents passed, he got me this job. He's a difficult man to impress, and he wasn't particularly fond of the idea of me and CJ, but he's always made sure I have everything I need to be successful.

He nods curtly and leaves, but Jameson and I remain inside the conference room, the air thick with tension. The other employees have scurried back to their offices, probably sensing the impending doom of this situation.

I close my eyes, shoulders inching up toward my head with each breath. "I guess we should get this over with."

"Stella." Jameson's voice makes my heart stall like I'm a newbie driving a stick shift, and my body betrays me by turning toward him.

"What?" I drag my sweaty hands over my skirt to quell my fluttering stomach. His eyes have somehow turned onyx in the span of time I've been ignoring him. His angular jaw is tight, and his hands are clasped together on top of the table, the veins bulging. My insides respond by turning into a puddle.

"If we're going to be working together," he says, "we should start on better footing than we did this morning. Maybe get to know each other a little."

I snort. "I know all I need to know about you."

From his flashy watch to his diamond-encrusted cufflinks, he screams privilege and control. Someone who hasn't had to work for anything in his life, the type of man used to submissive women.

He stands and approaches me, tight black Oxford stretching over his chest. "Well, as my secretary, you should know how I like my coffee."

Oh, no he didn't.

"Excuse me? I am *not* your secretary."

His brows furrow. "Then what are you doing here? I thought you were a funeral manager?"

Anger simmers at the base of my spine as I lean on the table. In his defense—not that he deserves defending—our meeting earlier didn't provide the opportunity I needed to divulge that information, nor did he hear Mr. Weston say I was an advisor. I swallow my snarky retort and fix a chipper smile on my face.

"I'm an advisor here, and I also help my grandfather run his funeral home."

"I bet business is struggling if you treat everyone like you treated me this morning."

My face heats. I normally pride myself on my customer service, but I allowed the hangover and Jameson's arrogance to put me in a sour mood. Even now, his smug face makes me want to punch him...or kiss him. Ugh, I hate hormones.

"I don't treat everyone like I treated you."

"So you saved your best charm for me?"

I roll my eyes and exit the conference room. "Don't flatter yourself."

Jameson follows as I give him a quick tour. The sooner I get away from him and the smell of his cologne, the clearer my head will be to make a game plan. Getting the promotion was important before because I could help Pop-Pop, but now that I'm competing against Jameson, I want to shove my victory in his face.

"You know, there's no shame in bowing out now," he says, stopping in front of the break room. His eyes are light, and he's got a playful grin on his face. "Not everyone is cut out for investments."

I lean against the door and laugh. "Not a chance. Guys like you never measure up to the hype. Your colleagues might've praised you in the U.K., but it won't be long before Mr. Weston sees what a disappointment you are."

Darkness creeps into Jameson's gaze, and I feel the shift from playful to predator on a molecular level. "I'm not the one whose performance is lacking. You seem to be disappointing him already without my help."

Digging my nails into my palms, I turn to him. "Has anyone ever told you you're a pompous asshole?"

His dark smile sends a shiver down my spine. "Thanks for the tour, Stella. I look forward to working closely with you."

He spins on his heels, ambling toward Mr. Weston's office. Fear creeps up my neck. Will Jameson tell him I was less than helpful? That I should be fired immediately?

"You and he can battle it out for that promotion," Mindy says from her perch beside the break room door. "I don't want the headache of dealing with a magnate. But I'll take a tumble in the sack with him if you aren't going to try."

I snort and head to the elevator, pressing the down button more times than needed. I was only required to be here for this meeting, and I'm not staying here any longer than necessary. "Have at it."

"You're still coming to my party, right? You haven't RSVP'd yet."

"I'll be there," I reply.

A ding sounds, and I back up to let a few coworkers off before I hop inside and head for the parking garage.

In my car, I instinctively dial CJ, like I would if we were still together. The rational part of my brain realizes it's a mistake to reopen communication and ends the call just as an email from Mr. Weston pings my phone. I quickly read it, making sure there's nothing he needs before I get on the road.

After the day I've had, I need dinner and lots of drinks to get Jameson Brooks off my mind.

Chapter Four
Jameson

As far as first days on the job go, mine went well. If you don't count the confrontation with the firecracker otherwise known as Stella Daniels, I'd say it went perfectly.

I don't remember the last time a round of verbal sparring got me this exhilarated, or frustrated. Had I known I'd be working with her, I would've been prepared for the smart remarks and playful jabs, but she has an uncanny ability to strike where it hurts most.

I'm not proud of how I baited her, using her family's business, but I've learned the best way to defeat an enemy is to know their weakness. And by no fault of her own, Stella Daniels is my enemy.

She's an enemy to my focus, to my discipline, and a distraction I can't afford.

"Have Stella give you the rundown of the area and our current clients," Dad says, strolling into my office. His gaze crawls over the artwork, and my chest inflates as he stops in front of one of my favorite paintings from an artist I represented in the U.K. The colorful geometric shapes morph into a chaos of swirls amidst the pressure of the paperweight on the banker's desk. I've loved art for as long as I can remember. It was my solace when I couldn't express my emotions, but it's something he's never understood.

Dad frowns, and my small blip of pride deflates.

"Can't someone else do that?" I ask.

"The more familiar you are, the easier it'll be to determine what accounts we need to prioritize when you take over."

He runs through the list of accounts to help me acclimate to the needs of my potential team and leaves with a reminder to get in touch with Stella.

It won't be long before Mr. Weston sees what a disappointment you are.

Her words stick with me far longer than I want them to. I spend the rest of the day setting up my office and hanging more artwork, hoping to dispel the tension she notched into my stomach with that jab. I need to find a way to work with her, to show her I'm here to stay, without letting down my defenses.

"What did you do to Stella?" Patty asks from the doorway of my new office.

"Who?"

"Stella Daniels." She rolls her eyes and holds her hand up in the air. "Five-seven, high cheekbones, brown skinned beauty who flew out of here all flushed earlier."

"I don't know what you mean."

She leans against the door frame. "Jameson."

I stand and gather my stuff to go home.

Patty moves to one of the chairs as I finish tidying my desk. "What happened this morning at the funeral home?"

I look at her. "What did she say happened at the funeral home?"

I thought I did a great job of ignoring her until she escorted me to the viewing room. That peach colored skirt was tight enough to give me a heart attack, but it wasn't her body that got me.

It was the fire behind her eyes.

The bite in her words.

Admittedly, I shouldn't have appraised her body so blatantly before I left, but I hadn't imagined I'd ever see her again and wanted to imprint her in my mind.

Patty lifts a shoulder. "Nothing. But with your reaction, and the fact that your face is flushed just talking about her, I'm thinking that may be a lie."

I grit my teeth. "If you weren't Landon's wife, I'd ask my dad to fire you."

She waves off my comment, heading to the door. "You couldn't get rid of me even if you tried. Who else would put up with your shit?"

I grab my gym bag and go downstairs to the building's pool to destress and regain control of my emotions.

It's near seven o'clock and most everyone has left for the day. A few stragglers are finishing up on the power racks, but the pool is completely empty.

Exactly the way I like it.

At the changing room, I open the door and listen for signs of another person. My phone chirps inside my bag, and I fish it out, frowning at the text.

Cameron: Can't wait until Dad sees the mistake he made. Might as well book your ticket back to London now.

My grip tightens on my phone. Dad wanted me to make a good impression on everyone, but my plan fell apart when Stella came through the door with her sharp tongue. Blood pounds in my head as I push Cameron's words out of my mind, replacing his comments with positive affirmations.

After the stress of moving across the ocean, dealing with the cremation, and starting a new job, I need to make time to find a therapist here, or at least get on the line with my old one, but I have to get settled in my new position first.

Me: I bet it's tiring carrying all that jealousy. I'll make sure you get time to rest when I take over as CEO.

After responding to Cameron, I slip my phone into the bag. As I grab my jammers, I stare at the gnarled skin on my thighs. My thumbs travel over the scars, a wave of shame crashing over me, thankful the material covers them. I fasten the swimsuit at my waist and head back out to the pool.

Cool water rushes against my skin as I coast down the lane again. Swimming laps has always calmed me, but each time I push against the edge, propelling back through the swells, the simmering heat of Stella's eyes unnerves me. Unable to find my usual solace, I shower and head to meet Mike and the gang at a new rooftop bar.

Friday night on the Riverwalk reminds me of Canal Street back in Manchester, a place I miss terribly. The scenery here is beautiful and refreshing, a river lined with restaurants and shops and people crammed together at too-small tables.

When my mum got sick and needed someone to take care of her, Dad offered me a job with Thompson on an interim basis. He knew I wouldn't want to stay long-term, but he also knew I wouldn't pass up the opportunity to impress him if given the option. It was just my shit luck that Mum waited until I'd already quit my job and taken on a lease in the States to die.

The low sun casts the Tower of Americas in burnt orange against the backdrop of downtown San Antonio. A homeless man leans against the brick wall of the building, plastic cup in hand. Tattered trousers, his face dirty and unshaven. The sign he holds up no doubt paints a sob story about how he's down on his luck, but I don't read it as I pass.

He's done nothing to earn anything from me or anyone else.

Music thumps as I enter, searching the crowd for my mates. Picnic tables are set up in rows along the AstroTurf and the air is heavy with the scent of bourbon as people clamor around the bar for fresh drinks. I spot my best mate, Mike, and his friend Tom, standing by the bar with a couple of beers and two purses hanging off their arms. I approach and wave the bartender over.

"A pint of Guinness. Thanks." I turn to the guys. "You blokes look lovely tonight."

"You're funny." Mike drags a hand through his blond hair. It's the longest I've ever seen his hair, but the look suits him. "Wait until you're holding your wife's purse."

I snort and take a swig of my drink. It's not that I don't want a wife. But if anyone knew who I was, and what I struggled with, they'd go running for the hills. Being with someone long-term can't happen, and I'm fine with casual dates and sex. My focus should be on my career anyway.

Mike sets his ale on the bar top and turns to me. "How'd your first day go?"

"Quite good until—"

A high-pitched squeal cuts through the air as Mike's wife Christine launches herself at me. Her eyes are glassy, ivory skin tinted pink. "Jim! Where have you been? I want you to meet someone."

Mike chuckles against his beer bottle. "Haven't you learned your lesson yet, Chris?"

I shudder at the thought of her matchmaking. Her last effort forced me to change my phone number.

"I've apologized for that. Many times." She hiccups. "This one's different. She's super smart, totally gorgeous, and my sister says she's on the rebound."

Mike cups Christine's face, and his eyes narrow. "You're definitely drunk." He leans forward and kisses her on the nose.

"Beside the point." She slides out of his grasp. "She needs someone to show her the way she should be treated. Her ex-boyfriend," Christine leans forward and raises a hand to her mouth to whisper, "didn't like to go downtown."

I raise a brow. "Why does it matter if he travels downtown or not?"

Mike spits out his drink and a peal of laughter from Christine has me gritting my teeth. He holds up his finger and searches for something on his phone. His face turns red, and he leans over and speaks into my ear. "He doesn't lick pussy."

I shake my head, humiliated on behalf of the woman who had a wanker for a boyfriend. I gulp my Guinness, the froth coating my upper lip. "That's a shame, but I'm still not letting you set me up with her."

Christine huffs and crosses her arms, her bottom lip protruding. "Well, she's on her way here now with Melody, so at least be nice."

"I'm not making any promises." I signal the bartender for another pint.

Melody breaks through the crowd, her arm stretched back as she drags her friend. The woman's head is turned toward the stage, so all I can see is her long curly brown hair and a slim, curvy frame. She turns, and my pint slips from my hand, shattering.

Christine jumps away from the river of Guinness heading toward her feet. "Shit, Jim. These are my new heels."

"You've got to be kidding me." Stella's words are slurred like she's had one too many pints.

Words evade me as I stare. The pink blush to her cheeks, the unruly curls slick with sweat from dancing, the peach-colored skirt she still has on from earlier. A cocktail of arousal courses through my veins.

Stella is the friend Christine wanted to set me up with. The one whose beau...I shake my head, clearing the thoughts of Stella's unmet needs, her sexual deprivation.

She walks away from the group.

"Stay." It's all I can manage to say past the lump in my throat.

Stella stops.

Sideways glances bounce around our group as everyone waits for an explanation.

Stella looks at Melody. "He's the guy I told you about earlier."

Melody's jaw drops. "Jim's the asshole?"

"Arsehole?" I smile at the flames I imagine flickering in Stella's eyes. "What did I do?"

A round of 'oOo's' sound from my mates as Christine and Melody cross their arms, their platinum brows pinched together.

Christine's voice is no longer high-pitched but stern as she says, "Explain, Jim."

"I've got no clue what she's talking about." A thrill of arousal shoots down to my trousers when Stella's dark eyes find mine.

"You have no clue?" Her words are clipped, no longer drawn out by the liquor. She holds up her hand, licking her lips and nearly making me groan.

"You were rude to my Pop-Pop." She puts her thumb down. "I had to use PTO to deal with you at the funeral home this morning." Her pointer finger lowers. "You left your mom's paintings and expected me to deal with them." Her pinky goes next.

"Dude," Mike interrupts. "Why didn't you tell me your mum painted?"

I roll my eyes, chuckling when I refocus on Stella and her nostrils flare. "You said I was bad at my job." She drops her ring finger and stills. The fire behind her eyes slashes through me, heat rushing down my spine as she gives me the middle finger. "And you killed my buzz."

I open my mouth to respond, but she's already leaving. Glass crunches beneath my feet as I follow her through the crowd. I've never once chased after a woman, yet I feel the need to prevent Stella from leaving. She stops abruptly when a server cuts in front of her, and we collide. Flush with her back, my cock stirs, and I inhale sharply.

"Stella," I grit out through clenched teeth and stop myself from pulling her closer. "I didn't mean to upset you. Come back to the group."

Her jaw clenches, and she cocks her head to the side. My heart jolts like a dart slams into it when she looks at me through her long lashes.

Chapter Five
Stella

He's so close I taste the malty sweetness of Guinness on his breath, the scent of bergamot and black currant wrapping around me. We're out in the open but we might as well be in a room with no windows or doors with how much space he takes up.

His gaze settles on me, and my core goes molten.

Remember he's an asshole, and you're not looking for a rebound.

"Don't make me ask again." His deep voice skitters across my skin.

His breath wisps the side of my neck, and I glare at him over my shoulder. "I'm not a dog."

He smirks. "You're right. Dogs are nicer…and obedient."

A server passes by and eyes us with a look of confusion.

I scoff. "You have such a way with words I'm surprised every girl here isn't lined up to be charmed."

His baleful chuckle makes my stomach knot. "I'm not here to charm you, Stella."

The veil of lust bursts and I remember the reason he *is* here. "I know."

"I was serious when I said we should get off on a better foot. My—" He drags a hand down his face. "Mr. Weston wants us to hold a meeting to go over portfolios and to get on the same page with our potential teams."

I didn't pay enough attention to Mr. Weston's email earlier. Had I been more concerned with work than getting away from Jameson, I'd be prepared instead of sitting here confused. I square my shoulders and pretend I know exactly what he's talking about. "Yes, and?"

"Let's squash this animosity between us now. For the benefit of the team."

Ugh. Why does he have to be so level-headed? And sexy. This tension between us won't help me succeed, and if I'm going to earn this promotion, I can't be ready to go to war with him any time he rubs me the wrong way. I've got to be smarter.

I lift my chin and give him my sweetest smile before I head back toward Christine and Melody. Jameson may assume we're 'getting on the same page,' but he's underestimating me. His charm and accent may work on everyone else, but I have more important things at stake, like ensuring my grandparent's business doesn't go into foreclosure.

"Everything okay?" Christine asks.

"Yeah," I say. "Everything's fine."

"Then let's get some more drinks," Melody says, herding me toward the bar and away from the men.

She and Christine crowd around me, shoulders bumping into one another. Warmth spreads down my back, and without looking I can feel Jameson's eyes on me.

"So." Christine arches her brow. Her vodka-soaked breath singes my nostrils as she leans forward. "What the hell was that all about?"

I lean on the bar top, reaching out to signal the bartender. "What do you mean?"

"You're gonna have that man chasing you for life." Christine laughs. "What did you do to him?"

I shrug. "Nothing."

"It's probably because most women don't walk away from him," Melody says, lifting her pink drink to her lips. "I bet he's a god in bed."

My breath hitches as I imagine *that*.

CJ was a creature of habit. Lube. Missionary. Focused on his climax. His need to relieve stress apparently meant he couldn't hold back until I got off. He used to at least offer to help me finish, but recently it'd been up to me. After four years together I expected a dry spell, but it was getting harder to lie that I was sexually satisfied.

The bartender hands me my drink and takes my money. The cool liquid hits the back of my throat, centering my thoughts.

"Being good in bed doesn't make up for being an insufferable dick."

Christine's eyes widen, alerting me to the block of heat behind me in the form of one tall, dark-haired, and frustratingly handsome jerk, who heard me discussing his sexual prowess.

"Still calling me names over here, I see."

I turn to make a snarky comment, but something like hurt flashes across his face, halting my words. Christine and Melody abandon me and scurry to their husbands.

Bitches.

I lick the salt on the rim of my margarita and ignore him.

He steps into my space, eyebrows knit together. "What will it take for us to move past this?"

My heart gallops inside my chest, and the flicker of emotion lingering behind his brown eyes has the alcohol pooling in my stomach. "An apology would be a good place—"

"I'm sorry." His lips pinch together as if the words physically pain him as he reaches out. "Can we start over?"

I snort, and my neck heats in embarrassment. He waits for me to accept his hand, and the sharp angles of his jaw tense. Why is it so important to him that we start over? He should want to get under my skin like I want to get under his, but squashing this beef means I can focus on what really matters.

Saving Pop-Pop's dream.

I clasp my hand around his. "Sure."

Jameson gestures to one of the empty picnic tables. "Are you hungry?"

I ate when I first arrived out of habit. That was at least something my good-for-nothing father taught me. Don't drink on an empty stomach or the hangover will be worse.

I nod. "I'll get something to go."

Ernie, the homeless vet who's made this his unofficial rest point, is outside and probably hungry. Seeing him always reminds me that being rich doesn't mean having money but having people around you who care and help when you need it. I know he'll appreciate a hot meal.

My stomach flips when Jameson's knee brushes against mine as we take a seat. *Whoa, down girl. It was barely a touch.*

The waitress takes our order, and I'm thankful for the distraction. I try not to focus on the way his lips move or the soft roll of his throat when he takes a drink of his beer.

Unsure how to converse with him, I sip my drink.

His eyes track my movements. "What made you get into finance?"

His question catches me off guard. I chew on my cheek to stop the prickling behind my eyes. "My Nunny."

"What's a Nunny?" Jameson folds his hands on the table, his attention entirely on me.

I pull my lips in, stifling a laugh. "It's my grandmother."

"Oh, your Nan." Stage lights strike his brown cheeks as he smiles. "Was she a financial advisor?"

"No." I take a deep breath. "She worked for a bank before she and my grandfather opened their funeral home. I used to get off school and hang with her until her shift was over."

Why am I telling him all this? He's the enemy. I flex my fingers and remind myself not to let him distract me with his charm. At least I haven't told him I was basically handed the job at Thompson when I graduated. He'd probably presume Mr. Weston is showing me favoritism.

Jameson nods, making me feel like he's actually interested in what I'm saying. "How long have you been an advisor?"

I hate this question. Most people would be further in their careers after eight years, but because I've had to help Pop-Pop, I haven't completed as many classes or certifications as I should've. I add that to my checklist of items to finish if I want this promotion.

"A while." I should keep the answers to a minimum. The less we know about each other, the easier it'll be when one of us inevitably becomes the other's boss.

From the moment Jameson strolled into the funeral home, my world turned upside down. He's arrogant in a sexy, and extremely frustrating sort of way, like he knows he'll succeed at whatever he puts his mind to because failure isn't an option.

In this case, failure has to be an option for him, because it can't be for me.

Allowing Jameson to get under my skin and into my head is a bad idea, one my twisting stomach reminds me of as a new band takes the stage, filling the silence floating between us. Focusing on the lyrics is made harder by the eyes boring into the side of my face.

The waitress appears with our food after a few songs, and I grab my purse to pay but she turns and leaves.

"Wait." I hold out my card.

"It's on me," Jameson says.

"But —"

He holds up his hands, cutting me off. "I said it's on me."

I bite my tongue, frustrated by his high-handedness. Taking a few bills out of my wallet, I lay them on the table for a tip. My phone pings, and a message from Pops is the perfect excuse to get far away from the weird feelings Jameson's presence produces in my stomach.

I stand and grab the to-go box. "This was great, but I've gotta get going."

"We haven't set up a time for the meeting. Would nine a.m. work? I need to let Mr. Weston know so he can email the teams."

I look around at the crowd smashed together by the stage as the band plays another song. I came here tonight to get the meeting with Jameson out of my head but ended up scheduling another.

"Sure, that's fine." I step away from the table.

He stands and grabs his to-go bag. "I'll walk you down."

My feet stop as if they're playing a game of red-light green-light. "I'll be fine. Go back to your friends."

He stares, chest rising and falling in time with my breaths. It takes a beat before I realize he's not going to respond, so I pivot toward the door.

Once out of the bar, I stoop by the front step and rouse Ernie from his sleep.

"What are you doing?" Jameson asks with a stern tone.

"Stelly Belly." Ernie sits up and brushes dust from his clothes. I give him the box. "Is this that barbeque tofu you brought last time?"

"Nope." I offer him plastic utensils with a smile. "I figured you'd like a variety of meats to choose from this time."

He eats a bite and closes his eyes, savoring the warm food. Reaching out to squeeze my hand, he says, "Wow, Ms. Stella. This is a treat. You didn't have to go to all that trouble for little ol' me."

Jameson clears his throat behind me.

"Is this your new bodyguard?" Ernie asks between mouthfuls.

I look at Jameson, his expression curt. "No. He's like a foreign exchange student from one of those really stuffy countries."

"Yeah. I know the type. Always seems like they've got a stick up their butts."

"I beg your pardon," Jameson cuts in, angry lines marring his otherwise beautiful face.

"We've got to get going, Ernie." I tug on Jameson's arm. "I'll see you next week."

Ernie waves his fork in the air. "Glad to see you got rid of that other dumbass."

His statement brings heat to my cheeks. CJ always called me gullible when I tried to help homeless people, like they were using me without my knowledge.

"If I knew your meal would be going to a vagabond, I wouldn't have paid for it," Jameson says behind me.

I don't stop or slow my pace. "If I remember correctly, I didn't ask you to pay. And when I tried to explain, you cut me off. So, if you have anyone to blame, it's yourself." My eye twitches, fueled by the anger pulsing through my body. I spin around, cocking my head to the side. "Why does it bother you that I gave him a meal?"

"Because he didn't work for it. All he had to do was sit there and hold up a sign. He could get a job but instead, he lies there all day."

"You don't have to work to be worthy of love and kindness." I cross my arms. "And besides, you know nothing about him. He's ten times the man you could ever be."

His face falls, then quickly turns to stone. "No one could ever be the man I am."

I snort and turn toward my car, leaving Jameson on the sidewalk. "I doubt anyone could ever be such a disappointment."

"As if you're the best judge of character," he mutters, following. "For someone so smart, you're quite prone to danger."

I straighten and turn toward him, nearly rolling my ankle. "What's that supposed to mean?"

"You've been drinking, you almost just broke your ankle, and you stopped to talk to a homeless man you know nothing about. You have no regard for your own safety."

I guffaw and Jameson gives me a sideways glance, the strong lines of his jaw taut. I curl my hands into themselves and keep my voice strong. "I've only had three drinks, and I do know Ernie."

He scoffs. "Just because you give him a few meals doesn't mean you know him. He could be a murderer or a rapist."

"So could you." I stop at a lightpost. "And not that it matters, but I met Ernie through a volunteer program at the VA."

"What's the VA?"

"Veterans Affairs. He was a soldier in Desert Storm back in the 90s. He lost his wife to cancer and moved here a year or two ago. Transferring VA benefits isn't easy. The government isn't worried about him now that he's done everything for them, and he fell homeless during that time. It's just like investments."

"How so?" Jameson asks, shoving his hand into his pocket.

"We're so worried about taking care of the new clients coming in that we forget about the old clients who have gotten us to where we are. Ernie's more like family now, and he deserves a whole hell of a lot more than a meal. Just because you can't see his scars doesn't mean they aren't there."

Jameson shifts, scratching the back of his neck. I stare at the side of his face, waiting for him to look at me, but his eyes stay glued to the ground, ignoring me.

I grab my phone and shoot Pops a text to let him know I'm leaving. I have a few messages from Rosay telling me she'll be back in town tomorrow and one from CJ.

CJ: I miss you babe. Please give me another chance.

I quickly close out of the message, realizing Jameson is still standing there.

"Why are you still here?" I ask.

"Are you always so rude?" he asks.

"Are you always so rude?" I mimic his accent. "That's grand coming from you."

"Give me your phone," he says.

"My phone? For what?"

He sighs, like dealing with my attitude is the last thing he wants to do right now. "I want you to text me when you get home, so I know you made it okay without hurting yourself."

Oh no. My heart is doing that stupid flippy thing. CJ rarely asked me to tell him I made it somewhere safely.

"Unless you want me to follow?" he asks.

My tongue sticks inside my mouth, but I force myself to swallow as I pass him my phone.

I shake my head, sure my cheeks are pink, but not because I'm embarrassed about where I live. It's an old brick one-story on the outskirts of the city, a tad different from the mansion I grew up in. But him following me home just feels too friendly for our situation. "I'll be fine, and I'll let you know when I make it."

He shuts the door with a nod and I drive off, somehow managing not to look in the rearview mirror.

Chapter Six
Stella

Dead people are the best listeners.

Though Mr. Shoal doesn't answer me back or offer any advice on what I need to do to earn this promotion, he does offer silence to work through my thoughts. If only I could stop my brain from veering off course and thinking about Jameson.

The man is one big ball of confusion, and every time he shows me there's another side to him, he changes back into the asshole I met at the funeral home. I shouldn't let it get to me. I've already wasted too much time deciphering his words.

I spent the weekend looking for any free finance classes I can take online or at the community college at night. If I have any chance to obtain this promotion over Jameson, I'll have to work harder than I've ever worked in my life.

"What time do you have to leave?" Pop-Pop asks, caning over to me.

I'd planned on spending the morning inventorying caskets and ordering more urns, but after Jameson's text last night to remind me of the meeting at nine am, I decided to come in early to make sure it was done. Pop-Pop's handwriting has been declining, and at eighty-eight years old, he's not as spry as he used to be. Maneuvering caskets is no longer a solo endeavor for him.

"The meeting is at nine, so I have about half an hour before I need to leave. I've already got Mr. Shoal set up." I pat the bald man on his cold, paper-thin hand. "He shouldn't give you any issues."

Pops rolls his eyes. "That's a relief. I was seriously worried."

Thirty minutes pass as we catalog and move the inventory. In need of a large coffee, I grab my phone, intent on ordering it through the app so I can pick it up before the meeting. I notice a missed call and messages from Rosay.

Rosay: Are you okay?

Rosay: Where are you? Mr. Weston is on a rampage this morning.

I quickly type back asking what she means.

Rosay: The meeting started at eight.

My fingers strain against the mahogany wood of the casket in front of me and sweat forms at the nape of my neck. It's got to be a mistake, right? Swiping out of her messages, I pull up the thread with Jameson. *That asshole.* I thought we made some headway but he played me for a fool, looking for an opportunity to make me look bad in front of Mr. Weston.

"I've gotta run, Pop-Pop. You'll be okay here by yourself?"

He nods, pushing his glasses back up his nose. "Unless one of these bills decides to give me a heart attack, I should be fine, Punkin."

I hug him and run to my car, nearly twisting my ankle again. Rosay thought it was hilarious I almost hurt myself while arguing with Jameson, but she was more interested in the potential for a rebound. I can't say the idea hasn't crossed my mind, but in my case, it would literally be sleeping with the enemy.

I can never trust him after this.

And if Pop-Pop's stack of bills isn't reason enough to keep me focused on getting the promotion, Jameson's underhanded tricks are.

Foregoing the coffee, I speed through early morning traffic on Interstate 10 and make it to the office in record time. If my car had lungs, it would surely be in an asthmatic attack right now with how fast I drove.

Out of breath, I push through Thompson's doors and rush into my office, dropping all my belongings onto my desk. I don't spare a look in the mirror at my haphazardly thrown-on make-up or my stubborn curls before I grab a notepad and pen and head to the conference room.

"Stella." Mr. Weston's voice is chilly as I take a seat beside Rosay. Her pink hair is pulled into a tight bun, and her ivory skin is tanned from her vacation. "Nice of you to finally show up this morning."

He turns back to the dry-erase board and anger sloshes my stomach like hot lava. Down the table, Jameson sits, fingers tented in front of him and sporting a sly grin.

That bastard.

I drop my guard and he takes advantage.

Rosay squeezes my leg and pushes her notes in front of me to copy.

"That'll be all," Mr. Weston says. "Stella, stay for a few minutes."

Rosay bumps my shoulder and tells me to stop by her office once I'm finished. I give her a doleful smile and make my way to the front of the conference room where Mr. Weston chats with Jameson.

"Good morning, Stella." Jameson's dressed in a navy-blue button-up and khaki slacks that accentuate his toned biceps and ass.

I hate how good he looks.

Gritting my teeth, I return his greeting. "Good morning. I thought the meeting was at nine?"

Jameson shoves his hands in his pockets, and the act makes me immediately zero in on his zipper. I rip my gaze away from the outline in his pants and refocus.

"You know how bad it looks when I tolerate your lateness, Stella," Mr. Weston says.

Jameson shifts beside him, lips moving like he's saying something to himself.

Mr. Weston speaks again. "Anyone else would've been written up multiple times by now," he pauses, "and I'm starting to wonder if you're still committed to being here."

Instantly, my mouth dries. I've pushed the limits of what's considered special treatment by needing extra days off or coming in at different hours, but I've always made up any time I've missed by staying into the evening or working on the weekends. I'm late today because Jameson's texts said nine am.

I grab my phone and bring up the message Jameson sent after I let him know I made it home. We exchanged a few funny GIFs of people tripping before he stopped responding. Thankfully, I didn't delete them.

"Per Mr. Brook's message last night, the meeting was set for nine am. I wasn't informed of the new meeting time."

Scrolling enough to hide the embarrassing clips, I shove my phone in Mr. Weston and Jameson's direction. A grin inches onto my face when Jameson's eyes dart to our boss. His shoulders slacken and his once delighted expression turns crestfallen. I bite down on my lips, so I don't laugh at the bravado he's lost.

Mr. Weston's deep inhale reveals his impending mood shift; he hates disorganization and excuses—as any boss does. If it wasn't for our past, I doubt he'd give me the leeway he has for the past few years, but since

Jameson's new, Mr. Weston will want to make it clear what he doesn't tolerate.

"My apologies, Stella." Mr. Weston turns to Jameson. "My office."

Without asking, I flee to Rosay's office.

"What the hell happened?" she demands I close the door.

I show her my phone. "Jameson told me the meeting was at nine, not eight. And I had the messages to prove it."

Rosay leans back in her chair and crosses her arms, a mischievous smile on her face.

"What?" I ask.

"Nothing." She shrugs and turns to her computer. "You said *messages*. Plural."

"So?" I draw out the word.

She pins me with an arched brow. "Trading cute texts with the sex god already?"

"No." My objection is too loud, and my cheeks heat.

She laughs, throwing her hands in the air. "No shame here. The tension between y'all is heavy, and it's not work-related. You should've seen how he was looking at you when you were copying my notes."

"Whoa, Rosay," I sputter. "Nothing like that is happening."

"Why not? You guys could hate bang and cut all that tension." She shimmies and waggles her eyebrows. "You're hot, and he couldn't keep his eyes off you."

Now it's my turn to laugh. "I bet he was thinking about the next way he can screw me over to get the promotion."

"I'm not so sure. More like he was thinking about screwing you in general." She shrugs. "I don't see what the issue is."

"He's the *enemy*." I rise from the chair. "I've worked here eight years, and this tea biscuit comes in like he deserves my promotion. Not happening. Pop-Pop is up to his head in funeral home bills, and I can't afford to get distracted by a chiseled face and tattoos."

"Tattoos?" She arches a brow. "How do you know he has tattoos?"

I wave a hand in the air. "That's beside the point."

"Well, I'm sure Jameson wouldn't think twice if you ever wanted him to get behind enemy lines." Her grin makes me wish she had a stapler on her desk I could throw at her.

After getting out of a long-term relationship, it's nice to know I'm still attractive to someone, even if I didn't feel desired by CJ. But the thought sours in my stomach because it's the foe across the conference table making me feel this way.

"Goodbye." I back toward the door. "I'll see you at lunch."

Smug because I bested Jameson at his own game, I make it a point to pass Mr. Weston's office on the way back to my own. The door is shut, but Mr. Weston's raised voice is unmistakable. I lean close to the wooden door and listen.

"This is not what I brought you here for," Mr. Weston says.

"I know, sir."

Someone clears their throat behind me. "Eavesdropping, are we?"

I turn and find Patty leaning against the wall. Her face is a picture of reproach, and I inwardly curse for being interrupted. I shrug and push away from the door. Spying on Jameson won't get me the promotion, nor will coming up with a way to make him look bad. If I beat him, it'll be because I'm a better advisor.

Chapter Seven
Jameson

Sparring with Stella promises to be one of the highlights of working at Thompson, but if I don't find a way to stop lusting after her, it'll only bite me in the arse. I figure, if she's mad at me for telling her the wrong time, then she'll stay away and I won't be distracted by her smart mouth anymore.

My father's strong reaction is, however, unexpected.

He paces his office and runs a hand through his disheveled hair. "This is not what I brought you here for."

"I know, sir." My voice shrinks, and when he doesn't respond, I timidly add, "It won't happen again."

"You're damn right it won't happen again." He shuffles the folders on his desk. "I've got enough on my plate, and you're supposed to be helping, not causing more issues."

His words are an elephant on my chest. Pain latches onto my throat, and the collar of anxiety almost makes me stumble. I struggle to remember how my therapist taught me to relax.

Breathe in for eight, hold for four, then out for eight.

"I'm sorry."

He slaps the desk, startling me. "I don't want your apologies, damn it. This is our legacy, Jim. Your brother is all but begging me to take over the reins, but he doesn't have what it takes to run this company."

Pride inches up my spine at his compliment but is immediately replaced with dread. He realizes my worth now, understands I'm a better option to run his company than my brother. One wrong move could make me lose it all. "I see a lot of me in you, but to be a leader you can't make careless errors like this."

Hearing this slows that drip of dread.

I've always wanted to be successful like him, and with his praise, I'm finally on track. Cameron can barely put on his shoes without instructions. I'm the one who will see this project through, and my father will finally realize I've always been the better son, more deserving of his affections.

But he's right.

If I get my head on straight, I have a chance to impact this company and usher Thompson into the next decade as the nation's top investment firm. I need to focus. I can't afford any distractions.

And everything about Stella is a caution sign made specifically for me.

"Don't embarrass me by being subpar or stooping to tricks again."

"I won't." My stomach pitches.

One-upping Stella by sending her the wrong meeting time only makes me look childish and worried that I can't beat her fairly. It's my responsibility to show him I'm committed to this job, and Stella is already burning the candle at both ends taking care of the funeral home and her clients here. It shouldn't be an issue to prove she's no competition for me.

"I trust you'll have a gameplan to go over with me for the clients you want to snag soon? If not, I'll have your brother draw one up with all the movers and shakers."

"I'll work on it tonight," I reply through gritted teeth.

"Good," he says. "I have an eight am tee time this Saturday with a potential client I'd like to introduce you to. Be at the Dominion by five-thirty."

With that parting command, I head back to my office.

I unwrap my client folders and slide the rubber band onto my wrist before logging onto the computer. I click through a few spreadsheets, taking note of the clients we have and the potential areas of opportunity. There aren't any galleries investing with Thompson, and that was my specialty at my old firm. Convincing one of the local art directors to sit down with me should be easy, and if successful, it'll bring many new portfolios to the company.

Taking out a piece of scratch paper, I scribble the names of other potential clients, ones my father would approve of, landing on Red McCombs as the one to go after. After what feels like an eternity, I settle on a game plan. Having someone who is familiar with the area, knows the markets, and has connections would be great to have on my team if I'm able to land his portfolio, and my mind automatically shifts to Stella.

A slight heaviness settles in my chest as I look back at the unread message I sent after the meeting. She's angry with me, and rightfully so. I've focused on work to distract myself from her radio silence, but I'm itching for a verbal tennis match with her. And I shouldn't be. The more attention I give her, the less I have for what's important.

The sharp knock on my door breaks my concentration. It swings open before I grant entrance, and in blows Stella with murder written all over her face. My lungs attempt to vacate my chest, squeezing as I hold my breath. Her hair is pulled into a tight bun with a few curly tendrils framing her face. Her brown skin is rose pink around her cheeks as if she's applied blush, but there's a dark smudge beneath her eyes like her make-up was re-done in a hurry.

I want to reach out and wipe away the dark mark, but I keep my hands clasped on my desk. Unbidden, an image of me smearing Stella's make-up as I devour her in bed pops into my head. I stiffen at the thought and refocus on her narrowed eyes and pinched lips. She's exquisite when she's on a mission to kill.

"Can I help you?" I feign disinterest though my heart dribbles inside my chest.

"I thought we made headway on Friday, but I guess your speech about 'squashing the tension between us for the team' was a load of bullshit."

"No, it wasn't." I clamp on my bottom lip when her hands rest upon her generous hips. Imagining her naked, draped in burnt orange silk as I paint her luscious brown skin, is not helping. I clear my throat and divert my attention. "I'm sorry for the miscommunication earlier. It won't happen again."

"You thought you were making me look unreliable, but all you did was show the others you're not a team player."

My bravado deflates, and heat creeps up my neck. I thought making her look incompetent would give me an edge and help rid me of these…feelings, but it hasn't. Seeing hurt in her eyes makes me sick to my stomach, and I don't like it.

Unconsciously, I snap the rubber band against my wrist. It stings, but it helps center me. I get up from behind the desk and saunter to the window.

"It wasn't my intention to make you look incompetent." I lie. "It was an error on my part, and my—Mr. Weston knows it's my fault. I hope we can move past this."

Stella leans on the edge of my desk. "I want to believe you, but thus far you haven't shown me you're worthy of my respect or forgiveness."

She uses her uncanny ability to find the small opening where my deepest worries lie, and then drives a blazing poker into the center of it. I move from the window and into her space. Her breath hitches at my closeness, and the scent of berries and vanilla floats into my nose, reminding me of my favorite childhood treat, an Eton Mess. It brings me back to a time when things weren't so complicated.

"You don't have to believe me, Stella." This close, I finally notice the light smattering of freckles dusting her cheeks. She's small, and when she looks up at me through those dark lashes my knees nearly buckle. An alarm blares inside my mind, reminding me this is the opposite of what I'm supposed to be doing, but I silence it and step closer into the cloud of sweet-smelling aroma. "I'll prove to you I'm worthy of it."

Chapter Eight
Stella

There should be a law banning emails or text messages on your day off. Squinting at the bright screen, I scroll through the bold text, highlighting which emails are junk and which are important. My breath catches on the name I've tried to avoid seeing or hearing the last few weeks.

From: Jameson Brooks
To: Stella Daniels
Date: October 1st, 2018, 8:38am
Subject: Market Connections
Good morning, Stella.

Let's set up a time to go over the market trends, and please send an updated list of accounts by tonight, so we avoid going after the same clients.

Thanks,

Jim Brooks.

I scoff and close the email, mumbling curses as I clear my eyes and hop out of bed. The audacity this man has to ask me for help on something after the stunt he pulled is flabbergasting. If he needs help, he can ask Mr. Weston.

My phone vibrates in my hand as I stretch.

CJ: Thanks for talking with me last night. You're going to the party today, right?

Stifling a sigh, I text back quickly and shove my phone into my pajamas pocket. I pad through the hall towards the smell of coffee and find Pops sitting at the kitchen table, papers stacked in neat piles on top.

Balancing the books is something I normally do, but a quick look at the calendar on the fridge shows me I'm a few days late. Inwardly groaning, I tense my hands at my sides before picking up the pile and going through it. Mindy's birthday party is today, but if I don't take care of this for Pops my stomach will be in knots.

"I can't remember the last time I was up before you," Pop-Pop says, handing me the checkbook.

"It was a long night." I yawn, scribbling out a check to the bank to cover our loan payment. CJ kept texting about how his parents wouldn't stop fighting over something to do with work, and after being together for four years, it's hard to draw boundaries where there were none. CJ's dad and my dad became business partners when we were in high school, so we were forced to spend holidays and celebrations as a family, weekends at Lake Travis, and summer bonfires where we stayed up and played cards. A relationship unfolded naturally between us.

I don't miss what we had, and I can't deny sleeping in a twin-sized bed in my childhood room is lonely, but I'm not sure I'm ready to put myself back out there so soon either. Rosay hasn't stopped sending me screenshots of her Tinder dates, urging me to download the app and 'see for myself' how many swipes I'd get in one day, but meeting someone that way doesn't feel natural.

"Work has been hectic, and I needed the rest." I pile the unpaid bills into one anxiety-inducing heap of paper.

"Speaking of work," Pop-Pop says. "Any word on a promotion or potential raise?"

The tiny people controlling my brain melt down. How do I tell him I've got to compete with the guy I was a total bitch to during his mother's cremation? And worse, that if I don't get the promotion over him, Pop-Pop may have to give up the business he and Nunny built together?

I'm the main provider for our little family of two. Pop-Pop has yet to retire, and my paychecks take care of the necessities for the house and funeral home, but with rising rent and the push toward bio urns, we're barely making ends meet, let alone repaying the loan we took out after Nunny passed. My throat aches as my gaze settles on the pile of bills on the table.

Owning a business as a black man in the south was unheard of when Pop-Pop was a teen. He and Nunny worked multiple jobs to open their funeral home, and my heart would break if he had to sell. It would've been nice if my parents had thought about the unforeseen things that could happen in the future, but if it wasn't about my dad and his businesses with Mr. Weston, it didn't matter.

I skirt the truth. "The meeting went well. We have a new team member, and if I can bag a mega client like McCombs soon, maybe I'll be able to get that promotion we talked about."

Pop-Pop pats the top of my hand. "McCombs is getting a little up there, isn't he?"

"I guess?" His comment sparks an idea. Jameson will probably waste his time trying to get a meeting with the patriarch to impress Mr. Weston, but I might have better luck with his kids. And if I'm lucky, one of them will show up today at the Dominion while I'm there.

"Either way you'll get the big fish. I believe in you." He gets up and washes his cup. "Can you take me to the church before you go to the party?"

"Sure." I finish my cup of tea. "Let me get dressed."

I throw on clothes and brush my teeth before I grab the bag I packed last night for the party and follow my grandfather to the car.

"I'm proud of you, Stella." Pop-Pop focuses on the cars passing by, but he reaches over and squeezes my hand. "You'll show your boss how special you are."

His words wrap around my heart. How he knew I needed to hear that is beyond me, but I'm thankful for his awareness.

"Thanks, Pop."

We drive past the church where Nunny and Pop-Pop got married. The country club looms over the small tabernacle sitting at the bottom of the hill, and we travel around back to the graveyard. It's the same graveyard my parents would be buried in if the authorities had ever found their bodies after the boating accident.

Pop-Pop still erected a headstone to honor my mother, and now he visits weekly to chat with the two loves of his life.

"If you text when you're done, I'll have Pastor Shew bring me up." Pop-Pop opens the door. "Have fun at the party."

I wave goodbye and take the car up the hill to the country club.

Tan bricks and vibrant mosaic tiles cover the front of the clubhouse as I pull into the parking lot. Sitting on fifteen hundred acres of land, the Dominion houses San Antonio's elite. I lived here in my dad's parents' guesthouse before my parents died and my father's parents decided they didn't want to raise a bi-racial grandchild. Thank God for Pop-Pop and Nunny. They raised me to be nothing like the people who frequent here, the ones who only accepted my mother because of who she was married to.

I didn't want to come today. The memories are still too vivid, too raw. It's even more awkward since CJ and I broke up. At least I have a chance of potentially seeing Charlotte McCombs, daughter of the richest man in Texas and the one client who could save my career if they decide to invest with us.

"Hey, babe." CJ appears at the car and leans in for a kiss before he pulls back.

Hearing him call me "babe" like we're still together grates. Although I know coming to the party means I'll have to spend time with him, most of my other coworkers will also be here, so it shouldn't be that bad.

His chest is bare, a light sheen of sunscreen covering his meaty arms. He's fit, but years of drinking and tailgating at football games have exacted a toll on the body he had in high school.

"How was work this week?" He pushes a strand of hair behind my ear.

I lean away. "It was okay. The new guy tried to make me look bad, but I turned it around on him. Your dad reamed him a new one."

CJ tenses. "What did he do?"

Bumping his shoulder, I say, "Calm down. I took care of it."

"If he gives you any more trouble, let me know. I'll kick his ass back across the Atlantic."

I glance at the determined look on his face. "How did you know he wasn't from here?"

"I, umm...heard some people talking about it in the break room."

"They were talking about him on the third floor?" I laugh, knowing there's no way a bunch of accountants sucked themselves out of their computers long enough to chat about Jameson's arrival. "CJ, I don't need you checking up on me."

"Just because we broke up doesn't mean I don't still feel protective of you."

I exhale and follow him up the cobblestoned path. "I know, and I appreciate it, but I'm fine."

Passing a red balloon arch, CJ leads me to a table near the heated pool. "Do you need to change?"

"Yeah."

His attention moves to the squeals coming from the pool area. "It's around the corner."

"I remember."

He flinches, as if remembering we were here the night before my parents died is an unwelcome thought. I ignore his sad eyes and head to the bathroom.

Pictures of the golf course cover the beige walls of the hallway. Outside of a few color changes, it's the same club as eight years ago. Distressed wooden desk at the front, wrought iron chandeliers, pro shop attached.

I used to run these hallways in search of friends. Dad would finally relax once he was around his golf buddies, a cold beer in his hand. And the light would return to Mom's eyes when she was able to laugh freely with frenemies she hadn't seen in weeks. But I never fit in like they did. I was the bi-racial kid, and even though my clothes were always 'in season' I was never good enough for the purebred money. In all honesty, even though I hated it, I would've lived here if it meant my parents would no longer hurt themselves and each other.

I push open the door to the bathroom but stop when I hear Jameson's name spoken by one of the women inside. Getting pulled into a conversation about how dreamy Jameson looks in suspenders is not something I want to do.

"Eavesdropping, are we?"

I startle, banging my toe on the door trim. The man of the hour leans against the wall, almost like uttering his name made him appear. "Damn it, Jameson. Don't sneak up on me like that."

He chuckles, and I rub the sore spot.

"Wait a minute. *Why* are you here?" He's not in swim trunks, so I know he's not here for Mindy's party. He's dressed in a dark blue polo, showcasing his toned forearms, and a wisp of black ink peeks out from his shirt sleeve when he leans against the wall. Compared to the refined older men in sensible shoes who usually golf here, Jameson stands out. It seems neither of us are successful at blending into the crowd, and when he tugs on his collar like he's uncomfortable, my core clenches.

He takes off the white hat he's wearing and swipes away a bead of sweat on his glistening brown skin. My breath catches in my throat watching the fluid motion of his biceps tensing.

"Last I checked, America is a free country." He smirks. "I'm exercising my right to play golf."

I roll my eyes and push away from the wall to put some space between us. "Har, har. I meant, what are you doing at *this* specific club? You either have to be a member or be invited."

His tongue swipes his bottom lip, and my body promptly responds with taut nipples and moist panties. "I was invited."

"Jim." A group of men, including Mr. Weston, arrive from the golf course.

Realization settles, weighing heavily on my shoulders. Jameson is here meeting with clients, and he has the backing of Mr. Weston. It shouldn't surprise me. With his pompous attitude and tailor-made suits, Jameson belongs here.

"Uh, I'll let you go," I grit out, and head into the bathroom.

Rosay and Mindy find me a few minutes later as I splash water onto my face, considering drowning myself in the sink. Rosay's hair is a brighter pink than yesterday, and I bury myself in her familiar rose scent. Her vacation tan has waned, but she keeps it alive with a hint of blush, bright eyeshadow, and a crimson stain on her heart-shaped lips.

"I'm so glad you're here."

"Me, too." She smiles and steps back to look at me. "What happened?"

"Jameson freaking Brooks."

Mindy's eyes widen, curious. I give her an account of what transpired between Jameson and me the day we met. I leave out the tidbits about how my body reacted to his touch when he tried to stop me from leaving, how I wanted him to press me up against the wall just now, and how I find myself looking for reasons to argue with him.

I'm not ready to sort through that clusterfuck of emotions yet.

"Damn, girl." Rosay shimmies and leans against the sink. "You put a spell on old Frosty the British man. Not that I blame you. Jim is gorgeous. I mean, the dark hair and broad shoulders, not to mention all that pent up frustration. Imagine what he's like in the sack. He drips sex appeal."

I choke on a laugh. "*Rosay*, I don't want to imagine what he's like in bed. Plus, he's an asshole. He sent me an email this morning with a list of questions he needed answered by tonight, my day off. Like I'm his personal secretary instead of his competition."

Jameson's made the last two weeks of my life so stressful with his demands, sitting in on meetings, reminding me he's here to steal my promotion.

It's suffocating.

"That's pretty shitty," Mindy says, "but I'm sure it's because he knows if he distracts you it'll be easier for him. He doesn't want you to get back to being the top advisor."

"I can only do that if I'm not dead from exhaustion. If Jameson doesn't let up soon, I may need to use one of Pop-Pop's caskets permanently. It doesn't help that Mr. Weston preens every time Jameson does something good. It's like the minute I broke up with CJ, he threw all his support behind Jameson."

I sigh and follow them to the pool. Even though it's October, the Dominion keeps its pool heated, so I can't even use the water being too cold as a reason I'm not swimming. Rosay, Mindy, and I lay on chairs beside CJ, who sunbathes as the partygoers play a round of water volleyball.

The sun beats on my skin as we tan and sip on cocktails. Switching between chatting with Rosay and CJ has my head on a swivel, but in the back of my mind, I focus on the men Jameson was meeting with.

I can't let Jameson get an inch ahead, and if I secure the McCombs account, it'll be hard for the board and Mr. Weston to dismiss my abilities to be the Project Manager.

On Monday, I must lock down a meeting with Charlotte McCombs.

Chapter Nine
Stella

After two hours of sunbathing, being splashed by the adults playing chicken in the pool, and dodging questions on why I'm not swimming, I head inside to order another round of drinks for the group. Mosaic tiles cover the front of the lounge, lit by lights underneath the lacquered bar top. Searching out an empty stool, I weave around the wooden tables filled with Stepford wife look-a-likes chatting about their tennis matches and businessmen clad in golf attire and find myself squeezed at the end of the galley.

Chatter fills the room, making it difficult to grab the bartender's attention. He finally notices me and tells me he'll be right over. Movement out by the pool catches my attention, and my eyes lock onto Mindy on top of CJ's shoulders battling it out with another coworker. With a hollow stomach, I tell myself it doesn't matter.

"Why the long face?" Jameson startles me and leans on the bar, effectively caging me between him and another patron. His forearms flex against the railing, and I fail at not following the bead of sweat that rolls down his temple, catching on the clipped strands of his beard.

"No long face here." I refocus my attention on the bartender.

A soft touch on my arm sends goosebumps cascading down my skin. My stomach tumbles, and I turn toward Jameson, noting the way his gaze drags up the length of my body and lingers on my bikini top before meeting my eyes.

"Why are you in here?" he asks.

I chuckle, waving my hand at the bar like a showgirl. "Ordering a drink."

His forehead creases. "There's a bar outside."

"How observant of you."

Laughter pushes inside through an open door, and instinctively my head whips around to watch everyone having fun in the pool.

My stomach sinks. Even Rosay's joined the game of chicken.

I push aside my sadness and look back to the bar, silently begging the bartender to return and put me out of my misery.

"You playing chicken next?" Jameson nods to the pool. "I'd pay to see that."

The pit in my stomach widens. An overwhelming desire to flee has me eyeing the exits and debating how awkward it would be to fake my death right here.

"Stella?" Jameson touches my arm again.

"I don't swim." Unbidden, the words rush out, hanging in the air like a dirty secret.

"You don't swim?" His forehead creases like he's solving an imaginary puzzle. "I thought Yanks loved barbecuing and swimming. It's kind of a hallmark of your holidays, yeah?"

If we were outside with the sun beating down, I'd be able to explain the wave of heat that takes up residence on my cheeks, but alas, we're not.

"Don't look at me like that," I say. I hate that he's gotten under my skin.

He rubs a hand along his beard. "I'll look at you however I please. But why—"

"I don't know how." The memory of sinking to the bottom of the pool one evening while my parents wined and dined their work friends edges its way into my mind. It wasn't their fault; someone had left the gate open, and I didn't want to ask if I could get in. They were too wrapped up in their own lives to even notice my absence, but thankfully another guest did. The irony that they were sucked into the depths of the ocean not long after sits in the back of my mind like a jack-in-the-box waiting for its moment to pop up again and terrify me.

Before Jameson has a chance to ask more questions, the bartender returns. I give him my order, and Jameson tacks his on with mine, handing over his credit card. I grit my teeth and thank him.

"You know," Jameson says, leaning forward into my space, the cedar scent of his cologne wrapping around me, "I could teach you to swim."

"What?" My laugh is breathless, my face too warm under his gaze. The flimsy material of my bikini top stretches over my now firm nipples, and blood whooshes in my ears.

Gah. I've got to either get laid or join a convent, because I'm not sure my lady parts can handle more of Jameson's backwards charm.

I cross my arms over my chest.

His breath wisps along the shell of my ear. "When you're ready to learn, I'll be here."

"Leave her alone, dickwad." CJ sidles up to me, skin glistening, trunks dripping water. "Are you okay, Stella?"

Jameson straightens to his full height, looking down at CJ. "I beg your pardon?"

"I beg your pardon," CJ parrots in a nasally voice, stepping in front of me. "I said, leave her alone."

"CJ," I admonish, pushing him away. He doesn't know Jameson is the new guy everyone's been talking about, and his dad may not be able to save him if Jameson goes to the board. "What's your issue?"

"Yeah, mate. What's the problem?"

"Get away from her." CJ pokes Jameson in the pecs, and the bar gets eerily quiet.

Anger boils beneath my skin, bubbling like a cauldron ready to tip over at his alpha male bullshit. Jameson's gaze tracks the water droplets down his shirt before he looks at CJ. He opens his mouth to say something, but Mr. Weston's voice cuts through the bar.

From my peripheral, I can see everyone else turned to look at Mr. Weston, but my eyes are locked with Jameson's. Something flashes behind his gaze. I'm not sure why, but the way I can tell he's straining not to look at my body thrills me.

"CJ, this is not the time." Mr. Weston stands between the two men.

CJ scoffs, "It's never the time," and stomps off.

"Stella." Mr. Weston tips his head toward me in acknowledgment before saying something to Jameson and ushering him toward the exit.

"Girl." Rosay pops up beside me at the bar. She takes what would've been Jameson's drink and we head back out to the poolside. "I have a feeling that's gonna come to blows at some point, so I suggest you take care of it soon."

I blow out a breath and shoot Pop-Pop a message to let him know the party is over. "I know, but what do I do? CJ knows we're not getting back together, and I can't cross that line with Jameson."

"I don't see why not." She lifts the beer bottle to her lips and gives me her signature shimmy. "One bang and it'll be out of your systems. Then you can get back to hating each other."

Her words marinate as I finish my mocktail. One night with Jameson doesn't seem like it'd be enough to quench this never-ending thirst I have around him, and my focus needs to be on beating him, not bedding him.

"I've gotta go meet Pops," I say, packing up my bag. "I'll message you later."

She hugs me, and I head outside just as Pastor Shew drops off my grandfather. I can tell from Pop-Pop's glassy eyes that he's been crying. Being here at the Dominion makes me feel like I could cry too, and I didn't even have a chance to look for Charlotte McCombs.

"You've got a flat," he says.

"Damn it." I bend over and inspect the tire. "How the hell did I manage to drive over a screw?"

"You've got a flat," a deep, accented voice echoes behind me, repeating Pop-Pop's words.

Awareness zips from my feet to my head. Where did he appear from? And why is my stomach a butterfly conservatory now that he's around?

"It's the asshole," Pop-Pop whispers, smiling at Jameson.

"I thought you left already," I say, examining the car instead of the man in front of me. His toned muscles lift the fabric of his shirt as he places his golf bag on the ground.

"Good afternoon, Mr. Daniels. It's good to see you." Jameson turns to me, the corner of his mouth tilted up in a small smile. "Got a spare?"

I stammer, scratching my head. "Umm...I don't... I don't know."

"Open the boot," he says.

My brows knit. "The what?"

He chuckles and knocks on the trunk. "The boot. Open it."

I roll my eyes, a small smile tugging at the corners of my lips. "Trunk. People don't call it a boot here."

He blinks a few times as if he hopes I'll disappear. My cheeks flush and I head to the front to pop the trunk. Pop-Pop clears his throat and asks Jameson how he's doing since his loss.

My ears strain to hear as they speak in hushed tones like old friends. When it's clear they're being intentionally quiet, I interrupt. "The trunk is open."

Pop-Pop gives me a clear look of disapproval, bushy eyebrows and pursed lips included.

"Do you always golf on Saturday?" I ask Jameson, redirecting the conversation.

He ignores me.

My inner child stamps her foot, but I press on. "Did your meetings go well?"

Again, silence.

"Or not, asshole," I murmur under my breath.

"You guys work together?" Pop-Pop asks.

I suck in a breath as if I can bring the words back inside my mouth. I nod and scamper to the back of the car, tripping over one of the decorative pots lining the parking lot. My ankle twinges, but I ignore it, smothering the pain under my guilt.

I should've been honest with Pop-Pop this morning. There wasn't any reason I couldn't have told him Jameson is the new guy, but the more I think about it, the more real it becomes. I don't want him to be my competition. I don't want to feel constantly on edge around him. And I definitely don't want to keep imagining him doing things to me that a boyfriend should be doing.

Jameson's eyes flit to me, an amused smirk on his face. "The meetings went fine." He lifts the carpet inside the trunk, unearthing the spare tire, jack, and lug wrench. His biceps bulge as he pulls out the tire, and saliva pools in my cheeks.

I reach for the tire, a nervous smile on my face. "Thanks. I can take it from here."

He wheels the tire back toward him and lifts it over his shoulder, rolling his eyes as he steps to the side of the car.

Pop-Pop snickers as I follow Jameson, my lips pinched together. "I can do that."

He pulls out the lug wrench, twisting off the nuts with a few pumps of his arms. Arousal and irritation swirl in my core.

"Jameson, I'm fine. I can do it."

"I have no doubt of your abilities." Butterflies take off inside my stomach until he adds, "But I'm faster at it."

Those bright yellow Monarchs drop dead at his words, reborn into angry, buzzing wasps. His muscles flex as he replaces the tire with the new one and wipes his hands on his khakis.

"You're good to go." He throws the jack and wrench into the trunk. "Get that changed to a real tire today."

I grit out a thanks and hobble toward the driver's side, my ankle now screaming.

"That cocktail must've been strong," he says.

"It was non-alcoholic," I reply sardonically.

"You shouldn't be driving if you can't even walk on two feet while sober."

Contempt simmers into a boil, and I fling over my shoulder, "What are you gonna do? Spank me?"

Pop-Pop's mouth drops, but Jameson bursts out laughing.

The sound of it freezes me in place.

My chest tightens, and my face and neck burn.

If I could run away and never look back, I would.

"I'm sorry. That was completely inappropriate."

Jameson's shoulders rise with a deep breath, and a shit-eating grin is stuck to his face. He wipes his hands on his pants again, and my gaze is drawn to his clearly impressive package.

Eyes up, Stella.

He clears his throat, and my cheeks flame. I struggle to cover awkwardly checking him out by saying, "Why are you wearing pants?"

Oh my god. Why are you so awkward?

His forehead creases, a devilish smile tugging at his cheek. "What makes you assume I'm wearing any pants?"

"Because I can see them?"

He looks down, and a beat passes before he promptly begins to laugh again. "Oh, you meant trousers."

I smack my forehead. "Yes, uh...trousers. Why aren't you wearing shorts? It's like ninety-five degrees, you weirdo. Scared someone's gonna laugh at your pasty legs?"

"No." His fingers tense, digging into his thigh like I've upset him. He opens his mouth like he's going to say something else, but instead he abruptly turns, picks up his golf bag and leaves without another word.

I drop into the car and stare out the window, confused about what just happened. My fingers grip the wheel as Pop-Pop opens the door and sits. His silence makes me jittery as I flip on my blinker and head toward home.

"Want to talk about what happened back there?"

I exhale. "Not really."

He clasps his hands in his lap and sighs. "Stella. You were with CJ a long time, and I know you wanted to get married and have kids."

"Pops, I don't need a lecture right now."

"I'm just saying, it's okay to move on and start living your life for you."

I rear back, surprised by his candor. Pop-Pop's opinion is important, and he never voiced any concern about my relationship with CJ, but I doubt he'd be supportive of me exploring the chemistry between me and the man who could potentially derail my career.

"What are you telling me?"

He raises his hands. "I'm not telling you anything. I want to see you happy and thriving," he pauses and then adds, "and loved the way you should be."

I bristle. I used to be happy and thriving, hopeful about the direction my life was going until CJ refused to move forward. Now, the only person my body wants is the one person I should stay away from. It's a recipe for disaster. I need to manage my career better than I've done with my personal life.

Chapter Ten
Jameson

Wineries and farms line the highway I take to my dad's Hill Country estate. I've only ever been to his home in San Antonio. He's invited me here before; I've just never wanted to visit. Nor would it have been a particularly warm welcome as his bastard son. If potential clients wouldn't be at this dinner tonight, I wouldn't have agreed to attend.

Since the unfortunate incident at the Dominion with Stella, I haven't been able to cope, and with each passing day the coil inside my stomach tightens. It's getting more difficult to complete the breathing exercises, and each time I've scheduled an appointment with a new therapist I've had to cancel because of meetings my dad set up for me.

I pull up to the main house, a European-style chateau surrounded by hills, somehow the perfect blend of old and new. Sunlight bathes the mansion in a soft yellow glow. Purple asters and perfectly trimmed bushes line the walkway, making it feel cozy.

I'm sure my dad's wife Colleen oversees the landscapers.

The scent of apples and cinnamon hits when I step inside. A man sits at the bottom of the winding staircase playing a grand piano as people chat and admire the view out the bay window overlooking the lake. My eyes flit around, noting the vaulted ceilings with exposed beams, the marble countertops, the butlers handing out champagne, and the fireplace inside the formal living room adorned with a fall-themed wreath hanging below a family portrait.

One I'm not included in.

I shrug off the exclusion and head into the next room to find my dad. My phone buzzes in my pocket, and I steal a look at the email on the screen. A list of clients and a brief overview of market trends stare back at me.

Stella hasn't blanched at the emails I've sent trying to get under her skin. She answers every query, responds quickly, and attaches any pertinent information I'll need, anticipating questions I haven't even asked. I can't say I'd do the same if the shoe was on the other foot, and I'm not sure if it's because she's looking to impress my dad or if she's *that* good of a person.

Cameron ambles over to me, in a white button down and a suit jacket straining to its limits to stay buttoned. He kisses the tall, lanky blonde on his arm before she begs off and he plops into the chair at my right.

"Leave her alone." He waves over the bartender.

Confused, I ask, "Who?"

"Stella." He orders his beer and turns to me. "She'll never want you."

Hearing her name is like espresso pouring into my veins. My heart races and my cock stirs. Had her grandfather not been there the other evening I would've taken her up on her offer to spank her, or at least take her to dinner, but my own weaknesses as a man ruined the conversation. I couldn't bear to stay any longer, and I still haven't been able to face her.

I lift my beer to my lips. "Sounds like a challenge."

"Stay away from her." He deepens his voice as if it'll scare me. "Why would she want the spare when she can have the heir?"

I snap the rubber band around my wrist, willing it to give me a morsel of calm. I should've put it back on the folders, but sometimes the sharp pain centers me when the breathing exercises fail. Cameron, like Stella, knows how to get under my skin. The difference is his words are intentionally directed at the fact that I'm 'the bastard'. The kid that wasn't planned, wasn't wanted, and was sent away the first time I made a mistake. I learned to play by my dad's rules if I wanted attention, and Cameron learned to shift the blame for his shitty life onto the fact that I was born.

"Jim." Dad waltzes into the room dressed in a sleek black tuxedo followed by Colleen in a red floor-length dress.

Everyone's dressed as if they're attending the Oscars.

My white oxford paired with a brown suit jacket accentuates my darker skin tone and fits in fine with the event. I don't need fancy clothes to impress when I have wits and a charming smile.

Dad extends his hand, and the heavy scent of liquor burns my nostrils. "Glad you could make it."

As if I had a choice. He would've reamed me out had I not shown.

"Follow me." He releases Colleen's arm. Although she frowns, she doesn't dispute him, not here. She knows her place. Cameron stands, but Dad holds up his hand. "Not you."

His face falls, and schadenfreude bubbles within. I smother my wicked grin, pretending to smooth my beard. For years Dad has chosen him over me. If Cameron did better in sports or school, Dad's attention stayed on him. But I've always bested him when it came to business. Cameron may be good with numbers, but I'm good with numbers *and* people. I follow Dad to the patio where a group of men smoke, mind still focused on what Cameron mentioned.

"Jim." My dad takes a seat and lights our cigars. "Sit and chat."

My lungs expand with a satisfying breath as I puff on the tobacco, a plume of smoke billowing into the air. I imagined this day many times as a kid, when my dad would see me as worthy to sit beside him. It feels like I've finally crossed the finish line of a race I've been running for years.

"How was your first month?" Rodney Lewis, a potential investor, asks.

Intense. Exhausting. Thrilling. "It went well enough."

"Let's talk about your game plan to increase Thompson's investments." Dad cuts straight to the chase.

Rodney Lewis sits forward, stoking out the ember on his cigar as he faces me. I wasn't prepared to be put on the spot in front of potential clients, but I need to show my dad, and his business associates, that I'm serious about the job. Rubbing elbows and talking shop will help me use that network to the fullest.

Under the table, I wipe my slick palms on my trousers and do my best to speak slowly so I don't sound nervous as I convey the areas of opportunity we're missing, concluding with, "My coworker Stella gathered a list of available real estate investment trusts on the private market, and with that I'll draw up a more in-depth plan."

"Stella Daniels." Dad aims a pointed glance to the graying man beside him. "You remember my late business partner Robert. Apparently, his daughter is just as *helpful*." I'm not sure if it's the alcohol, or if he's suddenly been reminded of a memory, but his face contorts with a surprising dose of hostility. "She's dating my son."

Whiskey burns my esophagus, choking me. Dating? Stella is dating Cameron? That's not the woman he was kissing tonight. No wonder he didn't want me to talk to her at the pool the other day. How did that piece of shit ever land an amazing woman like her?

"Are you okay?" Mr. Lewis claps me on the back.

I hold up a hand and clear my throat. "I'm fine." My voice strains. "Whiskey went down the wrong way."

"Good," Dad says. "Any other areas of opportunity we're missing?"

Fuck, I can't concentrate now. "Umm." Stuck on the tip of my tongue, words refuse to formulate.

"Yes?" Dad squints at me like he's seeing double.

Businessmen clad in tuxedos that cost more than a car stare me down as I gather my thoughts. Even if I wasn't drinking or smoking, I'm sure my face would tell how embarrassed I am. My dad's face surely shows how ashamed he is of me.

"I...Well, I found that..." Stumbling over my words like an imbecile, I stop and take a slow drag of my cigar.

"Jameson?" The bite of my dad's admonishment snaps me into focus. His posture is rigid, and his glazed eyes hold a storm. He doesn't use my full name ever, so I know he's cross with me. "Where are our opportunities?"

"Sorry about that." I release the smoke into the air. I'd wanted to speak in private with my father about potentially bringing over some of my work from my old firm, but his imploring gaze throws me off kilter. "We don't have a foothold in the arts division. I've spoken with a few galleries, and they're willing to—"

"Artwork is the same whether you buy it from a gallery or from Walmart for twenty bucks," Dad retorts. His gaze is furious, and it's reminiscent of when he told me my dreams were childish and that being an artist wasn't a real job. Because of that, he's potentially losing an opportunity for immense growth. "Our clients want to invest in important things, like real estate, businesses, and retirement homes."

The men at the table nod, and my dad's forehead creases with disappointment. Dread pours into my stomach, and the whiskey I drank pushes up my throat.

"How do we get the younger population to invest with us?" one of the men at the table asks.

Finally, something I can answer. "Stella reminded me that we've been so focused on finding new clients that we're forgetting about the ones we have. Clients who feel appreciated, like they're family, are more likely to recommend the companies that make them feel this way. If we're treating our investors like a number, they'll see us as a company they hire, not family."

Another one of my dad's business associates nods. "She was the top advisor in your division for a while, Jameson. You could learn a lot from her. She's extremely smart."

"Much smarter than her father," Dad replies, eyes glazed over.

My mouth slacks, and I stare at my father. The underlying ire in his statement confuses me, but before I have a chance to ask him what he means, the table prompts me for more ideas.

I finish my whiskey and stamp out the cherry on the end of the cigar. "We can invite current and prospective clients to the holiday party. Our team will learn more about them and their families in order to gain connections. They'll focus on setting up savings accounts for children and grandchildren, consider different holidays they might want to save for, and inquire about current real estate ventures. Families should know what's important to each other. And I believe we'll have more accounts at the end of the year."

"Set it up." My dad stands, slightly wobbling before he recenters. I follow him into the corridor, and he pulls me to the side. "I don't know what's going on with you tonight but cut that bullshit out with the art talk. You're not in London at some measly investment firm."

My mouth dries, heat crawling up my neck.

"We want clients like McCombs or Goldsbury, not some half-baked artist painting on the street." He runs a hand through his hair and pastes a smile on his face as people pass us by. "If we can get Lewis investing with

Thompson before the conference, it'll give some of the other magnates' confidence to invest with us too. Focus on that instead of chasing some childish pipedream."

Hearing him talk about art this way needles me, but he's right. I was never good enough, and he knew it. *This* is what I'm good at, where I can make the most difference if I get my head on straight. I itch to snap the rubber band but resist.

"I'll see if Lewis can swing by the office sometime in the next week or two. I want him to meet with you and Rosay. Don't fuck it up."

He strides away, and I head back inside to grab another drink. Cameron is at the bar, his hand resting on the blonde's arse, head nestled into her neck. Her midwestern accent grates my nerves and my fists clench at my sides, heat rushing through my body.

Stella doesn't deserve to be lied to and cheated on, but I also can't tell her without divulging why I know Cameron, or risk losing the chance my dad has given me. If people find out my dad wants his illegitimate son to run his in-law's company, their faith in him *and* me will be lost.

He'll blame me.

That can't happen.

Chapter Eleven
Stella

Two lists cover the table. One is clients I'd like to pitch Thompson's services to, and the other has upcoming classes to complete my master's degree. I've been working to the bone for the last month to outshine Jameson. Mr. Weston wants to see our action plan for nabbing the highest profile client at the weekly meeting, and this jumpstart is exactly what I need.

A man in a brown uniform exits the elevator holding a bouquet of roses and I cringe for the poor soul he's giving those to. I'm no expert, but I've seen every version of flower working in a funeral home, and the bigger the bouquet, the sorrier someone is.

Rosay plops on a chair in front of my desk, a tuna sandwich in her hand. "Who's getting the flowers?"

I shrug. "Some poor unfortunate soul."

"Maybe it's you." She shimmies and brushes crumbs off her top before stealing a water from my mini fridge. "Are we still working out later?"

"Not a chance," I reply. "And yes to the gym."

My eyes track the delivery man as he stops at one of the secretaries' desks, and a second later she points to my office.

"No," Rosay gasps, a smile cracking her face. "Who would've sent you flowers?"

"Who says those are for me?" I scoff. "She could've been pointing to you. Maybe Alex is trying to woo you again."

She scoffs, "Alex knows he can't handle all this woman."

My heart rate ticks up the closer the delivery man gets. I loathe flowers, and whoever might've sent these doesn't know me very well. CJ hasn't sent me flowers since we first started dating (outside of apology flowers, case in point), and it's not a special holiday.

The man stops outside my door. "Stella Daniels?"

"I knew it." Rosay hops up from the chair and takes the bouquet from the man. She frowns as she reads the card and she sets down the flowers.

"Who's it from?"

She hands me the card, and my forehead wrinkles. Jameson stops at my office like he has something important to say, but then his eyes settle on the large bouquet on my desk, and his face sours. A flash of anger speeds across his features before he schools it. He turns and leaves the office without saying a word, snapping a rubber band on his wrist.

"What the hell was that?" Rosay asks.

I shrug.

At this point, I feel like I'm in the twilight zone. Something is up with Jameson, CJ has gone off the rails, and my focus needs to be on getting this promotion. Pop-Pop and I have a loan extension meeting with the bank soon, and I need to show them we'll turn it around. Even if I don't get promoted, having the McCombs accounts would bring in the type of income needed to stave off foreclosure.

"I don't know what's going on with these men, but I'm not letting them get to me."

My phone vibrates, CJ's name flashing on the screen.

"I'll let you take that." Rosay scurries to the door. "Good luck. I'll see you at the gym."

I exhale and answer. "Hey, CJ."

"Hey, babe. Did the flowers come?"

"Yes, they did," I grit out, logging into my system.

"So?" He whispers. "Can I take you to dinner?"

My attention wavers, thoughts scattering when my inbox loads.

"Stella?"

"Oh, yeah." I stumble over my thoughts. "That's not a good idea. We're both feeling out this new friendship. It's probably best we don't blur the lines."

"Friends go to dinner all the time."

He's not wrong, but I can read between the lines. He's regretting his decision not to fight for us. "It's not a good idea, and I don't have time right now. I have to focus on work and the funeral home." I scan the email and my pulse quickens. "I've got to go, CJ."

I hang up and maximize my screen, staring at an email stating Charlotte McCombs can meet. Squealing, I get up from my desk and head to inform Mr. Weston.

"I haven't worked this hard for you to be a disappointment," Mr. Weston's raised voice stops me outside his door.

I lean closer to hear what the other person is saying but can't decipher their voice.

"I'm sick of the excuses. I've got enough to deal with right now, and you're adding to my stress."

A coworker startles me as they pass by. Figuring it's not a good idea to continue eavesdropping, I knock on the door and wait to be called inside.

"Come in," Mr. Weston says.

I open the door and still, surprised to find it's Jameson being reamed out by the boss. I figured after their buddy-buddy meeting at the Dominion the other day, they'd be thick as thieves right now. A blip of smugness rises in my chest. Jameson won't be happy to hear about my success.

"Yes, Stella?"

I snap out of my trance and look at Mr. Weston. "I've got some good news."

Jameson fiddles with something on his wrist as his jaw ticks, and I recall his reaction to seeing my flowers earlier. Is he angry with me for something?

"I've got a meeting with Charlotte McCombs."

I didn't think it was possible for Jameson's eyes to get stormier, but the minute Mr. Weston sighs, almost disappointedly, darkness encompasses Jameson's gaze, and the air in the room gets heavy.

"That's great, Stella," Mr. Weston grits out, his focus on the gloomy man opposite me.

He seems unhappy it was me and not Jameson who acquired the McCombs meeting, but I won't let their less than stellar reactions dampen my excitement.

"Well," I say, filling the awkward silence. "That's all I came to say."

"Thanks for letting me know, Stella." Mr. Weston drags a hand through his hair, his fingers massaging the back of his neck. "Glad to see someone takes this promotion opportunity seriously."

With that last jab at Jameson, I make my escape.

***

Running must've been invented by the devil.

After forty minutes of treadmill, all I've got to show for it is a cramp in my leg and a sports bra drenched with sweat. Rosay's on the elliptical, dancing to some techno beat thumping from her headphones as I stretch the aching muscle. I usually prefer to work out at home, but Thompson's gym is elite and has a great view of the pool.

I promised I'd get over my fear of the pool after the fiasco at Mindy's party, and I intend to start today. The entire run I spent pumping myself up to get into the water. I marveled at the people swimming laps inside the cordoned-off lanes and tried to visualize doing the same. Now, it's time to take the first step.

I wave to Rosay and head into the locker room to shower and change into my bathing suit. Everyone has left for the day, so hopefully I won't see any coworkers.

Water fills the cracks between the tiles, wetting my feet as I creep toward the pool. I shake out my hands, and swallowing becomes difficult the closer I get to the edge. *You can do this, Stella. You've got this,* I keep telling myself.

Realistically, I know there's no way I can drown if I'm standing, but three feet of water almost took my life when I was young. It's not as innocent as it seems.

My lungs freeze as I place my hand on the cold steel railing leading into the pool. The empty pit in my stomach clenches when I move to the first step, sending small ripples through the crystal-clear abyss. A bubble of glee rises in me at the small feat I've accomplished.

Feeling brave, I inch to the next step. I'm about to move when the door to the pool opens and Jameson storms inside, a black gym bag slung over his shoulders. He doesn't notice me at first, which is probably because I'm frozen in fear, half because of the water and half because he startled me.

He's snapping the same rubber band he keeps around his wrist, and mumbling like he's trying to calm down.

"Jameson," I say, slowly backing out of the pool. "You okay?"

"What are you doing here?" His voice is strained, his eyes wild as he looks over his shoulder.

"What's wrong? You seem upset."

He ignores me, snapping his rubber band and continues toward the locker rooms.

I follow.

"Would you slow down? You have like seven inches on me."

"Why don't you speed up? I'm a busy man."

"You're such an asshole," I murmur.

"I heard that."

I make it to the locker room as he's about to push open the door. "I meant for you to hear it."

"What do you want?" He steps close, our bodies nearly touching. His cedar cologne mixes with the smell of chlorine, somehow creating a lethal combination of danger and sex appeal.

"I—I wanted to..." I stutter when he meets my gaze.

"You want to what?"

We're less than an arm's length away from each other, nearly sharing breath. His throat bobs with a swallow and mine mirrors it, causing lust to roll through my center.

"Go on, spit it out."

"I wanted to know if you..." I stop, close my eyes, and inhale a deep breath.

He steps closer and I back up to the door. Leaning close to my ear so no one can hear him, he says, "Let me save you the trouble. I'm no damsel in distress, Stella. I don't need your help, nor do I want it. You should be focused on your meeting, not pretending like you care what happened in mine."

My mouth falls open and my cheeks heat. Whatever I expected him to say, that wasn't it. I'm not happy the meeting with Mr. Weston upset him enough for him to react like this. But I guess it's nice to know he's not a machine and beneath that cold demeanor are actual feelings.

He's not wrong though. I should be focused on my meeting, and even though I can tell he's struggling with something, he keeps pushing me away, afraid to let someone in. "I wasn't trying to help you, asshole."

"Fine." He steps out of my space. "Then what did you want?"

I look back at the pool, not meeting his eyes. "I was gonna ask if you'd teach me how to swim. But forget it."

I storm away from him and into the women's locker room. After changing back into my work clothes, I leave all thoughts of helping Jameson behind.

Chapter Twelve
Jameson

Concentrating on Excel sheets while hungover is made significantly more difficult by the sheer amount of people stopping by my office this morning. After a quick pop-in from Patty, I shut the door and retreat to my desk, groaning as my cell phone rings. Noting the caller, my shoulders fall.

"Hey, Mike."

"What the hell, dude? You were supposed to meet me at the bar to watch the game last night."

"I'm sorry, mate." My head throbs as I sit at my desk. "Work was a disaster and I guess I forgot."

"You forgot?" he asks. "When have you ever forgotten anything? You're like a walking calendar."

The lie leaves a bitter tang in my mouth. Mike is right. I never flake out on things I've committed to. "If you knew the week I've had, you'd understand."

"Well, it must've been pretty bad for you to miss beer and wing night."

The mention of alcohol makes my gut churn.

Mike's my best mate. He's the only one who knows about my past with self-harm, knows I sought therapy to help me cope better. If I tell him I'm struggling he'll freak out, and I'm already at the end of my thin rope.

Statistically speaking, I know I'm part of the thirty-five percent of men who self-harm to cope, but I went to therapy and got help. I'll never be cured, but I should be strong enough to withstand the pressure I'm under.

I was doing better before I moved to the States to take over this position, but now that I have it, I can't go back. I can't let Dad see I'm floundering or else he'll assume I can't handle the job and he'll give it to Cameron.

I need to be stronger, to fight the urge.

"I got sloshed last night and am paying for it now." I run a hand through my no longer greasy, vomit-covered hair.

"You got drunk by yourself?" His questioning tone makes me sweaty. "You sure you're alright?"

Why does he have to be such a good mate? Why can't he be like every other person I know who is too involved in their own lives to notice anything wrong in others? I drag a hand down my face and squeeze my jaw. If he was here with me, I wouldn't be able to look him in the eye.

"I'm fine, mate. Thanks for checking in on me. I'll see you on Friday?"

"Uh, yeah, sure. I'll see you then. Let me know if you need anything."

"Will do."

I squeeze my phone and force myself to put it in my pocket so I don't pitch it across the hallway. Snapping my rubber band, I count down from twenty and head toward the office bathroom.

Dark, sunken eyes stare back at me. I splash some water on my face and grip the sides of the porcelain sink, hanging my head in defeat. I was doing so well before this.

I had a plan to impress my dad by turning around Thompson's numbers, but I messed that up. Had Patty not given me the number for Stella's grandparent's funeral home, my head would be on straight.

Who am I kidding? I would've met Stella during the meeting at work, and my knees still would've gone weak. But it doesn't matter. She was probably so turned off by hearing my dad berate me yesterday she'll never look at me with those honey eyes again.

I've got to get over this fascination with her.

I enter the cubicle to use the toilet instead of the urinal. The idea of someone potentially seeing the scars at the top of my thighs causes my stomach to curl. I slide my hand over the bumpy skin, cursing myself for being weak in the first place.

The bathroom door bangs open as I'm debating whether I should cope by getting another tattoo. It's been a while, and I could use the stress relief.

How can you make it to a tattoo appointment but not a therapy appointment?

Cameron is leaning against the sink when I finish.

"Why are you standing there like a creep?" I ask. "Sod off."

"I know what you are doing."

Anxiety and frustration slide down my spine, mixing a volatile cocktail. He couldn't know what I was doing, right? Unsure of what to say, I use sarcasm to throw him off. "I thought it was rather obvious seeing as we're in the bathroom, but kudos to you for your observation."

"I can't wait to watch you crash and burn."

"What do you want?" I snap, feeling overheated and exhausted. "I'm busy."

"I know you're after her, but she isn't gonna downgrade like Dad did. You'd be a pity fuck like your mom was."

I'm not mad he called my mum a pity fuck; I know my dad didn't love her. Not even after she deserted me in high school and followed him back to the States. But nothing between Stella and I could be considered a pity fuck. I would worship her. Her flawless curves, the smooth expanse of neck I've imagined biting and kissing, the radiant brown skin I've longed to taste.

No, it wouldn't be a pity fuck.

It'd be explosive.

My patience unravels, and my fist collides with his mouth before I have a chance to consider my actions.

Blood trickles down his lip, and he touches it before looking in the mirror. "You split my lip, dickwad."

He spits blood at my feet, and I jump back. The wicked smile on his face makes me realize I've just given him ammo, and it makes my stomach spin.

"I'm sure Dad and HR will love to hear about how you're breaking under the pressure of the job," he sneers.

Fuck. He's right. This job, my dad's expectations, and Stella are all getting to me, and I'm spiraling. Had I been in the right headspace I wouldn't have hit Cameron. He's an arse, but he's always been that way. Too much stress is making me lose focus.

I chance a look at my knuckles. Thankfully, they're not split. If I have any chance to turn this around, here's my opportunity. I step into Cameron's space and bring myself to my full height. "Or, Dad will see how pathetic your attempts at getting his attention are. He's already put me in touch with his network, and you're still down on the third floor."

He sucks his teeth and wipes the blood away from his lip. "He's using you. He'll never actually love you." He skulks to the door. "Stay the hell away from Stella."

The door swings shut behind him. I take a few calming breaths and head to my office to gather my materials for the meeting. Checking my email, I find a response from a gallery I hope will invest with Thompson.

I know my dad told me to let it go, but when he sees the growth potential, he'll be proud I stood my ground.

I think about what happened in the bathroom, how I've started to unravel. It's time to make another therapy appointment. I can't keep pushing it aside anymore.

Breathing in the hint of berries and vanilla in the air, I stop outside a conference room door. I find myself drawn toward a soft murmur coming from the room. The door is cracked, so I pop my head inside. Stella paces the floor, her long brown curls floating behind her as she pivots. I tell myself to focus and show some restraint, but my heart trampolines in my chest the minute her silky voice floats through the air.

She steps past me with her head down and her scent floats into my nose.

I hold my breath, nervous she'll start yelling at me for how I treated her the other day, and also because I want that scent to become part of my bloodstream. I want to bottle it and diffuse it in my soul.

But I can't.

I won't.

I need to cleanse her from everything in my life if I want to show my dad I'm serious about leading this company.

She tugs on her lip, a deep line forming on her forehead. Who is she talking to? Is it Cameron?

I push through the door, and she startles. "Taking personal calls on company time?"

She murmurs into the phone and ends the call, breezing past me without another word. I follow, intent on apologizing for my comment the other day, but she's already back inside the main room where the rest of the team awaits. She doesn't acknowledge me when I sit beside her and instead focuses on the blank screen at the front of the room.

"You know, if you stare long enough something might appear on it."

She ignores me, but the muscle in her jaw twitches like she wants to say something.

"Let's get started." Dad enters and pulls up a PowerPoint. "We'll be holding the holiday party for our clients at the Hyatt Regency in December."

A round of oOo's and ah's fill the room. He clears his throat and gives the team an impatient stare. Once they're refocused, he hands out papers and waits for them to be dispersed.

"Remember, this is an opportunity to show your clients and the board you're invested in growing with us. Some of you may not be with us in the New Year."

The room falls silent.

My dad nods. "The conference will be held in December, so you have enough time to schmooze clients and increase accounts. Your future with this company will be determined by your success at the conference."

Stella scoffs and I tense, ready to defend her if my father unloads on her. He doesn't like being challenged or disrespected in any way, so I'm surprised when he moves on without comment.

"You're dismissed," Dad says. "Jim, stay after."

Stella murmurs, "No surprise there," under her breath and leaves.

A blip of nervousness rises in my chest. Does she notice the attention my dad gives me because she's my opponent, or does she assume something else is going on? Did Cameron tell her about our familial connection to keep her away from me?

My head spins as the last person closes the door. Feeling like now is the right time to tell him about my meeting with the art director, I open my mouth to speak but he cuts me off.

"You impressed Lewis the other evening at the party. He wants to meet next week."

Tension melts from my body. "That's great."

"Use Stella's idea about setting up accounts for the family. If it works, the team will be more supportive of you." This feels wrong, but I nod.

"Great." He gets up from the table. "You and Rosay meet with him. He wants to buy some real estate out in West Texas, and Rosay advises the oil tycoon accounts. She'll be a benefit to have on your team."

Uneasiness seeps into my mind and wrinkles my nose. "I thought you wanted me to go after a larger client."

He shakes his head. "You've been unfocused this past week. Impress me with this client, then we'll see about a bigger fish."

My heartbeat slugs around my chest, and the squeezing sensation in my ribs tightens. He's not outwardly saying it, but he's disappointed. He doesn't believe I have what it takes, and it's my fault because I've been distracted.

I snap the band around my wrist. "I'll get the meeting set up right away."

He leaves, and I count down as I stiffly walk to the door, trying to relax as I go on a search for Rosay. I find her in the break room laughing with Alex. "Can I speak with you?"

Alex glares at me. He must be on Team Stella, like everyone else. I'll win them over eventually, when I can concentrate on anything besides showing Dad he didn't make the wrong decision.

"Sure." She waves off Alex. "What's up?"

I'm too tense as I sit across from her, relaying the information my dad told me. When she doesn't tell me to get lost, I relax into the chair and take a deep breath. I was worried she'd tell me to beg off since I'm her best friend's opponent, but excitement spreads across her face.

Maybe working with me isn't such a terrible idea for everyone like it is for Stella.

"Why me though?" Rosay asks. "Stella is the real estate whiz.'

Stella is? Aligning the woman struggling to keep her family's funeral home open and the real estate whiz doesn't compute. And why did my dad suggest Rosay instead of her? He didn't even mention Stella's expertise. Unless he's still not sure I'm up to the task of being project manager and is considering promoting Stella instead.

The thought sours the tea in my stomach.

Faced with the knowledge and shame of disappointing him, I deflate. How am I supposed to defeat her when she's got the edge on me at every corner?

"You and I will work better as a team."

She laughs, and I swear the table shakes. "I'm not so sure about that. You and Stella have fire between y'all."

I huff. "The word you're looking for is disdain."

It's a lie, and I know it the minute I say it. I don't have disdain for Stella. Quite the opposite. I want her, so badly it's the only thing I can think about some days. Anytime I can get a rise out of her, to make her notice me in some way, my attraction grows deeper. Our verbal banter and her cutting remarks make my heart race. Sure, it's usually with anger, but at this point, I'll bask in anything other than self-loathing.

"Y'all can keep telling yourselves that, but everyone else sees it."

Is Stella telling herself the same thing? My breathing slows, and my heart beats in my throat. I shouldn't care if Stella feels the same way, but I do. It doesn't matter though. One of us will get the promotion, and the two meetings I've set up today will ensure it's me who ends up on top.

"I'll send you the details for the meeting."

We leave the break room, and as I'm returning to my desk, Stella exits the supply closet.

"Hey," I say.

She nods but doesn't answer, her focus solely on the folder in her hand. I follow.

"Can we talk?" I ask.

"About what?" She doesn't stop.

"Stop, Stella." I place a hand on her shoulder, the warmth of her skin burning through her white blouse. A shiver zips through my core and heads straight to my trousers. She shouldn't have this effect on me.

She shakes me off and spins around. "What do you want?"

Unsure of what overcomes me, I tilt her chin up, forcing her to look at me. "Stop ignoring me."

Her breathy gasp makes my stomach clench, and one by one the organs in my body combust. Heat rushes up my back, and my mouth dries as she turns and enters her office. I follow like cattle to the slaughter. Stella stands behind her desk, her shoulders slack and head down as she takes a deep breath.

"About the other day." I knock my fingers on the door jamb, trying to gather my words. "I shouldn't have—"

"Shouldn't have what?" Anger replaces what I thought was lust. "Been a dick to me when it was you that offered in the first place? Save yourself the ego pet. My feelings are fine."

"That's not what I was going to say." My shoulders slump, and I perch on the edge of her desk, toying with the band on my wrist. "I'm sorry for how I acted. It was rude, and it won't happen again."

She rolls her eyes.

I could stop speaking and hope all would be forgiven, but my mouth refuses to shut. "I had a shit meeting, and I took my anger out on the first person I saw. I'm truly sorry."

Her tongue darts out to moisten her lips, and I nearly groan at the sight. "I appreciate the apology."

"Good." The tension in my stomach dissipates. "Now back to this whole swimming business."

She waves a hand in the air. "Forget it."

I step close and force her to look up at me. "I'll teach you."

Her dark lashes flutter. "No, Jameson. Don't worry about it. We both have more important things to be doing."

"I told you I would, and I meant it. Next Thursday night. Six o'clock. Don't be late."

My words are sharp, delivered in a deep voice that leaves no room for rebuttal as I back out of the office.

Chapter Thirteen
Stella

After working all day, I set up meetings with two clients and register for an eight-week derivative marketing class that meets in the evenings. It may be a struggle between helping Pop-Pop with the funeral home and getting my schoolwork finished on top of my actual work, but when it's all said and done, I'll be better equipped to go after the bigger clients.

I'm determined to start checking off things on my list.

A knock on my office door steals my attention. "Come in."

CJ enters and plops into the chair in front of my desk, playing with the candy in the bowl. "Your birthday is coming up."

"Yes?"

He cocks his head to the side. "Could I take you out for lunch…like old times?"

I exhale and clasp my hands on top of the desk. "CJ, I told you the other day it wasn't a good idea for us to blur the lines."

He slumps. "What if we go out with a group? We can invite Rosay and some of the other coworkers so it isn't a date."

"I'm not opposed to that idea. Let me know a date, and I'll check my calendar."

He smiles, but his cheeks don't touch his eyes like they normally do when he's happy.

Regret swirls in my stomach.

The four years we spent together weren't bad, but we were on two different pages of the same book, and both of us were scared to turn the page. I'm glad I mustered up the courage.

We both deserve better than what we were giving each other.

"Sounds good." He disappears out the door.

Jameson passes and gives a half smile on his way to the conference room for our daily meeting. He's dressed in all black, shirt sleeves buttoned at his wrists to hide the tattoos I know are there. My mind wanders, picturing what other images are etched onto his beautiful brown skin.

Why it's always the assholes who are the hottest is beyond me. The more I learn about Jameson, the more I'm attracted to him, and the more attracted to him I am, the angrier I get with myself. My body shouldn't immediately perk up when he's near, and my vagina definitely doesn't need to roll out the red carpet for him when he speaks in that deep English accent. It'll take herculean effort to focus during our swim lesson if I can't get him out of my head.

I sit beside Rosay in the conference room. It's her team's day to present the market updates to Mr. Weston and the board. Stealing glances at Jameson helps me pass the time, but when my phone goes off in my back pocket with Pop-Pop's vibration pattern, I know something is wrong.

He never calls.

Excusing myself, I pretend I need the restroom and slip out the door.

"Hey, Pop-Pop." My heart beats in my throat. "What's up?"

"Stella," he sighs. "We have a bit of an issue."

My ears perk up, palm pressed to my now speeding heart. "What kind of issue? Is everything okay?"

My mind runs haywire, imagining all the worst possible things that could've happened. Was there a fire? Did someone break in and steal all the caskets? Is there a dead body…that we didn't get from the morgue?

Pop-Pop halts the doomsday train running through my head. "A pipe burst, and flooded the first viewing room."

Uttering a soft curse, I sag back into the bathroom wall. "Thank goodness it wasn't worse. I'll head right over."

"No," he says. "Stay there. I just wanted to let you know what happened."

He says no, but I can tell by the waver in his voice that he needs me. Pop-Pop is a proud man, not willing to ask for help.

"Don't worry about it. My work is done for the day." I lie because the last thing he needs is to worry about me. I'll feign needing to buy feminine products, and the men will be so uncomfortable they'll shoo me away.

"Punkin, I can handle it."

"I know you can, Old Man." I leave the bathroom and head back toward the conference room. "I'll be there soon."

His goodbye is cut off by me dropping my phone as I run into Jameson.

"Where are you going in a hurry?" He bends to pick it up, a zing of heat spreading up my arm when our fingers brush.

Why does my body react to him this way? It would be so nice to see him as my enemy, the man who can ruin my life and squash my Pop-Pop's dreams, but I don't. He's a nuisance for sure, but the draw to him is like fire to kindling.

"Sorry for running into you, but I've gotta go." I take the phone from him and turn to leave.

A warm hand wraps around my wrist. "Is everything okay?"

My eyes fall to his long fingers, and the heat I felt earlier spreads between my legs. "Yes," I mutter, breathless. "A pipe burst at the funeral home."

Shit, shit, shit. Already messing up my lie.

"Do you need a ride?" he asks, genuine concern in his voice. "Anything I can help with?"

My heart threatens to explode inside my chest at his offer. I admonish the stupid organ and refocus on my task. I need to show him, and everyone else, that I can handle both.

"No, I'm fine. Thanks for the offer, but I've got it."

He nods and releases my hand. "Let me know if you need anything."

I curl my fingers into my palm, sad at the loss of heat as I speed towards the elevator. At this point, I'm not sure if I'm running to Pop-Pop or away from Jameson. One feels dangerous, and the other feels like I'm being pulled underwater.

I speed across town. At the funeral home, a plumbing company van is parked in front of the entrance.

"Pops?" I yell, stepping through the door.

"In here, Stella."

I follow the large hoses snaking through the funeral home to Pop-Pop chatting with a man in a gray uniform. Pop-Pop's dark skin is pale, but his eyes still light up when he sees me.

"What happened?" I ask.

"Looks like one of the cremation pans was knocked over and clogged the drain." His shoulders slump.

The plumber supplies a more in-depth answer. "All the water was diverted to the drain underneath the first room, and it flooded."

A slow, rhythmic thumping starts in my head. "How bad is it?"

"Don't you worry about that, Stella," Pop-Pop says. "I've got insurance."

I rub my temples and take a deep breath. "Our insurance covers fires, not water damage."

The hand wrapped around Pop-Pop's cane tightens, and the dark lines of his face pull into a frown. My gut churns, and my mind spins on how to fix this. With the water removal and the plumbing bill, we're probably looking at thousands in damages, not to mention having to cancel the next two days' cremations.

"We'll figure it out, Pops." I turn to the plumber. "Can we work out a payment plan?"

He gives me the information for their billing department and packs up his supplies. Pop-Pop and I head to the office in silence. At the desk, I bring up the accounting spreadsheets and add this bill to the mix. Watching the cells automatically total calms me, but also ticks up my anxiety. I practice some breathing techniques to calm my racing heart.

Pop-Pop needs me to be strong and to have a plan.

"Maybe it's time we look into selling," Pop-Pop says, disappointment evident in his strained voice.

My mouth falls open. "Absolutely not. You and Nunny built this business from the ground up."

"But Stella—"

"No, Pops." I close the spreadsheet and look at him. "This is your dream. We can't give up yet."

"I don't want—"

I shuffle through the papers on the desk. "I can do the two cremations we need to push if I arrive at three instead of five. I'll also reach out to the county morgue to let them know we'll be open on Wednesday when we're normally closed. We can recoup the money we're losing by opening on my normal off day."

"But you have things you need to focus on at work."

"I can do it all, Pops." I get up and put the folders away. "I have a big meeting coming up next week that will hopefully secure me that promotion, and I've already added a client to my portfolio. I'll be fine."

"We have that loan meeting on Wednesday."

I sigh.

The dreaded loan meeting.

When Nunny passed, we were drowning in grief, and surrounded by it. She was the rock of our little family, the glue that held us together. Her last few months, Pop-Pop spent most of the time at her bedside while I handled the funeral home part-time and worked remotely. I was so overloaded I didn't realize we'd gotten behind on bills. The result was taking out a loan to catch up, and we're still paying that with the interest.

Had I been entirely focused on either job, I wouldn't have made so many mistakes. But I'm aware of my failings now, and better prepared to handle the pressures of both obligations. With Pop-Pop back, we've fallen into a good rhythm.

"I can get the cremations done and make it in time for the loan meeting." I take off my heels and slip into a pair of flats I keep hidden in the desk drawer. "Let's pull the carpet out into the parking lot and I'll rent a shampooer."

He nods and heads to the viewing room. Passing through the hallway, I swipe a hand along the picture of Pop-Pop and Nunny in front of the building when they first opened. Their smiles are wide, their eyes filled with excitement and love.

My heart squeezes inside my chest.

I'll do whatever it takes to keep their dream alive.

Chapter Fourteen
Jameson

Phone calls, emails, and Zoom chats fill up my morning schedule as I attempt to get in contact with someone at the McCombs empire. If I can somehow land an in-person meeting within the next week or so, my father won't push back on the deal I'm working with the Witte Gallery. Managing that and meeting with some of my coworkers to get a feel for their work ethic and goals as advisors, has me feeling ready for when I become Project Manager.

Sitting in my office, I fail to keep my mind off Stella. The door is open, and each time someone passes by my chest tightens. I'm looking for her, but I shouldn't be. I tell myself to focus and show some restraint, but my lungs expand with my held breath each time I hear her voice.

My intercom beeps and Patty whispers, "Your father is on line one, and he doesn't sound happy."

My stomach knots. I drag a hand down my face, squeezing my jaw. Answering the phone is the last thing I want to do, but I know I need to take the verbal lashing that's about to happen like a man. I'm not sure what I could've done, but these days he's more on edge than usual.

"Brooks." I answer formally.

"Jim." Dad's voice is terse. "You didn't pack me the folders I asked you to, and now I'm stuck in a meeting without them. I'll text the address I need you to bring them to."

I straighten, my whole body tense. I don't remember him asking me to put together any folders for him, but I've been so distracted with setting up my own meeting and keeping away from Stella that maybe I forgot. I glance at my watch, checking I have enough time before my next meeting. Even if I'm a few minutes late, Rosay can start, and I'll jump in when I arrive.

"Okay, I'll go up now and get them."

He hangs up, and a minute later my phone pings with the address.

I ask Patty to unlock his office. She huffs like I'm inconveniencing her, but opens the door.

Stark-white walls filled with awards greet me as I enter. As a kid, I used to imagine Dad would display my artwork here. I painted canvas after canvas, perfecting my technique. It wasn't the beautiful cottage by the ocean, or the typical farmhouse brimming with stacks of hay and cows. Looking back now, I can see the darkening clouds dashing the sky, the imminent storm, and the crashing waves I drew for what they were: the chaos inside of me. I'd always been attracted to the dark, the avant-garde, but he didn't appreciate his son playing with paints like a child. He promptly showed me by tearing my canvas and throwing away my brushes and oil paints.

I walk straight to his desk, feeling like I'm intruding. An array of folders, each a different color, sit stacked in neat piles. He didn't mention which folders he needs, but a quick peek at his calendar to see what meeting he attends helps narrow it down. In my haste, I knock over another set of folders, sending papers flying and floating to the floor. I gather the papers, looking at each name to make sure they go back in the right folder.

A familiar name catches my eye, my usual curiosity at anything involving Stella firing in a heartbeat.

I shouldn't scan the documents, but I do, my stomach churning when I find a blind trust of two million dollars where my father is the trustee, and a land trust for a home out in the Hill Country. I tilt my head, hoping to make sense of what I see. Stella's name, along with my father and another man I assume is Stella's father, have access to this trust. But if Stella has two million dollars sitting around, why is she working here? And why is she so stressed about the funeral home?

A tingle at the base of my neck fills me with a sense of unease. Does my dad's Hill Country property belong to Stella? Because the trust is blind, she may not know it even exists.

It's my dad's fiduciary duty to inform her.

If I ask her about it, she may wonder why the boss is letting me have access to those types of documents and cause more questions to arise than I have answers to. Unsure of what to do, I decide to ask my dad when I drop off the folders.

"Jim?" Patty's voice draws near, and I shove the rest of the papers back into the folder and place it neatly on the desk.

"Coming." I grab the stack of documents my father needs.

The drive to Boerne isn't terrible now that morning rush hour is over. Passing Six Flags and La Cantera mall, I make my way up Interstate 10 and pull into the parking lot of an engineering composite company.

Dad meets me at the entrance. His face is pulled into a frown as he snatches the folders from me. "Took you long enough."

"I wasn't sure which ones you needed."

His gaze narrows, and it's on the tip of my tongue to ask him about Stella's trust, but someone calls his name from inside.

"Come to the house this evening," he demands. "I have another client for you to meet."

I open my mouth to tell him I have an appointment tonight and can't make it, but I know he'll probe me for details. Any mention of therapy when I was a kid was met with a laugh and a brush-off, citing men who needed therapy as weak-minded. That's the last thing I need him to think about me.

"Okay."

He spins on his heels and leaves. Back in my car, I shoot a text to inform Rosay I'm on my way and that I'll most likely be a few minutes late, and call to cancel my therapy appointment.

Again.

A few minutes turns into twenty as I drive into gridlock. My phone vibrates in my pocket as horns sound in the distance and a fire engine passes. I answer it, assuming it's Rosay. "What?"

"Where the hell are you?" My dad's voice bleeds with anger. "Lewis showed up for the meeting and your advisor isn't there and neither are you."

"I'm on my way, there's an—"

"You should've been back twenty minutes ago." He cuts me off, voice lethal and cold. "I put you in this position because I thought you could handle it, not to make me look stupid."

"I'll fix this." I grit my teeth.

Offering an explanation is pointless. He'd see it as an excuse. I call Patty to help do damage control.

Once the traffic clears, I arrive at the Thompson building in record time, running up the stairs instead of waiting for the elevator. I stop to catch my breath and fix my suit before I push through the door and rush to Rosay's office. I bump into Stella midway down the hall, grabbing her hand to stop her.

"Where's Rosay?" My voice is clipped.

She opens her mouth, but the elevator dings and Rosay exits, her pink hair a tangled mess on her head.

I march over to her. "Where the hell have you been? If you've cocked up this deal —"

"I got stuck in traffic." Her face flashes with a wave of anger before she smooths out her features. "Give me a few minutes and I'll meet you in your office."

Hearing she was in the same gridlock I was softens my anger and makes me feel like a wanker. Patty hurries over to me. "Mr. Lewis is in your office with a cup of coffee and a muffin. I told him you were held up in another meeting."

I breathe a sigh of relief, snapping my rubber band as I head to my office.

***

"How do you think that went?" Rosay asks.

We finished our nearly three-hour meeting about viable real estate options with Mr. Lewis, and although I thought it went well, he asked for time to consider.

"Eh, not too bad."

Lewis is a hard man, one who prides himself on the way he does business. Being late made us look unprepared and disorganized. I can't let that happen again if I want my father to see I'm ready to go after the big clients.

"I bet it went well." She grabs her folders and stops at the door. "Or at least I hope so."

My phone vibrates on the desk, Dad's name flashing on the screen. Rosay remains at the door, and I don't want to have this conversation in front of her. "Anything else?"

"We're all going out to lunch for one of the co-worker's birthdays tomorrow, if you want to join."

Lunch with my coworkers could help boost their confidence in me, but I've got a lot on my plate with the meetings Dad has set up for me and don't want to be bogged down by plans. The phone screen darkens, and my heart rate ticks up. Missing his call will cause trouble. I need to hurry her out of my office.

"I'll pass, thanks."

"Okay, I'll let Stella know."

"Stella?" My head snaps up so quickly I jerk my neck.

Shit.

Rosay's smile widens. "I knew it."

I rub the back of my neck. "Knew what?"

"You're hot for her."

My jaw tenses, and I walk to the door, shutting it. "Goodbye, Rosay."

"Douchebag," she murmurs from the other side.

The phone screen illuminates again, the vibrations of the desk tickling my hand. I swallow and close my eyes. "Brooks."

"What the hell happened?" His voice is pure venom.

My vocal cords constrict. No excuse will make a difference, even if it wasn't my fault but his for forgetting the folders. "An accident held up traffic. Patty chatted with Lewis while we got set up."

"How did the meeting go?"

"It went well." I pull at the hairs on my arm, letting the pain calm me as I recount our meeting.

"I'm holding you personally responsible if this doesn't pan out."

A tightness grips my chest.

My mistakes make him look bad.

Weak.

He vouched for me, and I failed.

Regret swells in my stomach. "Yes, sir."

"I'll reiterate the benefits to Rodney," he says, a tightness to his voice. "You better have your shit together for the meeting tonight."

I purse my lips, drawing in a deep breath. "Yes, sir."

I don't wait for the screen to go dark before I throw my stapler at the wall.

Patty rushes in, her hand splayed across her chest, her eyes wide and questioning. "What the hell was that? Are you okay?"

I press my knuckles into the desk, my voice low and deadly. "I'm fine."

She glares at me for my tone but quickly leaves. I pace my office floor, snapping the rubber band. The skin on my wrist is raw and broken, slashed with angry red lines. Inhaling and exhaling isn't working, and the control is quickly slipping from my grasp.

"Buck up, Jameson," I say aloud.

My dad's reputation.

The company's reputation.

All of it hinges on whether I'm good enough to run it once he's gone.

The blood pulsing against my eardrums, the quick rise of my chest, the tension flooding every muscle and making me stiff. They're all signs my control is slipping, and I need to get it back. I can't break down when my dad needs me the most.

I go to the pool to gain some clarity and peace before the meeting tonight.

Chapter Fifteen
Stella

Pop-Pop is a creature of habit.

He's up by six every morning, has his morning cup of joe, showers, and makes it into the funeral home before I even get out of bed. Today, my hair is straight, my make-up perfect, and my red pencil skirt accentuates my curves and makes me feel like a boss. Even though I have the day off for my birthday, I dressed up for lunch with my coworkers.

Keep telling yourself that, my conscience laughs.

I doubt Jameson will attend my birthday lunch. Mr. Weston has been pulling him into his office for secret meetings every day, so I can't imagine he'd find the time to stop by his enemy's soiree.

When I pull into the funeral home parking lot, there's an unfamiliar car parked in my spot. Pop-Pop takes the bus every morning because he likes to chat with his friend who drives, and he so sweetly wants me to be able to sleep in instead of getting up to drive him. I grab my keys to unlock the front door, but it swings open before I reach the entrance.

"Mr. Garcia?" I step forward and hold the door open for him. He's in his early sixties, greying, but still fit as a fiddle. He's carrying one of our extra cremation pans in his hands. "What are you doing in our neck of the woods?"

He and Pop-Pop share a look I can't decipher before he turns back to me. "Hi, Miss Daniels. I was just...coming to borrow a pan."

"Did something happen to one of yours?"

"No." He glances at Pop-Pop, and the hairs on the back of my neck stand. "We have a lot of cremations this week and needed an extra. Your grandfather graciously offered to let us borrow one."

Swallowing becomes difficult as I read between the lines. They're busier than us.

"Oh." I rub my arms even though I'm not cold. "Well, it was good to see you."

"You, too."

Pop-Pop escorts him to his car, and I stare out the window as if I've suddenly gained the ability to read lips. They shake hands, and Mr. Garcia leaves.

"What was that all about?" I ask.

He takes a seat at his desk. Bank statements cover the top, and Pop-Pop peers down through his chunky black rimmed glasses, creases etched into his dark skin. The phone call after the meeting with the bank must not have gone as well as I'd hoped, and as a financial advisor myself, I feel like a failure. I should've remembered how chaotic life gets after a loved one passes. Bills are the last thing on a grieving person's mind, yet if they lapse, it's hard to catch up.

"The bank gave us one more extension." His shoulders heave with a large sigh. "It's the last one. I figured we might look into…other options."

Rubbing my temples doesn't give me the relief I need. "You mean selling to Mr. Garcia."

He shrugs. "It's an option I want to keep. Mr. Garcia runs successful funeral homes in the east and south parts of the city."

"That's because more murders happen there," I grumble.

He whacks my ankle with his cane. "Stella Rae."

I purse my lips as I look through the loan documents. "If I forego night classes and change back to a salaried position instead of a commissioned one, we can maybe turn the month around."

Pop-Pop clasps his hands on top of the desk. "You need those classes, and you're not going back to a salary. You've been working too hard to get promoted to end up back at an entry level position."

I chew on my lip, knowing I shouldn't say what I'm about to say. "Well then, I could always ask Dad's parents."

"No way, Stella." He pushes the papers away and levels me with a hard stare.

"But—"

"Absolutely not." He holds up his hand, cutting off another retort. "We made it this long without needing their money. I'd set fire to the funeral home before I'd take anything from them."

Pop-Pop is right. I'd rather sell the funeral home than beg for their money. Besides, they refused to help Mom years ago when she tried to get away from my dad, so I doubt they'd help me.

"I'll change positions. I haven't signed any big new clients, so if I switch to salary then at least I'll have the opportunity for bonuses and incentives without the constant stress of commission. And I can take classes next semester."

He shakes his head. "I don't like it, Stella. I should be taking care of you."

I chuckle. "You've always taken care of me. I'm returning the favor. You're my favorite Pop-Pop."

He ambles over to the coffee pot. "I'm your only Pop-Pop."

"That's beside the point." I gather the paperwork and push it back into the folder.

Forty-five minutes pass while I'm working on inventory before I take a break and text Rosay to see how her day is going.

Rosay: Stuck in meetings up until lunch. Can you swing by and pick up a coffee? I'll be forever thankful.

I drive to the cafe to grab her order. My phone chirps in my purse with CJ's ringtone. I haven't spoken to him outside of a few texts since he asked me about a lunch with coworkers.

"Hey, CJ." I rush into the cafe, looking through my purse for my wallet. "What's up?"

"Hey. I tried to call your work phone, but you didn't pick up."

"I took off today." I step forward as the line moves.

"Oh, okay. I might be a little late to your birthday lunch."

A ding sounds behind me and the scent of cedar and soap floats in on a breeze. I close my eyes and inhale.

I love that scent.

"Dad needs me for some big work thing," CJ says. "I'm sorry."

"You're late for work," a deep voice says behind me.

The phone slips from my hand, and I realize why the cedar smell seemed familiar. I pick it up and tell CJ I'll call him back later. I turn around and meet Jameson's smile. "You scared the shit out of me."

He chuckles. "Why are you late?"

"Why are *you* late?"

"I'm not late. I'm the boss."

I roll my eyes, a slight smile on my face as I turn around. "In your dreams." The heat of his gaze on my back thrills me. The barista calls for the next person in line and I step forward.

Jameson steps beside me, and I turn to him. "What are you doing?"

"Hi, Jim." The barista smiles up at him. "Your usual?"

She's taken with him and I'm a forgotten statue. "Yes, and a cinnamon dolce latte for Rosay."

"For Rosay?" I ask, incredulously. "I'm supposed to be getting her coffee."

He gives me the side eye. "She asked me to stop by and pick up her coffee."

Realization dawns.

Jameson rubs his temple and the muscles in his jaw work, but he says nothing.

"Why are *you* getting her coffee?" I ask.

He pulls his phone out, furiously typing with his tongue pressed against his cheek. "I had some smoothing over that needed to be done." He's making it up to her for being a dick the other day. That's so...sweet? A weird smile spills across my face, no longer upset that the barista skips over me. He slips his phone into his pocket and turns toward me. "What are you having?"

An aneurysm? An orgasm just thinking about you? Butterflies flutter inside my stomach. "Yorkshire tea, please."

He does a double take. "You like Yorkshire tea?"

"Yes?"

He hums. "Well, they don't sell it here, so you'll have to pick something else."

I laugh. "Yes, they do."

He crosses his arms, apparently prepared to battle over my tea selection. "No. They don't."

I wet my lips, blowing out an exasperated breath. "Have you ever asked if they sell it here, *Mr. Brooks*?"

He steps closer, encroaching in my space. His breath warms my neck when he leans forward. "Don't call me that. And no, I've never asked."

The low timbre of his voice peaks my nipples beneath my shirt, and arousal clogs my throat, making it hard to swallow. "Sometimes all you have to do is ask." I turn my attention to the now wide-eyed barista. "I'll have a Yorkshire tea with milk and honey, please."

"Coming right up."

I open my wallet and hand her a twenty. Her eyes ping pong between us. He hands her his card and turns to me. "Don't start."

I grit my teeth and wait at the pick-up section. My phone vibrates, dissipating some of the anger I'm feeling at Jameson's high-handedness.

CJ: We could always push your lunch to Thursday.

I start to respond but remember Jameson's offer to teach me how to swim.

Me: No, it's fine if you're late.

CJ: I guess so.

His response is no surprise.

It's my birthday, but if we aren't doing what he wants, when he wants, he's passive-aggressive. It doesn't matter. We're not together, and nothing will change that, no matter how hard he tries. He was fine with the break-up, so I'm not sure why he suddenly feels the urge to change the status quo.

"Espresso with squirty cream, cinnamon dolce latte, and a Yorkshire tea for Jim," the barista yells.

"Squirty cream?" I say with a British accent and a snort. "What the hell is that?"

He deadpans like he's been asked this a million times. "Whipped cream."

"How posh."

Jameson's jaw twitches. He steps forward, grabs the cup holder from the barista, and leaves. I follow him, confused.

"Can I have my drink?"

He picks up his pace, leaving me to damn near run after him. "Most people would say thank you."

The whiplash of his sudden demand has me on edge. "You just want me to drop to my knees and praise the ground you walk on, don't you?" I say. "Newsflash. I didn't ask you to pay. I could've paid, but you have a habit of butting in where you're not wanted."

He licks his lips, and his dark eyes turn stormy. "Well since you don't want anything from me, I guess this drink I paid for is mine." He smirks and shakes his head before opening his car door.

I wait for him to laugh and say he's joking, but he doesn't. "Are you kidding?"

He turns slowly, his attention fixed on my body. "And Stella, if I had you on your knees, it wouldn't be to praise the ground I walk on."

I gulp.

Literally.

Air refuses to enter my body and my brain fizzes out.

He drives away, leaving me wistful and without my tea. I head back inside and reorder, this time paying for it myself. The barista lifts a curious eyebrow but doesn't ask. I'm not sure what I'd say if she did.

Tea in hand, I spend an hour reading the class curriculum in my car before I meet up with the small group of coworkers waiting for me at the restaurant.

The music and conversation on the Riverwalk grate against my brain as we sit at the Hard Rock. It's not my favorite place to eat, but it's CJ's favorite restaurant and close enough to work that my coworkers can attend on their lunch break.

Wilted, brown lettuce and congealed cheese stare back at me from a plate riddled with water spots. CJ was thirty minutes late and has spent the entire time complaining about how his dad didn't choose him for a big project while the other coworkers chat.

I nod at the right parts, but my mind is focused on the one coworker who *isn't* here. Not that I wanted him to be, but I figured he wouldn't miss an opportunity to mess with me. With the conference happening in a few weeks, I need to have my ducks in a row.

"How are things at the funeral home?" CJ asks. "Were you able to get out of the hole yet?"

The funeral home issues are the absolute last thing I want on my mind right now, but he's attempting to fill the space I've created.

CJ isn't a bad guy.

We just never progressed to where we needed to, and I thought he understood that, but ever since Jameson came into the picture, it's like CJ has this need to prove I'm his.

"We'll get there." I stab the salad with my fork. "If I get this promotion, we should be able to catch up fast."

"If we were still together, you wouldn't have to worry about money."

Bread nearly lodges in my throat at that thought. "Well, we're not, and I don't need your money, CJ. You know that's not why I was with you."

He pops a fry into his mouth and shrugs. "I know, but it's not like you're making a whole bunch of money right now since your portfolio is light."

My gut hardens, a swell of anger inching up my neck. Our coworkers glance awkwardly at each other, averting their eyes. I'm sure my face is tomato red. Ignoring the fact that he casually dropped us getting back together into the conversation, like we didn't spend four years stagnant, I latch onto the comment about work. "What the hell is that supposed to mean?"

"Nothing, Stella." He swipes a hand down his neck. "Forget it."

Apparently noticing the tension, Rosay finishes her conversation with Alex and sits beside me. "I'm so glad Mr. Weston gave everyone off after this morning's meetings," she says, throwing an arm around my chair and defusing the situation.

"He gave you off?"

She nods. "Some big client wanted privacy for his meeting, so everyone got the day off."

"A big client? Maybe that's why Jameson didn't come." The statement slips through my lips before I can stop it. My cheeks flame up, embarrassed I let them see my reaction to his absence.

CJ's eyes widen, mouth parted in shock. "You invited him?"

"I did," Rosay chimes in.

"Why?" CJ asks. "Stella doesn't want him here."

"Don't speak for me," I scold.

Someone at the table sputters a cough after choking on their drink.

"Oh, so you're sad he's not here?"

I struggle to find words, and Rosay squeezes my knee under the table for support. "It's my birthday, and I can invite whomever I want."

"And you wanted him here?" CJ chews on his cheek.

"That's not what I said."

"But it's what you meant, right?" He scoffs. "I just thought our friendship meant more to you."

"What's your issue with Jameson? You haven't even given him a chance." My jaw clenches, and my fingers tense under the table as I exhale through my nose. It's typical of CJ to make me feel bad, but I'm not having it today. "We are friends, and if you wanna continue being friends, you need to change your attitude. I'll be friends with whomever I want to, regardless if you like them or not."

"I'm sorry." His shoulders slump. "I shouldn't have said that. I just don't want you to fall under his spell like my dad is."

With the last portion of his statement, understanding settles over me. CJ has worked for his family's company since he was able to get a work permit. He went to school for accounting, like his father wanted, so he could take over the business eventually. His dad promised he could swap to advising investments, but it never happened. Now, Jameson is here, and his father praises the ground Jameson walks on.

"I won't," I reply, turning to Rosay and the rest of my coworkers. "I appreciate y'all coming out to lunch, and I hope you have a great day off."

We say our goodbyes, and Rosay lingers by my car. I pull her in for a hug. "Thank you for setting up this party."

"It was nothing." She waves my words away. "I'm sorry he didn't show."

I shrug, deciding not to remind her I saw Jameson when she set me up to get her coffee. But the little pin pricks behind my eyes surprise me.

I didn't *want* him to come…did I?

The minute I ask myself, I know the answer. I did. I thought our banter was school yard picking on your crush, but maybe I read too far between the lines, and he was distracting me. "It's fine. We had more fun without him."

We embrace once more before I get into my car. Staring into the rearview, I tell myself not to cry, not to let everything going on with the funeral home, the promotion, CJ, and Jameson break me. I'm stronger than this.

I wipe a few stray tears away and shift my car into gear. I've got a massage and nail appointment planned. If I'm lucky, it'll be late enough that no one will still be at the office when I get there. I need some uninterrupted time to focus on inputting my client's info into the new system, reading through my notes for my meeting with Charlotte, and making sure I'm as far ahead of Jameson as I can be.

Chapter Sixteen
Stella

The elevator doors open to a darkened office. My massage was exactly the relief I needed, but my normal nail tech was double-booked, so my pedicure took longer than expected. I pass the rows of cubicles and inch towards the advisor's offices, my stomach turning when I notice a light still on in Jameson's office. I creep past and hope I don't alert him to my presence.

"Stella?"

Fuckkkkk. "Hey." I spin on my heels.

Jameson's suit jacket is off. The top two buttons of his oxford are undone, the white sleeves rolled up to his elbows. My gaze lingers on the tattoo that stops below his collarbone, and saliva pools in my cheeks. He stands, and I curse inwardly at how sexy he looks leaning against his desk.

"What are you doing here?" he asks, appraising my body with hungry eyes.

I'm still in my red pencil skirt, though the humid Texas air has done a number on my straightened hair. I step into his office and stand in front of him with my hands on my hips. "I could ask you the same thing."

His tongue swipes along his full bottom lip, and I swear I can feel it between my legs. Heat leaps to my chest, making me itch to open my white blouse to get some air.

"I'm working," he says. "I thought you took off the day for your birthday lunch."

So, he did know about it. He just didn't want to come.

"I've got some catching up to do." I shrug and turn away. "Might as well do it now."

"You should be out on the town with your boyfriend."

I laugh, but it's stale. "I don't have a boyfriend." I reach the door and turn around to find him with a perplexed look on his face and his eyebrows scrunched. "What?" I ask.

"Aren't you dating Cameron?"

I bristle at the use of CJ's first name. I haven't heard him called that in years. "No, I'm not. Not anymore."

Jameson makes a humming noise as if this is news to him. When he doesn't say anything else, I make to leave.

"I didn't think you'd want me there."

I stop and lean inside his office door. "What do you mean?"

He doesn't look at me as he sits at his desk. "At your birthday lunch."

"Why wouldn't I want you there?" My heart does a little dance inside my chest.

He fidgets with the knife on his desk. "Because of this morning. I didn't realize you weren't coming in today, or I wouldn't have taken your tea." He runs a hand through his hair, messing it up in the sexiest way possible. "It was a joke, but when you didn't email me back, I figured you were upset."

"Email you back?" I grab my phone and open my email app.

My heart simultaneously explodes and withers when I see his apology email. For someone so arrogant, he's frustratingly kind. Why he hides it, I don't know. It would only add to his attractiveness if others knew he wasn't a total dick.

"I didn't check my email. But if I had, I probably would've told you to screw yourself." His eyes go wide. "I'm kidding, Jameson."

He visibly relaxes, and a smile pulls at the corner of his mouth. His lazy grin sets my stomach on a roller coaster, speeding down the highest peak and giving me the thrill of my life.

"You look beautiful today," he says with a wide smile.

He's devastatingly handsome, and the more I see this side of him, the angrier it makes me that he puts on a show for everyone else. "Thanks. You're much more attractive when you're not being an ass."

He arches a dark brow. "You think I'm attractive?"

Stifling the urge to move further into his office, I smile and tell him I'm going to get some work done. I don't miss his dark chuckle as I hightail it down the hallway. I've got to get away from him before the slickness between my thighs disintegrates my panties.

In my office, I spend an hour uploading my client's information into the new software and confirming my meeting details with Charlotte McCombs. I spend another half an hour imagining Jameson laying me out over his paperwork and eating me for dinner.

It's safe to say that half hour was not the most productive, but it was needed.

Jameson knocks on my door, and I jump, banging my knee on a drawer.

"Are you okay?" He rounds the desk as I'm rubbing my knee.

My skirt is pushed up my thighs, and his stormy eyes turn hungry when they land on the light pink underwear between my legs. I readjust my skirt, and Jameson snaps out of his trance. I get up from the desk and land chest to chest with him.

"I'm fine," I say, nearly breathless. "You startled me."

He retreats behind the guest's chairs, giving me some space. "I bought dinner," he rubs the back of his neck, "to make up for missing your birthday lunch."

"You didn't have to do that." I blush. "That's really nice of you."

He grips the seat in front of him. "I hope that's okay?"

I gnaw on my lip. "Yeah, of course. You didn't order seafood though, right?"

His hand splays across his heart like I've shot him. "You don't like seafood?"

I laugh. "I know, I know. Pops makes fun of me because I don't eat it."

"I guess it's a good thing I didn't order seafood then."

Jameson stands beside me. His shoulder brushes mine, and the heat of it sends a shiver down my spine. His minty breath on my neck makes my nipples taut beneath my shirt as he hands me his phone, showing me an order from my favorite Mexican restaurant. I look at him, but his eyes are closed, nostrils flaring like he's inhaling a deep breath. He hasn't backed away, and somehow, he seems closer than before.

"How'd you know I like this place?" I ask.

His eyes snap open, and they're dark and dangerous. "A little birdie told me."

"Rosay?" I ask.

Damn her and her match-making, and damn Jameson for knowing to ask her. My voice sounds too light and airy for how I actually feel. My skin is clammy and my heart is racing, but I find my feet glued to the floor when I try to back out of his space.

He clears his throat and retreats to the door as if he's worried he might do something if he doesn't get out of here as soon as possible. "Do you want to eat in my office or in here?"

"Wherever is fine."

"My office it is."

"I'll be right there," I say, packing papers into folders.

He returns to his office while I lasso my runaway heart. A few minutes pass before I muster the courage to follow. Inside his office, the table is covered with tacos, rice, tortillas, and the rest of the fixings.

My eyes land on him, and he shrugs as if to say 'Rosay' without ratting her out. I smile, thrilled that he went to all this trouble. "Thanks."

He sets our plates down, and I notice he served us the same thing. "You like chorizo, too?"

He shrugs. "I've never had it before."

The little niggle in my chest is back again. "Why did you order it if you've never had it before?"

Another shrug. "I trust your judgment."

He lifts the taco to his mouth.

"You shouldn't. That's skunk shoulder."

His mouth falls and he reaches for a napkin.

I laugh, lifting my hand to stop him. "I'm kidding, I'm kidding. It's pork sausage."

"Hilarious." He glares, but a hint of a smile forms on his cheek.

Clamping my lips—and my legs—shut, I nod and dig into the food. I watch Jameson take his second bite, waiting patiently for his thoughts. "So, what's the verdict?"

"It's bloody good," he says.

I sag with relief and dig into my food.

"Do you always make noises like that when you eat?" Jameson asks.

I pause, taco midway to my mouth. "Like what?"

"Like you're having an orgasm."

I snort. "That's not how I sound when I—"

A shadow passes over his face, and a muscle ticks in his jaw. I swallow, but my mouth is too dry, so I end up looking like I'm gulping in air. "Stella."

"Forget it." I hurry to shove more food in my mouth. "Let's talk about something else."

He sits back in the chair, working something over inside his head. I force myself not to look at him, scan his office instead. Uniquely shaped sculptures sit atop his window sill, and Jameson's degree and certificates line the wall behind his desk, but they're overshadowed by the beautiful paintings on each side of the guest chairs.

"Who painted these? I ask.

"One of the clients I worked with back at my old firm."

"You represented artists?"

He shrugs, but his gaze is downcast and focused on his food. "It was my area of expertise. I loved art."

I don't miss his use of past tense, but I can tell from the way he won't meet my gaze that it's a sore subject. If my mom was an artist and didn't trust me with that knowledge even though I'm experienced with it, I'd be upset too.

I finally understand his reaction at the funeral home.

He shifts in his seat and pulls at his undone collar. Black lines curl around his collarbone, and my mouth waters following the curves to see where they connect. When he appraises me, I take a bite of food to prevent myself from saying something I'll regret.

Chapter Seventeen
Jameson

My defenses around Stella are as weak as a wall of marshmallows, the comfort between us making me say things I wouldn't.

Things I usually keep to myself out of fear for how they'll be perceived.

Most people don't notice artwork in business offices, but Stella notices everything I want to hide. Clamoring for control, I veer the conversation to something different.

"If you're ambitious enough to work on your day off, why didn't you gain a new client this year?" I ask.

She leans back in her chair, her white blouse stretching across her chest. My body heats, and my eyes linger a moment before I look back at her face.

"I'm busier than most normal advisors," she says.

"Helping your grandfather at his funeral home?"

She nods and sips her Jarritos, a fruity beverage Rosay mentioned she loves.

"If you don't mind me asking, where are your parents? Shouldn't they be helping your grandfather instead of you?"

She brings a shaky hand to her forehead as if fighting off a wave of light-headedness.

"Are you okay?" My breath catches as I take her face in my hands, and she latches onto my raw wrist, sending a zing of pain through my arm. "Breathe."

I curse my body for pining for this woman's touch. I shouldn't want to know what her hands feel like on other places on my body, but I do. Desperately.

"I'm fine," she croaks. "I drank too fast and the cold went to my head."

I don't believe it for one second, but I won't call her out. My closet is filled with things I'm not ready to talk about. "I'm sorry. I didn't mean to pry."

"No, it's okay." She waves me off. "I don't normally talk about my personal life at work. No one likes a sob story."

A heaviness settles on my chest at her admission. "You don't strike me as the type to have a sob story."

She shrugs. "My parents weren't the greatest. My dad was an abusive alcoholic, and my mom loved the lifestyle she had too much. By the time it got bad enough to leave, it was too late. They went out on a boat one weekend, and my dad crashed the boat. Neither survived."

My gut hardens. "Bloody hell, Stella. I'm sorry."

"It's okay." She blinks like she's clearing away the memories.

Hungry to learn as much as I can about her, I swallow the uncomfortable knot in my throat. "How did you complete university?"

"I took night and online classes and worked at the funeral home during the day." She shrugs like it's no big deal, and I frown. "What?"

"I imagine that was a lot to handle."

Another shrug. "My grandparents helped a good bit until my Nunny's Alzheimer's took a turn, and then I stepped up at the funeral home when she passed."

A strange feeling snakes its way into my chest.

"See?" She laughs. "Sob story."

I shake my head. "Not in the slightest. You are strong to have taken on all that responsibility."

She absently worries her bottom lip, and my cock stirs in my trousers as I continue.

"Even with all of that going on, you stayed diligent and completed your degree."

I lean forward, discreetly adjusting myself as heat rushes up her neck at my compliment. I don't want our time to end, and our swimming lesson tomorrow feels too far away.

She gathers our bins from the desk and throws them into the trash. "So tell me something about yourself."

The high I was feeling shutters in my chest. Swallowing is painful as I debate how much I want to tell her. She already knows more about me than even my father, and the deeper I go with her, the sooner she'll find out I can't give her what she needs.

"What do you want to know?" Needing to move, I get up and round the desk, leaning on the edge.

"What about your family?" she asks. "Got any siblings? Overbearing parents?"

The minute she makes the comment, I can tell she regrets it. Her cheeks pink, and she winces like she's in physical pain. I'm sure our meeting at the funeral home is crossing her mind like it is mine, but she surprises me by huffing out a laugh. "Insert foot in mouth."

"I don't want to talk about me, Stella." I move closer, and my stomach lifts like I'm on the London Eye, staring out over the Thames. "I want to know more about you."

"What do you want to know?"

"Anything," I breathe as she inches closer. "Everything."

Our fingers touch on the desk, and my breath stutters.

"Hmm..." Her pause is like a moan, and needing to touch her, my thumb swipes along her knuckles. "I love to read, and I love yellow cake with chocolate icing."

"What do you like to read?" I ask, watching as her elegant neck bobs with a swallow.

"Suspense," she rasps. "I like the excitement."

My lungs are working double time, desperate to catch up with the breaths I'm restricting. "No romance or fantasy?"

She chuckles. "Romance *is* fantasy."

I brush my fingers along her arm and a thrill shoots through me when goosebumps raise on her arms. "Why do you say that?"

"There's no such thing as romance in our day and age." Her gaze lands on where I'm slowly stroking her soft, brown skin. My trousers tighten when her eyes lock with mine. "Back when my grandparents were together, people worked through issues. They didn't give up when things got hard, but now people are giving up left and right. Flowers are no longer a symbol of love but of assholes apologizing."

Recalling the flowers she received the other day, and how she was probably not happy about them, makes me happy, but sad. She deserves to be cherished. "Wow. You've really given that some thought."

"We don't have to invest time getting to know someone because it's all in our bios. Everything we like, hate, want to do or see, and even what our dreams are. Fake love is what's in style. Not romance."

Her closeness and the sweet scent of her perfume thrums through my body, and I find myself pulling her between my legs. When she doesn't shy away from my touch, I brush my thumb along her cheek. "You deserve so much more than he could've given you."

She leans into the touch, and my charged nerve endings beg to devour her. I swear my cock is yelling obscenities I've never heard before. I run my nose along the expanse of her neck, groaning as she arches closer to me, and her breasts touch my chest.

Our quick breaths mix, and I brush my lips across her soft cheek. When she moans, my mind goes haywire. Feverish heat floods my core, making my cock jump and highlighting the areas where she's now touching me.

"Stella." My voice is a gravelly plea, and the hard length of my arousal presses against her thigh.

"Hmm?" She tilts her head, eyes closed like she's waiting for me to kiss her. I can tell we both want this, but who will be the one to cross enemy lines?

Her breath puffs against my lips, and her fingers tense on my arms, pulling me closer. To steady herself, she grabs my thighs, squeezing the area where my scars are. I tense and let out a soft gasp, worried that she feels the gnarled skin beneath my trousers.

The ding of the elevator pops the bubble we're in, and the loud rambling of rap music floats into the space between us. I blink like I've awakened from a dream, and my hands fall from her waist. I inhale deeply to stifle my arousal.

"I'm sorry." The custodian stops by the office on his way down the hall. "I didn't know anyone was still here. I can do another level if my vacuuming will bother you."

Needing some space, I back away from Stella. "No, mate. You're fine."

Her forehead creases, and I can tell I've cocked this up by saying that. It's probably for the best, because if this would've continued, I'm not sure I would've had the strength to stop. She would've found out about my issues, and I know she would freak out. I'm not ready to have her look at me that way.

"I've got work I need to finish," she says, moving from the desk to the door. "Thanks for dinner."

I could tell her to stop, to return and finish what we started, but something holds me back. "I'm sorry," is all I say before she disappears.

***

Shame is a hell of a thing.

Sometimes it can bring humility or disgust, other times it brings clarity.

I lay in bed, wondering how I got to this point, how my parents' actions left such an impression on me as a child that I carried the weight of it with me well into adulthood. I should've been waking up beside Stella, with the warmth of her body pressed against mine, but she's not here. I thought it was strong to push her away, but it was weakness. I'm too much of a coward to do what we both wanted.

Part of me thinks I imagined her labored breathing and the slight tilt of her head. If I kissed her, things would've snowballed into more, and I'm not ready for the questions when she sees my naked body, the things I've done to myself.

I close my eyes and am sucked into the memory of the first time I realized my mum was a monster.

My dad had told me he'd fly out to see me if my team went to the championship basketball game and I aced my report. I did neither. I wasn't as smart as some of the other kids and needed extra help. My low marks and failure meant there was no chance of him coming, and the report inside my backpack weighed me down the entire way home.

I knew what my mother would say. "It's your fault he's not coming. If you'd done better, he'd be here."

I wanted to believe it was the pills that made her say those horrible things, but deep down I knew it was my fault he stayed away. I was too needy. Too weak and dumb. Not worthy of his love.

She blamed me for his absence the minute I came inside, like she expected me to fail. My caretaker, Cara, hung her head when my mother berated me. She, like Dad, knew Mum wasn't in her right mind most of the time because of the pills, and we just had to wait it out until she calmed down and passed out.

This time, she didn't.

Tension crept up my spine, lifting my shoulders to my neck when she told me to get the belt. Cara's remorse-filled eyes darted to me. She knew what my mum was about to do, but she couldn't do anything about it.

My knees hit the ground with a thud. I unbuckled my trousers and leaned over the glass table in my white underpants.

I was too scared to look back.

To see the face of the demon who possessed my mother as she started to hit me.

Words caught in my throat, battling to force themselves out between the harsh blows she continued to deal.

I didn't understand why she wasn't stopping.

Sweat coated my skin as I held onto the table legs, bracing for the next blow. Pain from the glass digging into my legs washed over me, morphing into a sense of strength. I could almost pretend I wasn't being hurt by someone who was supposed to love me, could almost pretend withstanding the pain made me into a kind of superhero.

I wasn't weak.

And I would never be again.

My buzzing phone cuts through the haze of my memory, ramping up the pounding of my heart. The vision was so vivid and real, like I was right there watching in sick pleasure.

My lips are dry, mouth sticky with the whiskey I spilled last night. I drag a hand down my face, feeling dampness on my fingertips. I reach for the nightstand, wincing as I pull the lamp cord.

What the hell?

Blood covers my fingers.

I throw the sheets off the bed, eyes landing on the crescent-shaped imprints on my thighs.

Fuck.

I look back at my fingers.

I didn't do this.

Did I?

My heart thrums in my head recalling last night.

Stella.

Her name is like Narcan for my memories. Everything I pushed aside or tried to forget forces its way back with one thought of her. I had paced the floor all night with a glass of whiskey, convincing myself I could be strong like Stella. After she told me about her life after her parents' deaths, mine seemed easy. How strong could I really be if her touching my thighs made me tense like I was back in the room, covering the table as my blood marred the clear glass?

This is the last straw. I need to make time for therapy.

It was easy when I was far away from any triggers in the U.K., but ever since I've been back around my dad, the pressure keeps building. This fear I have of disappointing him follows me daily, and I know I'm one step too close to falling over the edge.

Something has to change.

Needing to do something with my hands, I find my sketchbook. I recall the dark amber eyes, silky brown skin, and pouty lips I missed out on last night. As I sketch curved lines, shading as I go, Stella's beautiful face forms on the page. Slowly, the tension in my body melts until I can take a breath without weight pressing on my chest.

The electric kettle I set last night whistles, and I pour the steaming water into a cup, steeping my tea while I get ready for work. The black Oxford shirt I select fits me like a glove, highlighting the muscles I've worked hard to attain. Muscles I've imagined Stella mapping with her tongue.

No. Stop.

I complete the outfit with my charcoal grey trousers, a pair of suspenders, and black wingtips. My eyes snag on a dark glint of metal on the closet floor and I reach down to pick up the item. Smooth blue epoxy, sleek curves. My heartbeat throbs all over my body: my head, my throat, my fingertips as I palm the knife my mother gifted me for my fifteenth birthday. It's heavy in my hand, and a sense of foreboding settles in my chest.

My still buzzing phone snaps me into focus, and I slip the knife into my pocket for safekeeping as I head to my car. Dad usually sends me a to-do list every morning, so I prepare for the orders sure to be on the screen. I'll be late, but the last thing I need is for him to flip out because I left his text unread. Yet when I read the message, the tightness in my chest dissipates, and I smile.

Stella: Thank you for dinner.

I tap my fingers on the wheel, unsure how to respond. Is she being polite? Or is she as angry as I am that I chickened out and didn't kiss her? After typing, deleting, and retyping again, I settle on a cordial 'it was my pleasure,' and head to work. Stella's swim lessons are tonight, and I'm already dreading touching her soft skin again.

I had a singular goal when I moved here: showing my dad he made the right choice in choosing me to be his successor. But that lens is slowly starting to widen as I get to know Stella.

I can work to the bone, but if I don't have anything to show for it, what's the point?

Chapter Eighteen
Jameson

"Jim," Dad says. "Glad I caught you before we head into the meeting."

Like a bad habit I thought I'd kicked, fear of his disappointment floods my system.

"I spoke with Lewis, and he'll be calling you to set up those accounts."

I exhale into the chair, my whole body relaxing with that statement. I knew we did a good job with the meeting, but nothing's ever definite in business, especially not in finance. I've been having trouble getting a meeting with Red McCombs, so this is a win for me. I've got to stay ahead of the game.

"Good to hear." I smooth out the wrinkles in my shirt. "I'll gather the materials to send over when he calls."

"Great work," he says, and a bubble of pride rises up in me. "Let's meet at the cigar club tomorrow evening."

My chest swells. Dad has never invited me to the club before. "I'll be there."

He nods and closes the door behind him as he leaves. I excitedly smack my leg before remembering the divots I made in them last night. Pain radiates around the marks as I grab my gym bag and take out the bottle of pain reliever, popping a few tablets in my mouth.

At ten, I head to the break room, convincing myself it's because I want a cuppa before the meeting. It has absolutely nothing to do with the fact that I'll get to pass Stella's office on my way. I stay calm and pretend like everything is okay and we didn't almost kiss last night, but the minute I see Cameron my stomach plummets to the floor.

Heat spreads through my chest reaching all the way to my fingertips. He's beside her, crouched over her desk, pretending to help her with something. His hand is on the chair, too close to her shoulder.

Stella's normally curly hair is still straight, falling far past her shoulder blades. A small part of me misses the unruly curls, but the image of her straight, dark hair wrapped around my fist makes my heart pound. Her almond-shaped eyes are outlined with dark liner, and her crimson lipstick sends my mind down an unsavory path.

I wish I could paint her likeness.

My heart gallops inside my chest at the thought. Sketching doesn't give me the thrill painting did, but after the last portrait my mum ruined, colors became muted, and the talent slipped from my hands. The sunlight caressing Stella's face makes me itch to pick up a brush again.

I'll swing by the store and grab a canvas and some paints after work.

Cameron's laugh grates on my nerves. Why is he helping her? She could've asked me for help if she had questions.

Needy. Weak. My mother's voice whispers into my ear, and cotton fills my mouth as I swallow past the lump. I used to be those things, but I'm not anymore. I'm stronger, and I go after what I want. And that happens to be Stella.

She deserves to be treasured and pleasured like the gem she is.

And I'm the man to do it.

I just need to find a way to balance everything else I've got going on in my life.

"Ready for the meeting?" I ask, smiling as a look of disdain crosses Cameron's face.

"Yeah." Stella bristles in her seat, a slight blush rising to her cheeks. "CJ was just leaving."

I school my features and mask my frustration at his presence. "It's a pleasure to see you again."

Cameron narrows his eyes and moves closer to Stella. He holds out a hand, a sly smirk on his face. "You, too."

I've got to give it to him. He's still the same master manipulator I grew up with. Able to turn on the charm with a drop of a hat. Too bad for him, I'm not our father. I know his games too well to fall for the act.

"Thanks for your help, CJ." Stella moves to her cabinet with a frown. "I'll see you at the meeting, Jameson."

Her chilly dismissal is like ice through my heart. How am I supposed to show her I'm sorry if I can't even get her to look at me? There's no way to forget how she leaned into my touch or how her lips parted, waiting to meet mine. She wanted this, too.

"I can walk with you," Cameron says.

She doesn't look up from her folders or turn around. "No, I'm okay."

"Are you sure, babe?" He reaches out for her arm again. "I don't have anything else to do right now."

"The lady said she's fine," I grit out.

"I heard her, *bro*." Cameron turns to Stella. "You want him to walk with you? Fine."

"CJ," Stella sighs. "Please don't start with that again."

Uncomfortable tension snakes around the room when I hear the strain in Stella's voice. Turning worried eyes to her, I ask, "Everything okay?"

Cameron scoffs and steps into my space. The anger behind his eyes fills me with the primal urge to destroy him, but I won't because Stella is here.

"It won't be long until she sees how much of a disappointment you are," he says.

"That's enough, CJ."

He leans in and lowers his voice. "Good for nothing but ruining others' lives. How long do you think it'll be before he abandons you like he did your mother?"

Like a balloon inflating, the small hole left by my father's absence expands inside my chest. I flip the knife open in my pocket, pressing the tip of my finger against the blade. Relief washes over me as it digs into my skin, and I'm able to feign disinterest at his jibe.

"Stop," Stella admonishes, turning around. "I don't know what the issue is between y'all, but this room is too small for both of your egos." She turns to Cameron and says, "you're gonna make me late for my meeting with your father. Go back to work." Her eyes pass over me, but she doesn't say anything.

Cameron has as much to lose as I do by divulging our connection, so I'm not worried about him telling Stella. I stop outside the door and say, "Don't forget our meeting at six."

"Your meeting?" Cameron shoots her a look of disapproval. "I thought you got off at five?"

Stella chews on her lip, her eyes ping-ponging between Cameron and me unsure of what to do. I leave and let her hash out her squabble with my brother.

If she wants to cancel, then she can come find me.

***

Her scent is what I first notice when I enter the conference room. It's a coma-waking scent. One I wouldn't be able to get rid of even if I lost my sense of smell.

Her laugh is second. The wholesome, hearty laugh shows she's actually happy and not laughing for someone else's benefit. She sits with Rosay across the table and doesn't acknowledge me.

Dad arrives, and the busy chatter ceases. "Update me on the newly acquired accounts, and the ones with potential."

Even though I have an account in the pipeline, the desire to flee the room still strikes me. If it wasn't for my dad's network, I may not have had anything to present at this meeting since I haven't locked in the meeting with the gallery yet. Mr. Lewis is a big fish, not quite the normal clientele I would've gone for had I been back at my old investment firm, but impressive nonetheless.

Art galleries were my specialty. Knowing why someone buys artwork is important to aesthetes, whether it's emotions, money, prestige, or actual love of art that inspires someone to spend millions on investing in certain artist's collections. I loved discovering their motivations. Maybe psychologically I was filling a void left by my own abandonment of my talent, but seeing, touching, and feeling artwork as I help create investment plans for galleries and independent aesthetes is what makes me...happy. Or it was what used to make me happy.

"Jim?" Dad's voice refocuses me. His eyebrows touch his hairline in a clear reproach.

I clear my throat and chance a look at Stella. She's doodling on her notepad, but the crease in her forehead shows me she's struggling not to look up. "Rosay and I met with Mr. Lewis the other day, and he's ready to invest with us."

A round of applause echoes inside the tiny room. Stella squeezes Rosay's hand and smiles at her before lifting her eyes to me. My breathing stills, waiting to see any type of real emotion on her face. Her smile is genuine but sad.

It's at this moment I realize I'm at a fork in the road. I want Stella. God, there's nothing I want more than her. But I can't have her and my career goals too. One path leads to disappointing my father, and the other to disappointing Stella. How does one choose between potential love and loyalty?

She's like a breath of fresh air when everything is dank and dreary. The person who makes me feel weightless when my dad's displeasure rests on my shoulders. Understanding me in a way no one else has, a future with her could mean peace. Something I can't have if I stay the course and keep pushing her away. The thought makes my stomach riot.

"For those who don't remember," Dad says. "Lewis is the fourth largest oil producer in our great state of Texas. He also owns the country's largest fleet of air-worthy World War two fighter planes."

Nausea swirls in my stomach at my dad's enthusiastic bolstering of my accomplishment. With each new praise, Stella's shoulders droop like she's failed. Frustrated I can't reach out and smooth the lines from her forehead, my fists clamp on the table. I want to tell her that she hasn't failed, that I've always had a leg up on her. When I first moved I didn't care about what would happen to the people already working here, but then I met Stella and it all changed.

I can't stand the sight of her defeat.

"I'm still having trouble getting McCombs on the hook," I say. "Have you had any luck with them, Stella?"

A dazed look of bewilderment takes over the sadness on Stella's face, and the knot in my stomach tightens. Did I stick my foot in my mouth?

What if she hasn't had any luck, and I'm now highlighting that fact right after my dad praised me?

Immediately, I feel like a wanker.

"Funny you'd ask." She perks up some. "I have a meeting with his daughter Charlotte this afternoon."

Coworkers 'oOo' and 'ah' at what they assume is hostility between Stella and me. When I first started working here, I would've been upset at being upstaged, but the small blip of happiness growing in my chest makes me realize there might be more to life than appeasing my father.

"A meeting isn't an account." Dad's hands squeeze the back of the chair. "Moving on. Let's talk about the conference."

The clear shift in topic from Stella's success has everyone sharing glances, including her and me. I want to tell her I'm sorry for how he's acting, to explain why he's so supportive of my endeavors, and why he *needs* me to be more successful than her, but I can't. The words are stuck in my throat as my dad's eyes drill a hole into the side of my face.

The hour passes slowly, and Stella shoots from her chair the minute my dad releases us to our whims. Like always, he asks me to follow him to his office.

"What the hell?" His voice is filled with ire when he shuts the door. "I praise your success, and you bring up hers?"

The excuse I want to give him is that making her happy means more to me than bolstering myself, but he'd say that's weakness. With that realization, I'm slowly starting to see there's something more between Stella and me. Something that if nurtured, could become more. *If she doesn't run away when she finds out about your issues.*

"I'm not sure if you've noticed, but Stella has the team's backing. Your praise of me must be equal with hers, or you'll start to look partial."

The implications of the picture I've painted unsettles him. He runs a hand along two-day-old beard growth and sits at his desk. It's not often he shows any emotion, but the frustration covering his face as he rifles through folders reminds me of what I wanted to ask the other day.

"Why does Stella work here anyway?"

He continues shuffling, not looking at me. "What do you mean?"

"Well, she has a trust fund," I say. "Was it a stipulation she had to work here for her to access it?"

Immediately his hands stop, gaze flitting over the folders before they land on me. "Why were you going through my desk?"

"I...I wasn't," I stammer, realizing the mistake I've made. "I had to figure out what folders you needed me to bring the other day, and I stumbled upon it."

He gets up from the desk and stands near the window, running a hand through his chestnut hair. A minute passes before his shoulders relax.

"Stella's trust is not for you to worry about, nor is it something she likes to speak about." He approaches me, his eyes narrowed like snake slits. "I'm not sure you know this, but her father and I were business partners. His death took a toll on both of us. I don't want you bringing up things that will be hurtful to her." His computer dings, and he redirects his attention while still addressing me. "She's aware of everything she needs to know. And you need to focus on impressing the board. This promotion isn't just up to me, and if you don't get your head on straight, you'll lose it."

His stern tone punctures my armor. His words echo what I've been fighting against this whole time. What am I risking by chasing something I'm not even sure I can have? A future with Stella is possible if I give up everything I've worked for, but I'm not sure I'm prepared for the fallout. I've lived my life under Dad's thumb for years, but he's the only family

I have left. Giving up this promotion would make me a disgrace in his eyes, or potentially a winner in hers.

Dad turns his full attention to business. "See yourself out."

An uncontrollable flush of heat creeps onto my face as I leave his office, and black dots dance around my vision as I even out my breathing with deep inhalation. I bump into a coworker in the hall, apologizing as I continue to my office and slam the door. Gripping my hair, I pull at the scalp and focus on the pain instead of losing control.

With Stella giving me the cold shoulder, and my dad disappointed in me, my stress level is near combustion. I decide to check out early and get some laps in at the pool.

Chapter Nineteen
Stella

The funeral home parking lot is empty when I pull up during my lunch break.

"What are you doing here?" Pop-Pop asks when I enter.

I shrug. "Where else would I be?"

He sits in one of the seats reserved for grieving families and clasps his weathered hands over his cane, nodding. Wrinkles fan out on the sides of his eyes, his cheeks drawn down by laugh lines and disappointments. He hasn't taken the best care of himself since Nunny passed away.

He leans back in his chair. "Don't you have that big meeting today? You should be getting ready for that."

"Yes, I do, but you don't have the necessary skills to apply make-up to Mrs. Fuller without making her look like she stepped off the set of *Beetlejuice*."

His eyes crinkle at the corners and a laugh bursts from him. "You're not wrong. But you shouldn't be working on your birthday." He takes his glasses off and rubs the smudges with the bottom of his shirt, lifting them into the air to inspect the cleanliness.

"My birthday was yesterday. It's a new day."

He rolls his eyes. "You worked last night when it was your birthday. You should go out tonight and do something fun. Like, maybe let someone take you to dinner?"

"Like who?"

He shrugs. "That young man who changed your tire didn't seem too bad."

I choke out a laugh, surprised by his insinuation. "No."

After the dismissal last night, I got Jameson's message loud and clear. He's not interested. It's disappointing, because now that I know he's not the asshole from the funeral home and that he's actually really sweet and caring, the rejection stings.

"Hmm." Pop-Pop nods and moves to the door, stopping a moment to look back at me. "So, what do you want me to do with this present out here?"

I clear my throat. "Present?"

"Yeah." He shrugs. "Arrived about five minutes ago."

Excitement lifts me from my seat, and I follow Pop-Pop like he's leading me on a quest, bouncing on my heels behind him.

A small green bag with white tissue paper sits behind the welcome desk. I have no reason to be nervous, but my mouth suddenly goes dry. Tremors take over my hand when I pull out the contents. Plastic crinkles reveal a slice of three-layer yellow cake with chocolate icing and a book. I clamp down on a smile before turning over the book and reading the title. I roll my eyes when I see it's a romance.

A tight coil springs in my stomach when I reach for the card.

You may not believe in romance, but you deserve it all the same.

The card isn't signed, but I know exactly who it's from. Only Jameson would be cocky enough to assume he could change my thoughts on romance. Why does he care? He didn't show me I deserved it last night.

Refusing to acknowledge the warmth spreading through my chest, I put down the book. He's giving me emotional whiplash with his Dr. Jekyll/Mr. Hyde act.

Pop-Pop snorts. "Gotta give it to the man. He's persistent."

I groan, realizing he's been reading over my shoulder. "You're too nosy for your own good. I'm going to do Mrs. Fuller's makeup before her family arrives."

Her body has been bathed, cleaned, and dressed for identification, but Mr. Fuller requested she be presented in full make-up. Apparently, she never left the house without her face on and her hair done.

The hardest part of running a funeral home isn't cremating bodies or organizing living donations, it's making sure the family is able to say goodbye in a way that gives them closure.

For some, it's simply saying goodbye and moving on. For others, it's dressing their loved one up in their favorite outfit, their most prized jewelry, or even reanimating them with the makeup they wore every day.

Studying a picture of Mrs. Fuller, I ensure every detail is as close as possible for her family before I head out to swap with Pops.

He handles the rest of the Fuller's service while I pay bills.

As awful as it sounds, holidays tend to be a busy time for death, and with Thanksgiving around the corner, I predict an increase in business.

I know it's bad form to curse the dead, but as I struggle to find money to make ends meet, I'm cursing my parents for their decisions. When Mr. Weston told me my father had invested his money into a new leisure company that tanked and bankrupted him, also tanking their partnership in the process, I was broken. Not only did I lose my parents, but I also wasn't set up to take care of myself. I didn't have any real-life skills or passions. My whole life was changed by my parents' decisions.

"Stella?" Pop-Pop ambles into the room I'm cleaning, rubbing the back of his neck like he's gearing up to tell me bad news.

"What's up, Pops?"

He clears his throat. "We, um, have to figure out what to do about those paintings your friend left here."

My friend. I laugh at his casual use of the word. I wouldn't consider Jameson a friend, but maybe I should. Maybe getting to know him better will help me get rid of the uneasy feelings pinballing around my body when he's near. "Okay."

After Jameson sped away on his motorcycle, I put his mother's paintings in another room. Her artwork was beautiful, and Jameson shares that same love of art. The way his face lit up in his office when we talked about his client's painting made me realize maybe he was upset about the paintings because his mom wasn't the nicest person. He loves art, and if her art made him react that way, then I want to help him get rid of it and make a profit in the process.

A thought forms in my head. I reach into my pocket and pull out my phone, searching through the contacts for an old friend who can tell me if these paintings are worth anything.

***

The hustle and bustle of the lunch rush reminds me why I usually pack a sandwich.

I stand outside The Pearl, one of San Antonio's historically rich districts, my gray dress pants sticky with sweat. Normally I'd be in a skirt, but the forecast called for rain that has yet to show.

I review notes on my phone as I wait for Charlotte McCombs to arrive. It's no surprise Jameson's having a hard time meeting with the head of the automotive group; he's ninety-four and will soon be leaving the company in someone else's hands. By acquiring a meeting with his daughter, I'm hoping she'll be able to whisper into his ear before that happens.

"Stelly Belly?" a familiar voice calls my name.

I turn, and a smile splits my face. He's dressed in a pair of denim jeans and a clean blue shirt. His silver hair and beard are trimmed shorter, and his eyes are filled with light like I've never seen.

"Ernie," I exclaim. "How are you?"

He pulls me in for a hug. "I've been great. Got a custodian job at one of those fancy high-rises, and my VA benefits finally kicked in."

"That's amazing." All my anxiety about Jameson and this meeting is replaced with elation, and I barely keep myself from jumping with joy for him. "I'm so proud of you."

He rubs the back of his neck and shrugs. "I couldn't have done it without you."

I wave away the sentiment. "Oh, hush. You can do anything you put your mind to."

"No, no, no." He raises his hands in the air, shaking his head. "If it wasn't for you introducing me to that guy, I wouldn't have known about the custodian job."

"That guy?"

"The foreign guy you were on a date with."

"A date?" I choke on my words. "Jameson?"

He nods. "Yeah. He's a funny fellow, that one. He came back a few days later and bought me some food then told me about the job opportunity. He set me up with a clean shave and a fresh pair of clothes too."

"That's great," I say, breaths coming in short bursts. "I'm so happy for you."

"Thank you." He checks the time on his watch. "I've got to get going. Don't want to be late."

"I'll see you around, Ernie."

He embraces me once more. "See you around, Stelly Belly."

His exit coincides with Charlotte McComb's appearance in the center of The Pearl's AstroTurf, and I have no time to dissect Jameson's actions.

With over two dozen restaurants to choose from, we meet at Kineapple, an eatery that features smoothies, salads, and light snacks. Charlotte slips into the seat, laying a napkin across her white pantsuit. "Thanks for meeting. I rarely get out of the office during lunch."

"I appreciate you making time for me. I know you're busy." I sip my smoothie, hoping it will cool the heat rolling off me. "I wanted to touch base and see how McCombs is looking to grow in the next ten years. With you poised to take over the company, I want to know what's most important to you."

A graying tendril of hair falls onto her alabaster face as she tilts her head, regarding me with cool blue eyes. "My father has his hands in a lot of different things, but I'd like to focus more on investing in smaller businesses with potential for widespread growth rather than already established companies."

I clear my throat, puzzled by her decision. "Of course, that's a great idea, though it does carry a significantly higher risk. What type of business are you interested in investing with?"

"I'd like to focus on car washes, storage facilities, and app development."

Her list of investments is unique, but not unusual. The biggest hurdle is being able to read the market and picking the businesses with the most potential for consistent growth. I tell her this in so many words, making sure I'm honest, but not brash. She's smart, and more than capable of growing this company.

"That's doable. Is this something your father would consider? Or is this something you'd like to tackle when you take over?"

She sits back in the chair, tapping her finger against her chin in thought. "Dad will be on board."

"Okay," I say. "I'd love to have you both at an event Thompson is putting on next month. I'll send you the invite."

"Sounds great. I'll mark it in our calendars." Her smile is wide and genuine. "It's lovely to meet another woman as ambitious as myself."

"Likewise." We say our goodbyes and I head back to the office, my feet a little lighter.

My phone vibrates once I'm inside my car. "Hey, Kami."

"Hey, girl. I found some information on those paintings you sent over."

"Already?" I grab a pen from my center console. "And?"

She laughs, and I can imagine the eye roll that accompanies it. "Well, I'm sorry to burst your bubble, but the curator for the Manchester gallery said the artist's name didn't sound familiar."

"The name?"

"Didn't you notice the paintings were signed on the inside of the frame when you took the pictures?"

I smack my forehead. "No."

"Yeah, someone named Jamie Brooks."

A puzzle piece slides forward in my brain, clicking into place. Jamie Brooks. Brooks. The surprise in Jameson's voice when I mentioned the paintings, and how harsh he sounded when he said his mom wasn't a painter finally makes sense.

Chapter Twenty
Stella

Water plinks against the metal grate surrounding the pool, each droplet ticking in time with my rapid pulse. I swallow against the lump in my throat as I slowly toddle toward the shallow end of the pool, thankful for the distraction from the dumpster fire that has become my life.

Last time I tried to teach myself to swim I was hopped up on anger. This time I'm fueled with a mixture of anger and celebration. Anger at Jameson for his confusing actions, and joy because my meeting went better than expected. Personally, and professionally, my growth is finally on the uptick, and competing against Jameson has given me confidence I can tackle this fear of water. It's kept me shackled for too long.

Jameson is swimming when I approach, tight cords of muscle no longer hidden by a shirt. I slow my pace and watch his tattooed arms part the water, his muscles flexing as it cascades over his body. He swims back to the shallow end and stands, allowing the full view of his shirtless form. My heartbeat is entirely too loud, and my fingers twitch, wanting to touch him. Broad and muscular chest, an eight-pack of abs, and two sharp lines that converge to make the sexiest no-no zone I've ever seen.

For as buttoned up as he is, I never would've expected him to be so...gritty.

My tongue darts across my lips as I stare at his torso. A Phoenix bursting with reds and oranges spans his back, the word *overcome* written above it in elegant script. Animated depictions of animals are inked on his arms, followed by rhythmic lines that wrap around his biceps. I gather my hair off my sticky neck and throw it into a sloppy bun on my head.

"I thought you changed your mind," he says, a cold blandness to his voice.

After our almost kiss, his chilly demeanor sets me on edge. I push those feelings aside and remind myself why I'm here. Anxiety stews inside me, and my fingers numb at the tips.

I'm so not ready for this.

I shake my head. "No."

Thick tension hangs between us, and I need to find a way to cut it before my lungs give out from holding my breath.

"Go get dressed then."

"Promise not to laugh. I lost my bathing suit, and this was the only one they had."

He crosses his heart. "Love, I would never."

The endearment hangs in the air like a pinata waiting for one of us to bat it away. Jameson moistens his lips, but he doesn't shy away from what he said. I swipe a loose tendril of hair behind my ear and give him a shy smile.

My footsteps slap against the tile floor five minutes later. Warmth floods my lower half when Jameson comes into view. His gaze tracks over my bathing suit with *Llamacorn* written across its front.

He cracks a smile.

"Not a laugh. I swear." He bites on his lip to prevent his smile from widening and diverts his eyes. "Ready?"

"Nope. I'm terrified."

"That's fine. We'll work up to that once you're comfortable by the water." He points to the side of the pool. "Now grab a towel and sit down."

"Sit down?"

He turns away from me. "Stop asking questions and trust me."

I do as he says, but my feet slow and my heart beats in my throat the closer I get to the side.

"Jameson," I squeak. "I don't...I don't think I can."

"Come here." Water splashes, and I watch him swim toward the edge. I take a deep breath, forcing back the fear. I can do this.

I *will* do this.

He reaches out, helping me slowly inch toward the edge. My knees shake when he takes the towel and lays it on the floor.

"Sit down, love." I oblige, and my entire body quakes like I've severed a fault line. Fibers of the towel scratch the backs of my legs as I lower to the ground, eyes firmly closed. My fingertips brush along the cold tile, raising goosebumps on my skin. He takes my hands and lays them on my stomach. "I want you to keep your eyes closed and breathe. Focus on making your stomach rise before your chest does. Okay?"

I exhale and nod. I can do this.

"Take a few deep breaths to calm down."

I inhale, and my hands rise on my stomach. My pulse slows and the fuzziness in my fingers abates. When I open my eyes, my breath catches in my throat. His hands are clasped together on top of his head, and his eyes roam over my body. I've always been self-conscious about my curves, but under Jameson's smoldering gaze I feel...sexy.

Slowly his gaze meets mine and a cocktail of emotions swirl inside my head. His jaw is tense, eyebrows knit, lips in a hard line. Nerves tighten my stomach and I turn away.

"Scoot up." He runs a hand along his jaw. "Put your feet in the water."

I swallow but do as he orders. The water cools the heat on my skin but does nothing to quench the fire burning in my core. My nerves ease, and the pressure from the water weighs down my feet as I move them back and forth.

"Good job." Jameson smiles. "Can you get in? We're only at three feet."

My muscles clamp up, my entire body paralyzed with panic. "Only at three feet? Three feet isn't some magical number where nothing bad happens."

Jameson's smile falls. "I'm sorry. You're right. But I'm here. I won't let anything happen to you."

A flashback of tipping over the edge and falling into the pool crashes over me and I shiver.

"What's wrong?" he asks.

"Just remembering."

His hands brush along my arms. "Want to talk about it?"

I shrug. "There's not much to tell. My parents were having a party and I wanted to swim. I didn't know how, but that didn't stop me from getting in. They were too drunk to notice I didn't have my floaties on."

He moves closer, gripping my arm lightly. "I'm sorry you had that experience. Do you want to try with me? I can help you in."

I chew on my lip and nod, even though my insides quake. "Yes, please."

Jameson closes the distance between us. "Can I touch you?"

Oh lord, please do. "Yes."

Warm hands wrap around my waist and of course, Jameson is tall enough that my breasts are right in his face. He tears his eyes away, and his head falls forward, shoulders rising with a deep breath.

"Are you ready?" he asks.

I put my hands on his shoulders, and his grasp on my waist tightens. He slowly pulls me off the edge but stops. "Stella, your entire body is shaking. We don't have to do this if you're scared or uncomfortable."

"I'm okay." I inhale and my heart thumps like it enters the game Jumanji. I shake the nerves away and stretch my neck. "I'm ready."

He backs up again and the water inches up higher on my legs. It smacks against the side of the pool with a splat, startling me enough I wrap my arms and legs around Jameson with a death grip.

He stills, his rapid heartbeat pounding against my chest.

My face is buried in his neck, the sweet smell of cedar comforting. He doesn't say a word and instead winds his arms around my back, pressing me closer as he moves around in the water.

"You're okay," he murmurs into my hair. "You're doing great." He walks around the shallow end of the pool and inches deeper into the four-foot area. The knot in my stomach tightens the closer we get. "You are brave, Stella. Look at you in the water."

I laugh against his shoulder and my heart hammers. "I'm clinging to you like a koala. That doesn't count as brave."

"You've overcome a portion of your fear. It'll get easier with time if you keep working." We return to the side. "Do you want to put your feet down on the bottom? I'll hold you."

I nod, urging myself to conquer this. To make myself proud. He doesn't let me go but instead lowers us down into the water together until the tips of my toes meet the pool floor. His hands glide up the backs of my thighs and around my butt, resting at the small of my back.

The thrill of my feet touching the ground is exhilarating. He walks me backwards until I'm against the side of the pool, his eyes closed and body flush with mine. He blows out a breath, lifts me to the side, and backs away slowly, shaking his head. How can just his gaze set my entire body on fire while I'm surrounded by water?

Chapter Twenty-One
Jameson

Even in a Llama bathing suit, Stella's still the most beautiful woman I've ever seen. I roll my shoulders to loosen the tension before I look at her again.

She rolls her eyes. "Where do you want me?"

Gritting my teeth against all the places I could list, I point to the stairs. "Can you make it there?"

It's a few feet away, and it'll give me a moment to collect myself and will my hard-on to wane. Giving her space is taking an excruciating amount of control, but I force myself to look away from her breasts. The white swimsuit does nothing to conceal the round buds I'd like to nip and lick.

"I could try." She moves to the railing. Her eyes flutter closed, and her mouth forms an 'o' like she attempts to meditate.

Cool air hits me as I move to the bottom step. "Open your eyes, love."

She bites down on her lip, shaking her head in protest. I inwardly groan, staring at her reddened lips. Why does she have to be my kryptonite? Why didn't I tell her I couldn't do this anymore? I'm too weak and vulnerable around her.

"I'm sorry about how CJ acted earlier."

Hearing his name reminds me that I'm keeping secrets from her. Things she'd be upset about if she knew, things that could help her out of the rut she's in but would demolish my career and relationship with my father. "That wasn't your fault."

"Yes, it was," she says. "He's jealous and wants me back."

"It's not your fault he doesn't make your heart pound like I do."

She laughs, and her eyes are pinned on me. I can feel her fighting against the pull right now, but she won't give in. Her tongue darts out to wet her lips and my cock jumps in my jammers. The images going through my head right now are not kosher for swim lessons. What I wouldn't give to take her upstairs and bend her over my desk, peeling that bathing suit off to feel the soft skin beneath.

"Are you sure I can fit in this pool with your ego?"

My laugh echoes off the tiled wall. "Probably not, but we can try."

"CJ shouldn't be an issue again."

Here's my opening to tell her.

My head buzzes as I muster up the courage to say the words that could ruin everything. Will she think I was only after her to spite my brother? Will she be angrier at him than me? Can I repair what's bound to break once she hears the truth?

If my father found out I was pining after my brother's girlfriend—well ex-girlfriend now—he'd laugh in my face. Like I'm too pathetic to find my own woman and need to latch onto someone else's. It doesn't matter if Cameron treated her poorly, or even if she deserved more. Westons are never second.

But I'm not a Weston.

I wasn't even worthy of the last name.

"What now?" Stella's shaky voice interrupts my inner tirade.

I snap my rubber band and focus back on her.

"You okay?" she asks.

I clear my throat. "Fine. I'm fine. Now give me your hands."

Everything about her touch sets my skin on fire. Dark green nail polish. Soft, lithe fingers that could wrap around my...nope. Refocus. Take a deep breath.

"I want you to go from this side to the other."

She shakes her head. "I can't."

"Yes, you can, love. We'll stay in three feet the entire time, and I'll go with you."

She puffs out her cheeks and exhales. I start to release her hand, but she grips mine tighter. Her touch is a noose around every erogenous part of my body.

"Please, don't let go." The soft whine in her voice makes me want to press her against my body and discover other noises I could have her make. *Her noises are my Achilles Heel.*

"I won't." My voice is strangled, but if she notices she doesn't say anything. Hand-in-hand we slowly wade through the water. Her body is rigid, and I swipe my thumb across her smooth skin to soothe her nerves. She doesn't look at me. Her focus is on putting one foot in front of the other.

I take the opportunity to drink in her features. Her long, supple neck. Full lips that purse when she concentrates. Toned arms and curvy hips that lead into a bum as round as a peach. My bones liquify as I imagine taking a bite of her juicy—

"I did it." Stella squeals when she reaches the edge of the pool. Her smile touches her cheeks, and I find myself mirroring her joy. What seems small to me is monumental to her.

"Yes, you did." I grab her hand again, seeking a physical connection. "Now let's do it another three times, and then I'll teach you how to float."

She frowns. "Can we talk and ask each other questions? It'll help me keep my mind off what I'm doing."

"Sure." I move forward, pulling her with me. She hesitates but follows after some coaxing.

We chat about how her grandfather started the business over forty years ago and kept it running through the recession of the nineties, but now wants to sell. She takes me through a day in the life of a funeral director, and I can't hold my surprise at how she's been able to do both jobs.

"You're amazing," I say.

"Why, thank you Mr. Brooks."

My nose wrinkles at her use of the proper name. "Don't call me that."

"Why do you get angry when I call you Mr. Brooks?"

"Because I love the way my first name sounds on your lips."

She stops, pulling her hand out of mine. "I'm being serious. Why? I'll have to get used to calling you that when you get the promotion."

Her words burn like acid, but her face holds no malice. She's not angry, just stating a fact, one my dad has made apparent, regardless of her efforts. I chew on my cheek, deciding how to phrase my thoughts. I've made it pretty apparent I'm attracted to Stella, but if she knew the type of power she wields over me, would she assume I'm weak too?

"Because you saw the real me. Not the cold businessman everyone else does."

"Why don't you show anyone else the real you?"

I run a hand along my beard. "Jameson is weak and needy. Mr. Brooks is strong, cutthroat. You tell me which one is needed to run a multi-million-dollar company. No one wants Jameson. They all want Mr. Brooks."

She shakes her head, her lips downturned in a frown. "I don't believe that for one minute. You don't have to split yourself into two different personas to appease people."

"That's easier said than done, love."

"I've met both Jameson and Mr. Brooks. Both are strong, and cut-throat..." she pauses, "a little arrogant at times, but helpful, nonetheless. Why wouldn't someone want both?"

My chest tightens as we reach the other side of the pool. I turn to her, searching her features for any hint of spite. When I find none, my lungs release the breath I've been stifling. "No one has ever wanted both. Not even my parents. They used each other, and me."

The realization crashes like a freight train, derailing the pathway of the past. I've never spoken about my parents so candidly, but Stella's transparency about hers makes me want to open up.

"Mum had me out of wedlock, and she used me to keep her hooks in my father. When I grew up and no longer needed her as a pathway to reaching him, she treated me like the grime beneath her shoes. She didn't care if I was successful. She only saw her tether to my father severed."

Stella's wide eyes make me want to gather the words I allowed to spill out and shove them back inside my mouth.

But it's too late.

My tongue is heavy in my mouth, parched though I'm surrounded by water. The look on her face shows she can see the cracks and fissures in my façade.

Chapter Twenty-Two
Stella

Not even his parents.

Jameson's words echo inside my head. How could his parents not see how great he is? How could they use him like that? A pile of word sludge sticks to my mouth while I figure out what to say.

I squeeze his hand. "Well, it's their loss because Jameson is as great as Mr. Brooks."

Creases form along his forehead before he snorts and rolls his eyes. "You called me an arsehole the first time we met."

My face blazes. I did call him that. I didn't even give him a chance, didn't extend an olive branch. "Sorry. You're right."

We amble silently toward the other side. Chatting with him keeps me focused on everything except the fact that I'm inside a pool and not drowning.

"In your defense," he says. "I was being an arsehole that day."

I shrug and put on my best Billy Crystal impression. "You were grieving. It's a process."

Darkened eyes settle on me and his lips thin. "The last thing I'd ever do is grieve that woman."

The thumping of my heart ceases, and my stomach decides it's a great time to cliff dive. I should've known from the way he acted at the funeral home. While he's being so open and honest, I muster up the courage to ask what I've been dying to know. "Are your parents the reason you stopped painting?"

He recoils like a crash dummy. "What do you mean?"

I try to swallow but it doesn't work. I wet my lips and try again. "The paintings have a signature on the frame."

He doesn't speak for a few moments. His throat bobs, the thick muscles straining as his head falls back. I wait for the silence to be broken, for him to confirm they're his.

"I thought she threw them all away." His voice is a strained whisper.

An odd sense of relief flows over me. I tamp down the excitement as another piece of his cold exterior melts. Jameson doesn't seem like the type to willingly share things about himself. I'm honored he trusts me enough to talk to me.

"They were beautiful. Why'd you stop?"

Another shrug. "It wasn't what young men did, according to my father. And if it wasn't paying the bills, it didn't matter to my mother. When Dad ordered her to toughen me up, she'd ruin my paintings. I got into some trouble in secondary for graffiti, and he sent me to boarding school in the U.K. Eventually, I got the picture and stopped."

My heart beats in my ears. I can't imagine how someone could look at something so beautiful and want to ruin it. "I'm sorry you had shitty parents. You're talented. The paintings are beautiful."

"Thanks." He starts moving again but this time he heads to the stairs. His posture is slumped, shoulders barely rising with a breath. I need to turn this conversation back to something lighter.

"I saw Ernie today."

"Who?" He tries to hide his surprise, but I see right through it.

"Ernie, my friend you met the night at the bar."

He tilts his head, pretending like he doesn't remember him. "Hmm...nope. Doesn't ring a bell."

"Ugh." I search his chiseled face for a hint of a smile. "You know, the homeless vet you found a job for?"

"Ah...Ernest." He nods. "Yes, I remember now."

I throw my hands in the air. "Jameson, why do you make things so hard?"

"Love, let's talk about what *you* make hard."

I laugh and shove his shoulders. Denying the feelings buzzing through my body with him around isn't easy, but unless he makes the first move, I'm not willing to act on what's brewing between us.

"He needed a job." Jameson props a foot on the step and moves me in front of him.

"You helped him. That's —"

"No. I didn't help him. I told him about the opportunity."

I snort. "You did more than that and we both know it. Why are you so against helping someone?"

He stretches his neck, rubbing his muscular traps. "Needing help is a weakness."

"Yeah, well, you helped him anyway and it proves you're a better person than you like to let on."

He scoffs and turns. "Not in the slightest."

I throw my hands in the air and start up the stairs. Warm hands land on my waist, sizzling the skin beneath. His fingertips dig into my sides with the best type of pressure as he draws me back to him.

"Jameson," I shout, squirming around to get out of his grasp. His front meets my back and my body melts into him. He releases me like I've burned him, and I spin to meet his fiery gaze.

He drags a hand down his face then pushes it through his hair. "Can we *please* stop talking about me? Get back on track."

I cross my arms. "Jameson."

"Love, I want to teach you to float." He sighs, and his head falls forward. "Please?"

His frown and reddened face show me I'm treading a fine line. One wrong step and he'll shut me out for good.

I swallow my questions with a silent promise to dig deeper. "Okay."

He relaxes and places his hands at the top of my back and behind my thighs.

Little pinpricks of fear etch their way into my skin as he explains he's about to lower me into the water. I scratch at my neck, the backs of my arms, and my scalp, desperate to rid myself of the feeling.

Tightness creeps up my throat, strangling me.

Everything is fuzzy and muffled inside my head.

I scan the room, hoping to find something to focus on other than the water sloshing around, smacking the side of the pool.

But I'm surrounded by it.

It's rising.

A lasso of fear wraps around me, pinning my arms to my sides as the water haunts me.

It didn't get me last time.

It wants me now.

Tremors seize my shoulders and firm hands latch onto my arms and squeeze.

"Breathe." The grip tightens. "Stella. Breathe."

A gasp rips from my closed throat and tiny black dots dance around my vision. Jameson's pinched brows and worried eyes come into focus.

"Breathe from your diaphragm," he coaches, laying a hand on my stomach. "In. Out." He mimics what I should be doing, then his fingertips lightly brush up and down my arm.

I close my eyes and focus on the feather-light touch coaxing me back down to earth. My head clears after a few moments. Jameson takes my wrist in his hand, two fingers pressed against my pulse while he stares at his watch.

"I'm fine," I croak.

He lets go of my wrist and tilts my chin up, eyes searching me. "Are you sure? You gave me a scare."

"Yeah, I promise." I nod and meet his stare.

He releases my chin and a little piece of me folds in at the loss of touch. "We can stop for the day."

"No." I shake my head. "I need to conquer this."

He arches a brow. "You nearly fainted on me a moment ago."

"I'm fine. Now tell me what to do."

He shakes his head but repositions himself to my side, chest nearly bumping into my shoulder. "Keep your hand on the railing here. Don't let go unless you feel comfortable. Do you understand me? I don't want you pushing yourself too far and backtracking on the amazing progress you've made."

I nod and swallow the fear.

I can do this.

The thumping in my chest matches a similar pulse in my lower half when Jameson scoops me up into his arms and lowers himself. I reach for the railing, wrapping my fist around it with a tight grip. Cool water hits my rear and I shiver, goosebumps breaking out all over my skin.

"Are you okay?" Jameson slows his descent, raising a brow at me.

Cobwebs fill my mouth making it sticky as I struggle to answer past the fear. Instead, I nod, urging him to continue. Rigid muscles slowly release as my feet and head touch the water, the waves slowly rolling beneath my back. Cool air skitters over the areas not submerged in the water, turning my nipples to peaks in my white bathing suit.

Jameson's eyes dip to my chest but quickly snap back forward. I bite down on my lip, knowing this was a bad idea. My body responds to him in a way it's never responded to CJ, and that lands him firmly in the 'stay far away from' zone.

"I'm about to rock you back and forth. Keep breathing. Your lungs are like little life jackets inside your body. If they stay filled, you stay up. Got it?"

I gulp. "Okay."

He moves me like a ship, water rolling under my legs up to my head. I close my eyes and listen, finding peace in the muffled sound.

"It's weird." I loosen my grip on the railing. "I feel...relaxed? Like the fear made me heavy, and now I'm light."

"That's what swimming does for me." He clears his throat. "It helps ground me when things get to be...too much."

Feeling brave, I release my hand from the railing, letting my fingers glide over the water as he rocks me.

"Tell me something." Jameson moves slowly around the shallow end as water cascades over my stomach.

I peek an eye open. "What do you want to know?"

He shrugs. "Tell me about your family."

"Well, you've already met my Pop-Pop. My Nunny was amazing. She took me to church every Sunday, taught me how to cook and sew, and made sure I knew I could do anything. When I found out I'd be living with them after the accident, I was...relieved. I knew they loved me.

That's why I need to make sure Pop-Pop has everything he wants. They gave up a lot to raise another kid."

"I'm sorry." Jameson looks down at me, conflict in his eyes. "Didn't your parents leave you with anything to help?"

"My parents left us with nothing. Any money they had went to paying off the estate and selling it. Mr. Weston actually helped me with everything, since he and my father were business partners."

Jameson's blunt nails brush against my skin, and his gaze sends a shiver through my body. I blink, trying to break the spell between us. "But that's enough boring you with my life details."

He leans down and pins me with a hard stare, his mouth so close we're sharing breath. "I'll never tire of learning about you."

His lips are right there. All I'd have to do is tilt my head to feel the soft brush of them against mine. My mind short circuits, and the air I've deprived myself of in the last few moments claws at my throat. I gasp and my head nearly goes under the water.

Jameson lifts me, placing my feet on the slick bottom of the pool, probably worried I'm about to have a heart attack, but it's him. His smell, his laugh, his full, pillowy lips that I want to taste.

"Are you okay?" he asks.

"Mmhmm." I cough to force the lust back down. We've learned so much about each other tonight, and the more he opens up, the harder it is to deny I'm falling for him.

Hard.

"Yeah, I'm fine."

He rests his forehead against mine, and his hands return to my waist. "Love, I'm trying very hard not to kiss you right now."

My lungs expand, and my breasts touch his chest. "Kiss me."

"Stella." His voice deepens and he nudges my chin up to look at him. He strokes my hair, his eyes hooded and pupils dilated. "Are you sure you want to do this?"

Does a kid want the biggest lollipop in the candy shop?

Hell yes.

I answer by reaching up on tiptoes and capturing his lips. At first, his mouth is firm, his body stiff, but slowly he melts. He backs me against the pool wall and his tongue swipes along the seam of my lips, begging for access.

Minutes pass in a blur as Jameson devours my mouth, my neck, my collarbone. Fire sizzles through my veins, igniting a stick of dynamite in my core. He catches my mouth with another kiss, groaning as our tongues tangle. I moan and let my head fall back as he explores my neck again, his beard rough along my skin.

The normal awkward tension of a first kiss isn't there. Our mouths coordinate like they were made for each other, our bodies forged in the same fire, destined to meld together in the highest heat.

"I wanted so badly to do this the other night." He pulls me closer, lips grazing my shoulder.

I'm a boneless heap against the wall.

"Then why did you stop?" My nipples harden when he captures my earlobe in his teeth. He lifts me out of the water and places me on the edge of the pool before standing between my legs.

"Because you deserve better." His voice is a hoarse whisper against my sensitive skin.

I grab his face and force him to look at me. His eyes are a dark abyss of emotion, and I'm quickly getting sucked in. "Don't tell me what you think I deserve. I make that decision, not you."

"But—"

I nip at his lip, stifling the argument he's ready with. My hands move to his shoulders, and I scoot closer to the edge, pressing my hot center against his.

Strong hands land on my thighs, softly kneading the flesh. Jameson doesn't push the line further, but his touch sets my skin on fire, and I find myself moving his hand up toward my aching core. His sharp intake of air sets off a river of goosebumps as his thumb travels beneath my bathing suit.

With CJ, I was never vocal about my needs. But the way Jameson is worshiping my body gives me courage to demand it.

"Touch me," I beg.

His thumb caresses my center, and I tremble against him, letting out a whimper. His dark chuckle raises the hair on my neck. "You like that, Love?"

"Mmhmm," I murmur.

He puts more pressure on the tiny nub, making small circles as he lazily kisses me. My hips move of their own volition as his lips make it down to my neck. "Words, Stella."

I dig my nails into his shoulder. He growls at me and shudders like he's gotten a cold chill.

"Yes," I say. "More, please."

"Good girl." His praise makes me whimper, and he groans as he brushes a knuckle against me. "Bloody hell, you're soaked."

I wrap my arms around him and move closer as he sinks his fingers into my wet heat. In the acoustics of the empty pool area, my moan echoes. Jameson uses his other hand to pull my top down so he can take my pert nipple into his mouth.

Chaos erupts inside me with the sensation of his teeth nipping and grazing and his fingers pumping slowly in and out of me. Our breathing is labored, and Jameson catches my cry with his mouth as I shatter beneath him.

He removes his hand from my bottoms and smears my release across his lips before his tongue darts out to taste his fingers. His erection strains against his trunks, and I reach forward to release his cock. Warm hands wrap around my wrists, stopping me before I have the chance. "We need to talk about something."

I take his hands in mine, swallowing my pride. I know what he's about to say. Mr. Weston most likely already told him he has the promotion in the bag, but I still have the McCombs account in the pipeline, and that's good enough for me. "It's okay, I know."

He shakes his head, and his eyes are downcast. "No, you don't."

Laughs resound from inside the gym, voices getting louder as they head our way. I cover myself just as a group of men arrive, and one cannonballs into the pool, effectively ruining any chance for the conversation to continue. I can't believe we let the cloud of lust make us forget we weren't alone.

Judging by how quickly Jameson moves away from me, neither can he.

Chapter Twenty-Three
Jameson

After spending the morning drinking a celebratory Bloody Mary for closing the deal with Rodney Lewis, my dad and I shared a cigar. For as long as I can remember, I've always longed to be on this level with him, for him to be proud of me and see me as an equal, someone worthy of his time. But all I could think about was how I cocked it up with Stella again, and that I'm no better than my brother.

As a child, I hated Cameron because he could spend time with our father every day. In all fairness, if people saw me out with his family, they would've asked questions. Questions my father and his wife didn't want asked. So instead, he took his real family out on the town and spent time with me when he came to London.

When my mum finally moved to the States, the summers I spent with my dad were intended for me and Cameron to bond, but I figured out early on that he loathed me as much as I loathed him.

My phone vibrates along the dash, and I hit the Bluetooth.

"Brooks."

"Good morning, Mr. Brooks," a voice too chipper for the early morning says. "This is Tanya, Mr. McComb's secretary, calling back about setting up a meeting."

"Oh, great." I pull into the office parking lot and head to my office. "Thanks for getting back to me."

Hearing Mr. McCombs is willing to meet with me is bittersweet. On one hand, my dad will be thrilled, but on the other hand, what does this mean for Stella's meeting?

This past week has changed so many things between us, and I'm not sure where we go from here. I want Stella, but I'm not in a place where I can give her what she deserves. She should be with someone who's strong, stable, and able to be in a relationship.

I can't give her that.

The pressures of this job and my dad's expectations are beating me down, and I'm worried about how to keep Stella from finding out about my cutting, while also making sure she doesn't learn about my connection to her ex and our father. Add in the fact that I now know my father is keeping her trust a secret for a reason I've yet to figure out, and it's an explosion waiting to happen.

The lies are piling up, and according to the therapist I had a brief chat with this morning before my dad interrupted the call six times, I can't expect to start any type of relationship with Stella when I can't be honest about all of that.

"Sir?" the secretary asks.

"I'm here." I snap the rubber band, letting the pain refocus me.

"Does Friday work for you?"

I check my desk calendar. It's empty except for Stella's swim lessons on Saturday. "Friday's great."

We set the meeting, and even though I should feel excited at the prospect of landing a client like McCombs, my stomach is in knots about seeing Stella again. I thought I'd be able to get her out of my system, but after last night, all I want is more. Wondering if she feels the same way is driving me mad.

After the daily meeting, I need to find her and feel her out.

I pull out my sketchbook and start a rough outline of the pool, remembering the gentle slope of Stella's body as the water rushed over her toned stomach. The droplets clinging to her bathing suit, the waves rippling out as I lowered her into the pool.

Everything about last night is etched into my mind. Her moans, her breathy gasps as I brought her closer to the edge. God, remembering the sound of her coming sets my body on fire.

"Hey dickwad," Cameron says, barging into my office.

Startled, I close my sketchbook and clasp my hands over top of it. "What do you want, wanker?"

He shrugs and plops down into a chair across from me. "I'm not allowed to check in on my brother?"

My eyes dart to the open door. When I look back at Cameron, he's got a sick smile on his face. I slip my hand into my pocket, gripping the blade I told myself to put away for safekeeping. I long to open it and press my finger along the sharp tip, but instead, I force myself to release it and focus on my breathing techniques.

"You know what would happen if anyone found out." My voice is soft but carries the edge I'd hoped.

He grins, and my stomach knots. "I know. I just wanted to remind you that one word from me and your whole life goes bye-bye." He waves his hand like a child. "Including Stella."

"Stella?" I press my feet onto the floor, urging myself not to make any movement. *Lie, or else he'll tell your dad.* "What does she have to do with anything?"

He rises and leans over my desk. For a moment, I consider stabbing him with the knife in my pocket, but he wouldn't be worth the jail time.

"I know you want her, but if I couldn't even keep her, what makes you think you can?" He scoffs. "No one actually wants you here."

I should be focused on the fact that he insulted himself, but my sick mind locks onto the bigger portion of that sentence. The part I've failed at convincing myself isn't true from the moment I met her.

I've spent years trying to show my dad I'm worthy of his love and attention, and I still haven't. I'm nowhere close to being deserving of Stella's love or attention, but damn if I don't want it with every fiber of my being.

Cameron's exit coincides with my dad's entry. "Jim." He shuts the door behind him, eyebrows nearly at his hairline. "What was your brother doing here?"

Anger simmers beneath the surface when I look at him. I hate when he calls Cameron my brother. Brothers are there for each other. They support, and sometimes rile each other up in good fun. Cameron and I are *not* brothers.

I lie. "He had questions about some paperwork I sent his way for the Lewis account."

"Okay." He considers the artwork on my walls and frowns as he stares at the colorful pictures of a mural I painted back in secondary school. He doesn't know the artwork is mine, but his expression would still be the same even if he did. It's on the tip of my tongue to let him know about the art director meeting I finally set up, but his eye roll evaporates the admission on my tongue.

"I want you to work on a plan for your team for when you take over. You may have to make some cuts to the department, but with the Thompson name on their resumes, they'll be able to find jobs with no problem."

"Cuts?" I ask.

"Soon enough you'll be showing the board how much revenue you can bring to Thompson, and the transition to VP will be easier."

"VP?" My voice pitches like I suck helium and I snap the rubber band a few times beneath the desk. The plan was for me to stay in the project manager job for a few years and work up the hierarchy, not jump immediately to running the company. "What are you talking about?"

He pins me with a hard stare. "I want you as my right-hand man. The board wants a fresh face to take over after Carlson retires, and this puts you in a better position to take over when I'm finished."

I gulp.

The more he talks about it, the bigger the knot in my stomach grows.

This is what I should be working toward, what his plans have been for me since I graduated university, but the conversation with Stella about my art keeps nudging at the back of my head.

Is this what I really want to do? Does my success have to look like my dad's? I was happy, and stable, when I was working in art investments back in the U.K. Since I've moved here, I've embarked down a path I know won't end well.

"I don't know if I'm ready for that," I say.

He opens the door and steps out before turning back to me. "You will be."

I breathe a sigh of relief into the empty office and rest my eyes, cycling through the anxiety checklist my therapist gave me years ago. My palm itches to find a dark supply closet and relieve this tension, but I've got to be stronger. I can handle the stress.

A knock at the door makes me groan out loud. Why does everyone choose the moment I'm having a minor breakdown to bother me?

I shove back from the desk and open the door, ready with harsh words on the tip of my tongue. "What?"

Stella's eyes widen. "I'm sorry. I didn't mean to bother you." She turns away, but I catch her hand.

"I didn't know it was you. I'm sorry." My fingers curl around hers and pull her toward me. Her shoulders ease from her ears and she looks at me with resignation. "Are you in a pissy mood? I can come back later."

The longer we stand in the doorway, the more chance we have of being seen. I'm not ashamed of what we did, but I don't need coworkers butting in and making their own assumptions before I know how she feels about it.

"We're drawing attention. Please, come in."

She gives up and waltzes into my office. I catch a whiff of her perfume, and my cock stirs. Following behind her to the chair is pure torture. Grey dress trousers for women should be outlawed. Especially when they're worn by exquisite beauties like Stella. Simply thinking of the slight brush of my body against hers sets my mind down a not so friendly path.

"What's wrong?" she asks.

I tug on the coarse strands of my beard, pretending like I can banish the thoughts of peeling the trousers off her, laying her across my desk, and sinking myself so deep into her she'll feel me for days. I struggle to banish the inappropriate thoughts, but her moans from last night are the soundtrack playing inside my head. "Nothing."

She squints. "Are you sure? You seem agitated."

"I'm fine, Love."

She shivers at my endearment, and a little bubble of glee pops in my chest before I realize she's probably here because of last night. I've been so focused on how she made me feel and what she let me do, that I forgot I started to tell her about what I've been keeping from her.

With the cloud of lust popped, I'm not sure it's a good idea anymore.

If I tell her about my cutting, I'd also have to tell her why. That would open more questions about my family, and I'd have to tell her about Cameron and my father. Not to mention, my father is the trustee on a blind trust she knows nothing about. After last night, I'm sure my dad is hiding something, but I haven't found the right time to snoop.

"Are you busy tonight?" she asks.

My trousers jump at the question, silently answering for me. I should be drawing up a plan like my father requested, but I'm willing to slack off in exchange for more time with her. "What did you have in mind?"

Her bottom lip is red from her nervous chewing. I lean back in my chair, failing at not letting her see the lust filling my eyes. She shifts in her chair, and her nostrils flare. "A few of us are going to dinner and a bar later."

Breathing is a struggle as I will my hard-on to stand down. "They don't have what I want on the menu."

Her tongue swipes along her bottom lip, and I ball my fists beneath the desk. I want to reach out and touch her soft skin, to trace my tongue along her elegant jaw, but we're not there…yet.

"Jameson," she laughs. "I'm serious. Do you want to come?"

Her cheeks flame when she realizes the double entendre.

"I'd love to," I say. "I can't make dinner, but what time are you going to the bar?"

"Around ten." She stops at the door. Her hair is tied back, but the curls of her ponytail swing side to side in time with her hips. I damn near keel over at my desk when she cocks her hip to the side and looks at me over her shoulder. "I'll message you the address."

***

By the time I finish copying the trust paperwork and making a rough outline of my grand plan to take over Thompson, I'm thirty minutes late to meet Stella.

Loud music vibrates the soles of my feet the closer I get to the bar. Stella's address brings me to a brick building right off the Riverwalk. A wrought iron sign hangs above the door, the words 'Howl at the Moon' scribbled across it with an accompanying wolf picture. The bar is dark but filled with neon lights, and Rosay's pink hair catches my eye. Mike and his wife Christine are at the table with Stella.

"Hey, mate," I yell over the loud piano music. "Didn't know you'd be here." My tone is cordial, but I'm sure my eyes convey betrayal.

"We were out on date night when Rosay texted us."

Stella has a large, colorful drink in front of her, and her attention stays focused on slurping down the contents. I lean down, next to the shell of her ear and whisper, "You look beautiful."

She releases the ribbed straw and looks up at me. Her fruity-scented breath makes my heart speed, and I long to capture her lips. My eyes fall to her parted mouth, nearly closing the distance, but I remember we're in public and she may not want anyone to know what's going on between us outside of work.

She smiles and pulls out the seat beside her. "Took you long enough."

My pocket vibrates, and I slip out my phone to make sure it's not my dad. A chuckle escapes when I see it's Mike. All the text includes is a confused emoji. I chance a look at him, and both he and his wife wear matching arched eyebrows. Stella and Rosay are focused on the band at the front of the club.

I type back a mischievous emoji with the words, 'I haven't a clue what you're talking about' and slip my phone back into my pocket.

Stella's hand slams down on my leg beneath the table. Her shoulders sway to the tune the pianists are dueling back and forth on, and her fingers draw little circles on my inner thigh. Simultaneously my body heats, muscles tightening the closer she gets to my upper thighs. I grab her hand before she reaches where my scars are, and entwine our fingers.

A few songs pass, and when the band takes a break, Mike steals me to get some fresh air. He doesn't bother warming me up. "What's going on with you and Stella? Christine is up my ass about it."

I lean against the balcony railing. "Fuck if I know, man."

"What's that supposed to mean?"

"It means I don't know what's going on between us." I turn to him and shrug. "She was dating Cameron."

"Cameron? Like your," he lowers his voice, "brother?"

I nod, and my knuckles turn white as I squeeze the railing. Mike and Cameron have never gotten along, and he's always been a good friend and kept the fact that we're siblings a secret, even from his wife.

"Yeah, mate. What fucking luck have I got if I'm not only falling for the enemy, but also for my arsehole brother's ex?"

"Falling for?" His eyebrows raise. "That's...wow, you're serious about her?"

I nod.

"Damn." He chuckles and scratches the back of his head. "That's the worst kind of luck. Well, what are you gonna do?"

I shrug. "What can I do? Only one of us can be the project manager, and it's looking like my dad will pick me. And when she finds out Cameron is my brother, she'll be furious."

"Have you asked her what *she* wants?"

I look back into the bar where Stella laughs with Rosay. She looks so carefree, not like the uptight woman I thought she was when I first started. Even with the weight of the funeral home potentially closing, and the promotion so close, she still can find something to be happy about. And I'm sitting here miserable because I'm too much of a coward to ask her to be mine.

"She deserves better than I can give her."

"That's not what I asked." Mike pushes my shoulder and laughs. "You can't make that decision for her. Stella seems like a great girl. Shit, she even somehow managed to get you to smile more times tonight than I've seen from you in the last ten years. "

I scoff. "You're being dramatic."

"I like that you're not the brooding jackass you used to be. Tell her how you feel. Before your brother wises up and realizes what he took for granted."

I down the rest of my drink and consider his words. Stella all but told me the same thing last night, but she doesn't know about my issues. Mike's been my best mate for years, but even he never understood the urges I have.

It took years of therapy before I understood it was the need for control that drove me to self-harm. Even though I still struggled, I was healthier back in the U.K. and could resist the urge when the stress wasn't high. How can I manage a high stress job and a relationship with Stella if there's already this much against us and I feel out of control?

"Let's go inside." Mike claps me on the back. "Figure out what you're gonna do soon. Stella's a catch."

Don't I know it.

"I didn't think you'd show tonight." She's still facing forward when I sit back down, but I know she's talking to me.

Inching closer, I speak into her ear. "There's no place I'd rather be."

Goosebumps break out down her arms, and she leans into me. How a touch that small can set off a chain reaction in my body is beyond me, but it does. I feel it in the way my chest expands to touch her again, how my toes dig into the ground to keep me in my seat, and how my hand tenses around hers.

I want her more than I've wanted anything in a long time.

"How's work?" Mike asks the table.

"It's been fine," I say. "How's that case you're working on?"

Mike's a hotshot prosecutor. He's been working on a first-degree murder trial that's been in the papers. "It got a little hectic the other day."

A warm hand lands on my thigh, and I watch Stella as she lifts her drink to her lips, letting the cool liquid stream into her mouth. "How so?"

Mike runs a hand through his blond hair, tugging at the ends. "A fight broke out on the defendant's side. Something about two mothers arguing over a ceramic angel that turned physical."

I respond with wide eyes, but it's not because I'm surprised at Mike's story. Stella's hand has made it to my cock, and she's teasing me with soft brushes of her thumb. Her eyes are dark and filled with lust when she looks up at me. Mike continues with his story, but my gaze is locked on the brown-eyed beauty in front of me. Her cheek lifts with a smile before she wraps her hand around my cock through my trousers.

I damn near explode at her rough palming.

She stops abruptly when a waiter stops at our table. I clasp my hands on the table, so it doesn't look suspicious, but I don't succeed in fooling Mike. His eyes are narrowed, and a hint of a smile appears on his lips.

To break the awkward tension, I reach for the glass of whiskey the waiter hands me. Stella grips my thigh tightly, and her fingernails dig into my leg at the wrong spot. Midway to setting the drink down, a sharp pain shoots through my leg and I drop the glass.

I wince at the ache and grab for some napkins.

"Are you okay?" Stella asks, brows scrunched together.

I nod and direct my attention to cleaning the mess. I can't look at Stella. I don't want to see the confusion and questions sure to be on her face.

As much as I want her, I'm not ready to be honest about my struggles. I need to get help before I pursue a relationship with her.

I slip my phone from my pocket and send off a text to the therapist I had to cut short the other day to see if I can schedule another call with her.

Stella doesn't touch me the rest of the night, and I don't blame her. I wouldn't want to touch a head case like me that blanches every time she gets near my cock. She can tell I have issues, and even if she doesn't know what they are, she's smart enough to realize I'm not worthy of her.

Chapter Twenty-Four
Stella

The soft click of a cane has me jumping up from the couch and heading into the kitchen to make my grandfather a cup of coffee. Pop-Pop shuffles the bills on the table, his shoulders slouching with a sigh. "It was fifty years ago we bought this house and the funeral home." He waves his hand around the room, a wistful look upon his face. "I miss her."

"Me, too." My voice breaks. "Growing up, you and Nunny were the only example of true love I'd ever seen. I always wished I could find love like that."

"You don't think CJ was true love?" The way he asks makes me feel like he already knows the answer.

"CJ and I loved each other, but something was missing. He wants to fix things between us, and I keep telling him we aren't meant for each other."

He peers at me through the glasses on the end of his nose. "You sure it doesn't have anything to do with Jameson?"

I've run the gamut of emotions the past two months with him. Half the time I loathe him, and the other half I find myself smitten. But he's flighty, not direct about what he wants. He pulls me in, then pushes me away when I get close.

After getting out of a long-term relationship, my heart should want a break.

But it doesn't.

The stupid organ wants more, and I'm not sure he's capable of giving me that.

I roll my eyes, frustrated I told him about my kiss with Jameson. Pop-Pop is my honorary best friend outside of Rosay. Taking care of him and Nunny didn't leave me with many friends, so he became my confidant. Unfortunately, that means he also calls me on my crap.

"I don't know, Pops. I thought CJ was it for me. We spent years together."

"But he didn't light that fire in you. He smothered it."

I rear back. "What do you mean?"

"You had to grow up a lot faster than other kids, and I couldn't help out more because of Nunny. You became a caretaker for everyone else, but when did CJ ever take care of you?"

I'm speechless.

He's not wrong, but I like being helpful.

When I don't speak, he continues. "Now, Jameson might be an ass, but he helped fix your tire, he's helping you learn how to swim, and he even got Ernie a job." He gets up from the table and pours the rest of his coffee down the drain. "I know it may not seem like the biggest thing in the world, but ever since you met him, the fire has been back in your eyes. There's passion between you two."

"Passion isn't everything. Look what happened to Mom and Dad."

He frowns. "What your mom and dad had wasn't passion. It was poison. And you can't live your life based on what happened in theirs, Stella. You've got to give yourself the best chance at happiness, and sometimes that's scary, but it's the only way you'll find love like me and your Nunny had."

My face heats and tears prick my eyes.

Damn, Pop-Pop.

***

I'm halfway home from dropping Pop-Pop off at the cemetery when my phone rings.

"Hello?"

"Hi, Ms. Daniels. It's Ron from Wynne City Caskets. We have a bit of a problem."

"A problem?"

"The caskets came in, and I don't have enough room to store them. We need to unload these today, or else they'll be stuck outside until we're able to fill the other orders, and it's calling for rain."

"Damn it, Ron. How did this happen?"

"I'm sorry, Ms. Daniels. It looks like someone couldn't read Mr. Daniel's handwriting and mistook a six for an eight on the date. I only just caught it when I saw the order."

I blow out a breath and flick on my blinker. Pop-Pop's handwriting has gotten worse the last few years, but he still won't change to electronic ordering. "If your guys can meet me right now, I can be at the funeral home in ten minutes."

He speaks with one of the unloaders. "They'll head over now."

We hang up and I call Rosay. I refuse to turn around and pull Pop-Pop from his anniversary date with Nunny. It's Rosay's off day, so if she can help me, I'll be able to get to work on time.

"Hey, Stella."

"Hey beautiful lady. Any chance you can help me out at the funeral home?"

"Oh, no. What happened?" she asks. "Is everything okay with Pop-Pop?"

People chatter in the background of the call, making it difficult to hear her. "Everything's fine with Pops. It's his and Nunny's anniversary, so he's at the cemetery. There's an issue with the casket delivery and I need some help."

"Darn it," she says. "Mindy asked me to swap shifts with her the other day, so I'm working. Hold on." Muffled voices and a weird clicking noise sounds through the speaker before she returns to the phone. "Sorry. I'll see if I can get an early lunch, but no promises."

My shoulders fall, and I puff out my cheeks. If I can't get the caskets inside by lunch time, I'll have to reschedule my meetings and call off work. Once again, I'm split between my career and the funeral home, and I don't know what to do. "Okay, thanks anyway, girl."

I pull up to the funeral home and go inside, touching the picture of my grandparents as I head down the hallway to open the back door. Ten minutes pass before the tell-tale beep of a reversing delivery truck echoes through the alleyway. Two men jump out and fling open the door, unearthing the caskets Pop-Pop ordered. I grab the dolly and push it toward them.

"Thanks for bringing these on such short notice," I say, giving them a smile.

The older man, Elias, grumbles, and the younger one shrugs, unbothered. We get the first casket down and inside as a loud motorcycle pulls into the parking lot. As I stroll down the ramp, Jameson parks and pulls off his helmet.

Dark hair, corded, tattooed forearms, a black t-shirt and denim jeans. Lava sludges its way through my bloodstream, setting my skin on fire as he stalks toward me. "Wh...what are you doing here?" I ask.

"Rosay said you needed help." He opens his arms like he's offering a present. "Where do you want me?"

Underneath me? Behind me? Take your pick. My heart pitter-patters in my chest, and an alarm goes off inside my head. How long will it take for him to pull away again?

"I guess right here?" I motion to the back door where the two men are.

"Can we get this done?" Elias says. "I have things I need to do."

Jameson's jaw tenses. "Don't speak to her like that."

I stifle the urge to remind him he spoke those exact words to me the first day we met, and instead relish in the fact he's standing up for me now.

He showed up, even though I didn't ask him.

Elias's head snaps up. "You guys could at least help."

I reach for Jameson's hand as he steps toward Elias, snapping the rubber band on his wrist. My eyes fall to the red skin, and an uneasiness settles in my stomach. Why does he do that?

"Ignore him," I plead.

His eyes pierce me, and he frowns. "He shouldn't be talking to you like that."

I pin him with a hard stare. "I've heard worse. Let's finish this and I'll talk with his boss later. We both need to get back to work."

The two men and Jameson finish moving all the caskets into the funeral home within the hour. A few months ago, I wouldn't have expected Jameson to be the one to aid me in my time of need, but here he is, my knight in a leather jacket. He knew I was struggling, and he showed up for me.

Jameson reaches over and closes the back door when the delivery drivers pull away. His cedar scent wafts into my space, enveloping me in the soft caress of his presence. My mouth waters when his toned muscles strain beneath his shirt.

He chuckles. "You're drooling, Love."

My jaw clenches in protest. "Am not."

"Do you need help with anything else?" He catches my hand and rubs a thumb over my knuckles. We're like magnets, one flip and we're pushed apart, another flip and we can't stay away from each other.

"No, I'm all done here. You didn't have to help, but I appreciate it."

He wraps his arms around my waist, pulling me close as I finish locking the door. "Don't mention it."

Soft lips meet the heated skin on my neck, and I wiggle out of his hold. "Jameson," I groan.

He leans against the reception desk with a smirk. "What, Love?"

"What is this?" I ask, motioning between us. "Because you're giving me whiplash."

He shifts on his feet and regards me with warm eyes. "I don't mean to."

"Then tell me what you want from me." Surrendering, I throw my hands in the air. "One minute you're all over me, and the next you're pushing me away like I'm a pariah. Am I doing something wrong?"

He slides a hand down his face, gripping his jaw. "God, no. You're all I can think about, but—"

"But what?" I ask. "Do you want a fling? I can do casual, Jameson."

I've never done it before, but I'd be willing to try with him.

He shoves his hands into his pockets. "No, Stella. I don't want something *casual* with you. I want more. I want it all."

"Then what's the issue?" I step toward him. "Is it the promotion? Are you worried what people at work will think?"

Challenging him about his stance on the job makes me think about mine. With Pop-Pop considering selling the funeral home, do I even still want the promotion? And would getting the promotion prevent me and Jameson from dating?

So many questions I can't answer on my own.

"Fuck what people at work will think." Jameson takes his hand out of his pocket and reaches for my hand.

Something drops to the floor.

My gaze lands on the knife at his feet.

It's sleek, covered in blue epoxy. It looks...dangerous.

We both reach down, but Jameson beats me to it and shoves it back inside his pocket. His expression is unreadable when I look back at him.

"I don't care about everyone else." He pulls me close, whispering into my ear. "Only you matter."

A weight lifts off my shoulders at the sincerity in his voice.

His chest puffs up with a long inhale, and his eyes close as he exhales. "But I need to talk to you about some things before you decide if you want to be with me."

"Like what?" I ask, my pulse racing. What secrets could he be hiding? A wife? Kids? Maybe he's an ex-con?

His phone rings, and he groans when he looks at the screen. "Damn it. I've gotta go, but we'll talk at the swim lesson later."

Dazed, I nod. "Okay."

He leans forward and kisses me on the cheek. "I'll see you in a bit."

Too many questions swirl around my head as I lock up and head out to my car.

Chapter Twenty-Five
Jameson

The cool metal of the knife in my pocket soothes me as I grab my helmet. Leaving Stella without answers wasn't my intention, but I'm already late getting on the road to my father's house. Somehow, she burrowed deep, like a termite into the rotting frames of my mind, chewing away at everything keeping me centered.

I slide onto the seat and exhale, gripping the handles with white knuckle force. The engine purrs to life and a jazz melody plays through the speakers. I go over my notes a few times to ensure I'm ready for any questions Dad might throw my way. He didn't seem upset when he messaged, but that can change by the time I arrive.

"Good afternoon, Mr. Brooks." My father's housekeeper greets me and leads me to the office. "You can wait here for him."

Anger bubbles inside me.

His staff treats me like a secondhand citizen when I'm technically part of this family, but I know it's how Colleen trained them. I didn't ask to be born, but she still sees me as a threat to her perfect family.

I pop out of my father's office and head to the loo to splash water on my face. Passing the kitchen, I overhear Colleen chatting with Cameron. Their voices are hushed, but I can tell it's not a friendly conversation. Without consulting me, my feet plant themselves in front of the door and I lean close to listen.

"This is all your fault," Colleen says. "If you would've gotten yourself together, *he* wouldn't be here."

I assume the *"he"* she's referencing is me.

"It doesn't matter," Cameron replies. "Dad might've gotten him the Lewis account, but he's not gonna get the McCombs account. Stella already has that in the bag. It won't be long before Dad realizes he doesn't need him and sends Jameson back to where he came from. He's here because of what Dad says he can do for the company, not because he loves him."

I fight the urge to open the door and tell them off. How Cameron plans to take over the company when he isn't even being considered for a promotion within his own department is beyond me.

"One can hope," Colleen says.

Disgust fills my stomach.

At one point in time, I'd hoped Colleen could become like a second mum to me. When we moved to the States, I thought I'd find a family, something I didn't have back home, but Colleen and Cameron made it clear I wasn't wanted. They hated me more than my mum did, and they showed me by ignoring me, alienating me, and making me feel like an inconvenience.

I wasn't allowed to go anywhere off the property with them, and my dad never challenged Colleen or stood up for me. But his love is all I've ever wanted, and he's all I have left.

"Jim?" My father startles me. "I thought you were meeting me in the office."

I wet my dry lips and nod. "I needed to use the restroom."

Dad spins on his heels, and I follow, my stomach uneasy as I take a seat in his office. "Did you bring your plan?"

"What plan?" Cameron bursts into the room with a can of pop.

"That's none of your concern, CJ." Dad's focus is on his computer.

I smile at the clear dismissal, but Cameron doesn't blanch. "He probably doesn't have it. He's too busy chasing my sloppy seconds."

My fists curl around the knife in my pocket. "I beg your pardon?"

"Your sloppy seconds?" Dad relaxes into his chair.

"He's been chasing Stella around like a love-sick puppy dog." Cameron steps into my space and smirks. "Isn't that right, bro?"

If looks could kill, I'd be handcuffed and in the back of a police car right now. It's not that I didn't want my dad to know I was interested in Stella, but I haven't even talked to her about what we are yet, let alone figured out the ramifications of dating your half-brother's ex-girlfriend while she doesn't know the boss is also your dad.

"Jim?" Dad prompts. "Is that true?"

Lie. Lie. Lie. "It's not chasing if she's not running, mate."

"You son of a bitch." Before I know it, Cameron's fist swings at me. I'm more agile than him, so he connects with my shoulder instead of my face.

"Get out, CJ," Dad's voice bellows, his hands smacking against the table. "Now."

Smug, I turn my back on him and sit in the chair. I know I shouldn't have antagonized him, but he had it coming. Stella is anything but sloppy seconds. Now, if only I could figure out a way to convince her I'm still worth it once she finds out all I've been keeping from her.

The door slams, and my father's lethal eyes settle on me. "Tell me he's lying."

My chest and throat tighten. "It's not how it sounds."

"Damn it." His voice raises. "Why her? Anyone else would've been fine. Hell, Mindy would've been a better option."

Have you seen Stella? There's no one else.

"It's not like I planned to fancy her." I shrug. "It just...happened."

"You'll stop seeing her immediately—"

"What?" I rise from my chair, pressure building in my chest, restricting my breath. He can't be serious.

"Your brother might've lowered his standards, but you're not."

My stomach churns, and the leash I've kept around my tongue releases. "Lower my standards? Like you did with mum?"

Anger flashes behind his eyes, but he doesn't take the bait. My dad is all about control, and even as I watch his composure almost slip, I see where I first learned the need to always be in control.

"Don't put pussy over power and legacy, son."

His crass use of the term grates on my nerves, and I long to reach across the table to silence him.

Stella is so much more than that.

Being with her makes me happy, makes me feel whole. Half the time I almost feel...normal. No job can make me feel half of what she does when she simply smiles at me. If anything, she's lowering her standards to be with me.

"Damn it," he says again, running a hand through his hair. "If the board gets wind of this, I may have to wait until the next big project to promote you. Why would you fuck this up? All my hard work is potentially down the drain because you can't keep it in your pants."

My stomach knots tighter.

I've cocked everything up I came here for. Dad's furious, I've potentially lost the opportunity for the promotion I'm not even sure I want anymore, and Stella will most likely tell me she never wants to see me again when she finds out who I am.

"Get out of my sight," my dad says. "And don't return until your head is on straight. Both of them."

My feet are like lead as I head back to my bike. I can feel eyes on my back, but I don't turn around to see who's looking. It's probably Colleen standing at the window with a glass of wine and a smug look on her face. I kick start the engine and peel out of the driveway.

Fresh air and the long stretch of highway between Boerne and Downtown San Antonio is exactly what I need to calm myself down before Stella's swim lesson and our talk.

Weaving in and out of traffic, I make it to Thompson right as the last few employees are leaving for the day. Inside, I pace my office floors, fidgeting with the Swiss Army knife in my pocket. I missed the tele-health call with my therapist again, and thus far, nothing has helped quell this burning need inside me.

My emotions are in a traffic jam, each one inching further into the other's lanes, trying to steal my attention. My dad's expectations, his disappointment, Cameron's hate seeping between everything I've worked for to show my dad I'm worthy of his love, and now Stella. They're all like cars honking at each other and screaming to be free.

Breathing exercises aren't working, and control is quickly slipping from my grasp. I can't let Stella see me like this, and I need to be entirely focused on her swim lesson. She's depending on me to help her, and my emotions are too chaotic right now to do that. I give it half an hour before I check the main floor to see if everyone is gone.

Grabbing my bag, I turn off the lights and head down to the pool to relieve some tension in the only way I know will work.

Chapter Twenty-Six
Stella

"Are you finally gonna bang him tonight?" Rosay's husky voice is at a volume too loud for open windows. I press the automatic window button so the poor old woman sitting beside us doesn't have a heart attack.

A noise somewhere between a scoff and a snort makes its way out of my mouth. "I doubt it. He's the king of mixed signals."

"The electricity popping off y'all last night was insane." She does a little shimmy as she opens a bag of spicy pork rinds. "I figured you'd go home together, but then he left early."

She leaves the rest unsaid, but it hangs between us like a bad smell. *What the hell happened?*

It's a question I've asked myself all night.

Both times we've made progress, sexual or otherwise, he puts a stop to it. At this point, I'd take the physical whiplash of a car accident over the one happening inside my head.

"I know," I groan. "I don't know what he wants."

"Do you even know what you want?" she asks, sucking down her water. "I mean, you said you didn't want a rebound after CJ, but now Jim is here, and he's after the same job as you."

My sigh is big and dramatic. "It doesn't feel like a rebound with Jameson. Or, at least it feels like it could be more, if he'd stop playing red-light green-light with my emotions." I rest my head against the seat.

"And now that the McCombs account is so close to being mine, I'm not sure I'll need the promotion to help Pop-Pop. If I get it, I'd be responsible for a team, handling client issues, handling employee issues, and that's on top of helping at the funeral home. I thought I needed it, like it should be mine because of my tenure, but I'm having second thoughts."

"Are you sure those second thoughts aren't because of your feelings for Jameson?"

I shrug. "I'm not sure. It already seems like Mr. Weston wants to give him the job, but none of it matters until I know how Jameson feels. I could be making all this up in my head."

"Do you really believe that?" Her white fingers are covered in orange crumbs, and she sticks them into her mouth to clean them.

I take a moment to consider, but I already know the answer. "No, I don't. Every interaction with him has felt authentic. I mean, sure he was a dick in the beginning, but after I yelled at him at the funeral home, I didn't expect it to be all roses for us. Add in the promotion, and it's understandable why we butted heads those first few weeks."

She makes a noise of agreement. "You need to tell him how you feel, and if he's still reluctant, walk away. You waited too long for CJ to get his shit together, and you deserve someone who's one hundred percent in it like you are."

"Thanks for the pep talk. I love you, girl."

"Love you, too. Now go make that man's knees weak."

She heads to her car, and I throw on some 80's pop to help take my mind off Jameson and our situation before our swim lesson. The gym is empty when I arrive. Inside the locker room, I quickly change into my bathing suit. Jameson isn't swimming laps like he normally is, so I decide to surprise him by getting into the pool.

I shake out my hands, and swallowing becomes difficult the closer I get to the edge. *You can do this, Stella. You've got this,* I keep telling myself.

I place my hand on the cold steel railing leading into the pool and move to the first step, sending small ripples through the crystal-clear abyss. Glee rises in me at the small feat I've accomplished.

Feeling brave, I inch my toes closer to the next step.

A loud crash inside the locker room makes me jump and I slip on the edge and fall into the water. Fear shoots up my spine and I cling to the railing, squeezing my eyes shut.

My heartbeat thrashes around in my head.

Don't breathe in. Don't let the water inside.

I hold my breath, waiting for water to flow over my head.

Nothing happens.

I open my eyes to find I'm still on the step. I wince as I stand, butt and legs drenched. My heart still pounds in my throat and my skin is alive with goosebumps. I head to the women's locker room and rush inside to check all the shower stalls and bathrooms but find no one.

Through the thin wall separating the men's and women's locker rooms I hear a painful groan then thump. Swallowing my fear, I leave the women's changing room and open the door to the men's.

I scan the rows of lockers, hoping I don't find whoever it is with their dick out. I shudder at the thought but then correct myself. *Who cares if there's a dick?* If someone's hurt, then I'm the only one here to help them since Jameson is late.

"Hello?" I ask. "Everything okay?"

Another groan from somewhere in the room raises the hairs on the back of my neck. The sound leads me to a running shower at the back.

A set of feet peek out from under a pulled-down curtain, the red-tinted water still flowing.

"Oh my gosh," I yell, lifting the curtain, ready to render aid.

I clamp my hand across my mouth, my body freezing mid-movement.

Vomit shoots up my throat at the sight of Jameson passed out, covered in blood. I force it back as I crouch beside him, water cascading over my head.

"Jameson." My voice breaks.

The pressure in my chest makes it hard to breathe. He doesn't answer, but his eyes flutter open and he groans.

I search for my phone to call an ambulance but realize I left it in the other room. *Idiot.*

I grab his face with both of my hands. "Jameson. Wake up," I cry.

"Stella?" His eyes are closed, his voice weak.

Blood pulses in my ears. My throat tightens.

I reach up and turn off the water so he can hear me. "Yes, it's me." I rub my hands along his beard, massaging his cheeks to rouse him and bring some color back to his face. "What happened?" I squeak.

"Huh?" He opens his eyes a little.

At the back of his head, I search for a lump or any cuts in case he slipped and fell and has a concussion. Once I'm satisfied his head is fine, I take in our surroundings.

A familiar blue knife lays in a puddle in the corner of the shower, surrounded by pink water. *Why would he bring his knife into the shower?* Thoughts about him being an ex-con pop back into my head. Maybe that's what he wanted to tell me the other day. Was he worried someone planned to hurt him?

No one else was in the room when I came in, but someone could've left while I was checking the women's locker room.

Something nudges in the back of my mind, and I look down at my feet.

Blood.

I blink.

Once. Twice.

My heart pumps so fast I'm worried it'll overwork and shut down. Where is the blood coming from? I follow the trail of the pink water to Jameson's thighs.

His legs are cut, surrounded by old scars.

I search around for any shards of glass but find nothing sharp in sight but...his knife.

Did he do this to himself?

My breath leaves me and a knot forms in my stomach.

All at once, everything focuses. The rubber band snapping, the breathing techniques he showed me to calm down during our swim lessons, his pulling back each time I touched his legs.

It makes sense, but at the same time doesn't.

He's a man.

A strong, arrogant man...who cuts?

I feel like I'm missing something. Men drink. They drown their worries in liquor. They don't take sharp blades to their skin. Women do. Or at least that's how the media always portrays it. Men are strong. Too strong to succumb to hurting themselves this way. Too proud to get the mental help they need.

Jameson has been putting on a front to seem strong.

I squeeze my eyes shut to regain control over my own emotions. "What did you do, Jameson?" My fingers tremble as I run them through his hair.

"Stella?" he asks again, more clearly.

"Yes, it's me."

His eyes snap open like he's a narcoleptic coming back to consciousness. "Get out."

"What?" I ask, taken back by the sudden switch.

He pushes me aside and tries to get up. "I said, get out."

"Jameson."

His voice deepens, the tone dark and dangerous. "I said, get the fuck out." He winces as he moves, pushing me away with one hand.

"I'm not leaving you here." I reach for him again, tears streaming down my cheeks. "You're hurt and need to go to the hospital."

"Stella." His voice sends a chill through my bones, paralyzing me. "If you value your job, I suggest you leave right now and keep your mouth shut."

I let out a harsh breath and stand, my teeth clenched so hard my jaw hurts. Embarrassed and worried, I leave with my hands balled into fists at my side. I make it back to the women's locker room and put on my dress before I leave, tears racing down my face.

I rush out to my car, wiping my cheeks before I throw my bag into the backseat beside the first aid kit I keep for emergencies. Looking back to the building, my heart is torn between helping Jameson and keeping my job. He has Mr. Weston's favor, and I'm already on thin ice since CJ and I broke up. I would never divulge Jameson's secret, even if he ruined my career, but my heart aches for what I've witnessed.

My Nunny always taught me to help people who are in need, even if they can't see or won't admit they need help.

With clarity, I grab the first aid kit.

Rummaging through the contents, I find a pair of gloves, alcohol, butterfly tape, and some liquid stitches. I don't know how deep his cuts are, but it's the best I've got.

Tears prick my eyes and I push back the sadness bubbling up inside me. *Why the hell would he cut himself?* Vomit roils in my stomach the closer I get to the building.

I inhale a fresh breath of air before I head back inside and creep into the locker room.

Jameson sits on the bench with his hands over a wad of paper towels stained red on his thighs. His head hangs and his shoulders rise with a shaky breath.

I bite down on my cheek and move closer, a mound of nervousness growing inside me.

"Jameson." My voice strains.

His eyes rise to meet mine and blood flows to every edge of my body, setting my skin on fire. In the craziness of finding him bloody and passed out, I didn't register that he was completely naked. *Focus, Stella.*

"I told you to leave." His voice is harsh, strained, and the wrinkle in his forehead deepens into a crevasse.

I tentatively step up to him, my hand coming to his shoulder.

He shakes it off, not meeting my eyes. "Go," he says. "I don't need your help."

I kneel in front of him, looking up at his pale face. He turns his cheek, and the muscles of his jaw tense. He flinches and closes his eyes when I lay my hands on top of his. "Let me see them," I beg.

"No." I open the first aid kit and lay my supplies on the bench. He opens his eyes but doesn't look at me. "I can do it myself."

I ignore him and put on the gloves before I uncap the alcohol and place my hand on top of his again, hoping he won't shake me off. When he doesn't, I move his hand.

Blood trickles down his leg the minute I lift the towels to inspect the cuts. I take a deep breath before I look down at the three-inch gash in his leg. My throat closes, a lump forming as I catalog at least twelve other faded scars.

How can he do this to himself?

I know from watching my dad drink himself into oblivion every night that asking why someone hurts themselves is futile and will only agitate and embarrass them more. "Brace yourself."

He sucks in a breath when I pour the alcohol on his leg. His brown knuckles are white, and he grips the wooden bench, his focus on the locker room door. My eyes keep floating back up to him, worried he may pass out or push me away again. I reach for the liquid stitches. "I'm not an expert, but I think you need actual stitches, Jameson."

His chin tips up and his eyes go to the ceiling. "You're right. You're not an expert and I'm not going to the hospital." The finality in his tone has me shaking my head in frustration.

"Fine," I say. "I need you to help me then."

"How?"

"Hold the cut closed while I put on this liquid stitch and bandages."

He licks his lips and finally meets my gaze.

Nerves fire from head to toe in a steady ripple as I'm sucked into the darkness surrounding him. I blow out a breath and look down, forcing myself not to focus on the other scars.

I uncap the stitches and Jameson's hands land on his thighs, cursing as he pinches the cut together. Slowly, I disperse the liquid and lean forward to blow on it. Goosebumps appear on his skin and mine tingles with an unfamiliar sensation.

"Keep holding it closed while I get the bandages ready." I grab the butterfly strips and place four across the cut. I run my finger along the stitch once it's dried to make sure I didn't miss a spot, then I tape some gauze over it in case it splits open.

When I'm satisfied, I turn my attention to the other side. "Next one," I say, holding up the bottle of alcohol. I repeat the steps, somehow managing not to throw up or ask any of the questions running on a loop inside my mind.

Little bits of our conversations run through my mental filter. When he said he needed to tell me something before we became intimate, was this it? Did he think I would freak out or shun him? The thought of anyone making fun of someone who needs help makes me sick to my stomach.

I don't want to push him deeper into whatever darkness consumed him enough he did this, so I keep my mouth shut.

"You're all done." I close up the first aid kit. "Get dressed and I'll take you home."

He leans forward, elbows resting on his knees, fingers tented at his lips. "Why don't you ever listen?"

I stop at the door and turn back. "Get dressed. I'll be waiting."

As the minutes tick by my heart rate increases. I check my phone. Ten minutes have passed. I have to trust that he didn't let me stitch him up just to reopen his wounds, knowing I'm out here waiting.

I lift my hand, ready to knock on the door. It swings open and Jameson steps out.

Relief floods me.

He's back in his navy chinos, the sleeves of his button-down rolled up.

"Ready?" I ask.

"You don't have to do this," he says. "I'll be fine."

With each step he takes, he winces, and a spiky ball of anxiety wells up inside me. Will he be okay once he's home? Should I call Christine and have Mike check on him?

No, I tell myself.

Jameson is a proud man, one who would be mortified if someone found out. I can't tell anyone about what happened or risk him falling deeper into whatever caused this.

The walk to the parking lot is painfully quiet. Each time I open my mouth to say something, the words get caught in my throat.

I've never known anyone who self-harms. I don't know what questions are okay to ask and which ones are more likely to lead to more negative feelings and shame. I remind myself to look it up when I get home.

"This is me," he says, standing in front of his motorcycle.

"You're not driving that," I say. "I'm taking you home."

Angrily, he runs a hand along his dark hair. "Stella, I'm fine."

I grab his keys from his hand and shove them down my shirt.

"That won't stop me, Love." He tries for humor, but it doesn't land.

"You're not fine, Jameson. You're pale and shaky. You don't have to talk to me, but I couldn't live with myself if you crashed on the way home. We're taking my car."

His jaw tenses, nostrils flared as the swirl of darkness abates. "Fine."

At the car, I mentally give myself a pep-talk. Tonight didn't turn out how I planned it, but I was in the right place at the right time for a reason.

Chapter Twenty-Seven
Stella

With a huff, Jameson gets into the car.

"What's your address?" I ask.

He spouts off numbers, and I take him at his word that it'll lead me to his apartment. The drive is spent in silence, while my head is flooded with a million questions.

From my college psych class, I remember a lot of self-harm has to do with feeling out of control. Bits of our interactions trickle into understanding. Moving here from the U.K., his mother's death, the promotion and Mr. Weston's berating him, whatever is going on between us. Those things would make anyone feel a little off kilter.

After my parents died, I had to go to counseling for a while. Everything changed in such a short span of time, and I wasn't able to adjust the way I needed to. Adjustment disorder is what they called it, and they gave me tools to help focus me when I'd spiral. I threw myself into helping Pop-Pop and school, and before I knew it, I was in a routine that worked for me. If Jameson doesn't have the tools to help, he'll always feel out of control.

"It's right up here." He points to a building, and I swing into the closest parking spot.

We get out of the car, and he doesn't argue when I follow. The elevator ride is spent much like the car ride, but we make it to his floor without incident. He faces the door with his hand out beside him. "Keys?"

"Oops." I dig into my shirt and place the keys in his palm. "Here."

He unlocks the door and leaves it open. I stand still, unsure whether I should cross the threshold. I don't know if my presence or my departure will upset him more. If I go inside, will he open up to me and help me understand? He's done nothing but push me away, and I don't know if I can break the shell he's placed around himself.

His voice cuts through my inner turmoil. "Do you want a glass of whiskey?"

"Sure," my lips say without thought.

Closing the door, I'm met with a surprisingly warm apartment. It's an open concept with a large kitchen island, beautiful artwork covering the walls, and sleek black furniture. I run my hand along the leather couch, my mouth parting as I stare out the balcony doors. He's got a breathtaking view of rolling hills.

"Here." He places a glass of whiskey in front of me and slings his back before wiping a hand across his glistening lips. My breathy gasp is loud. Jameson's chest rises rapidly, and his teeth sink into his lip.

With a shake of his head, he turns down the hallway.

I'm not sure if it's a dismissal or an invitation.

I stand outside his bedroom door for a minute before I gather the courage to go inside. The room is cozy and inviting, like the rest of the house. He has his own balcony, and a large king-sized bed takes up the majority of the space. His bedding is dark, like I'd expect from someone as intense as he is, but the accents of color make the room lighter.

Jameson stands beside the nightstand, his head hung and shoulders low. Chancing a rejection, I approach him and snake my arms around his waist. He relaxes into me and the tension floats from his body. "I'm sorry you had to see that."

"I'm glad I was there."

He spins and clasps his arms around me. His eyes search my face, for what, I don't know. When he says nothing, I perch on tiptoes and kiss him. I need to get his mind off it before he spirals deeper down the hole.

His body responds quickly, and before I know it, he's ravishing my mouth, hands tangled in my hair. Any questions I had vanish as Jameson distracts me with hot, wet kisses and his hard cock.

I work on unbuttoning his shirt, arousal brewing in my core as he nips at the taut skin on my neck. "Why are there so many freaking buttons, damn it."

"Stella," he pants, breaking the kiss.

Heart beating furiously all over my body, I stop moving. Caught up in the lust, I forgot how we got here, forgot how I found him passed out.

My stomach flips and my eyes fall to his legs to make sure he's not bleeding again.

"I'm sorry," I say. "I wasn't thinking. We shouldn't do this tonight."

He nudges my chin up with his fingers. His eyes are a storm of lust and I'm caught in the epicenter. "I *want* to do this, but if we do, there's no going back. You're mine."

Adrenaline courses through my bloodstream.

He brushes his thumb across my bottom lip and his words sink in. *You're mine.*

My breath catches on the words I know are true. Since that first day in the conference room, and if I'm honest, even at the funeral home, I knew I was a goner for Jameson.

"I'm already yours," I say breathlessly.

He runs a finger along my jaw and leans forward, our lips meeting in a promise. As I undo each button, our teeth, tongues, and mouths fight for purchase. I trail my fingers down to his waist, and his erection presses against my leg.

Should we be doing this? Probably not.

I should be helping him through whatever he's dealing with, but pushing him to confront something he's not ready to talk about isn't the way to go either.

I can't think straight with his fingers dancing along my skin. My lungs refuse to fill, and I'm lost to the sensations pulsing and spiraling into my core.

Jameson reaches behind me and unzips my dress, his fingertips brushing against my bare skin and sending a chill down my spine. My nipples pebble as he slips the straps down my shoulders and peels the dress off me. I swallow, nervously standing in front of him in my matching panties and bra.

"You're gorgeous." He bites his lip. "Smart, funny, frustrating."

My eyes fall to the bulge in his pants, hungry. He lifts me up, wraps my legs around his waist and presses his length against my center. I whimper and rock my hips, needing more pressure. He unclasps my bra, letting it drop to the floor as his eyes land on my small, dark nipples.

Cupping my breast, he nips at the bud, tongue lashing against the firm peaks. He thrusts forward, brushing his cock across my damp panties. The lazy drag of his mouth mixed with the rolling of his hips against my clit has me panting, near begging for relief.

It's in this moment I know sex with him will far surpass anything I've ever felt. It'll be sweaty and slick, demanding and passionate, and fulfilling in the most heavenly way.

"Jameson." I pull his mouth from my chest. His eyes are nothing but pupils, a dark abyss I want to get lost inside. "I need more."

His muscles tighten as he kicks off his shoes and drops me onto the bed.

He covers my body with his, making me dizzy with need. His knee brushes up against my center and I shamelessly ride it, whimpering as the friction draws out a moan. He groans and his lips trace a path from my neck to my breasts and back up to my mouth, kissing me slowly but passionately.

I tug hard on his hair, and his teeth close around my neck, nipping me hard.

"I've dreamed about this scent—" He runs his nose along my collarbone, inhaling deep "—wondering whether it was your shampoo, your lotion, or if God infused it into your skin on purpose."

He works his way down again, moving further toward my waist. My center clenches when he nears the elastic of my panties, muscles tense as his nose brushes along my thighs, inching closer to my core.

CJ was never a fan of reciprocating oral.

Jameson notices my hesitation and moves back to my stomach, letting me take a breath. The hunger in his eyes liquefies my insides.

"Hey, now. I wasn't invited to this no pants party alone," I say, hoping to gain a minute to calm my nerves while he undresses. Jameson's whole body goes rigid, and he begins to pull away.

"What's wrong?" I grab onto his toned arms to keep him on top of me. He won't meet my eyes and his cheeks are red, but not from the heat of the moment. Did I upset him? Was I going too fast? Being too forward? I can tell something's wrong, but a minute passes before he speaks.

"I haven't..." He closes his eyes and takes a deep breath.

He hasn't what? Had sex recently? Manscaped? None of that matters to me. He stays silent, chewing on his lip. It takes a few moments before I make the connection.

His scars.

My heart swoops in my chest—he's trusting me with something special. This moment, where he sheds the fear of being fully seen, the inside scars as well as the physical reminders.

Tears form behind my eyes, but I keep them inside. I don't want him to assume my tears are pity when they're not.

It's honor filling my chest.

"Jameson." My voice is soft, hands firm on his biceps. His attention is on my stomach, eyes downcast. "Look at me," I urge, tilting his chin up like he does mine. His worried gaze slowly moves to me. "You're safe with me."

He nods and slides off the bed.

I rise on my knees and watch him as my shaky hands reach his button. His focus is on the wall behind me, his chest rising and falling in double time just like mine. He inhales sharply when my lips meet the skin of his abdomen, my tongue tracing each individual hard pillow of his eight-pack.

I unhook his button and slide my hands around to his ass, tugging his chinos down over the firm mountains. He stills when I arrive at his thighs. His shoulders are tense, but I remind myself he's trusting me to get him through this, to show him it's okay.

I slow down and give him the chance to stop me. When he doesn't, my mouth moves down to the sharp curve of his hip diving down into his briefs.

"No one should have a no-no zone this perfect," I murmur between kisses.

He chuckles. "A what zone?"

I stop the swirl of my tongue and look up at him. "A no-no zone. My friend and I used to call it that in college."

He licks his lips and arousal swells in my core.

Being on my knees in front of him doesn't make me feel less than, like I'm supposed to be doing this because it's my job in the relationship.

I feel powerful, like a Goddess giving him a gift.

I refocus on undressing him, and he tenses when his pants hit the ground.

Kissing along his waistband, I begin to pull down his briefs. His hands fall to my wrists, and I halt immediately, hoping I haven't pushed him too far.

"I've never had someone..." He stops and inhales deeply, his fingers pinching the bridge of his nose. "...do that either."

My tongue darts out to wet my lips. "May I?"

Chapter Twenty-Eight
Jameson

Tension melts from my body as Stella's soft, full lips work their way down my torso. The image of her on her knees in front of me is something I've dreamt about since the moment I met her, but never dared to believe would happen, especially after what she saw earlier.

I thought she would've run as fast as possible, but she stayed, and she's in my arms.

With every tidbit of myself I've shown her, Stella's stayed when others would've bailed. The chaos inside my head, and the fear about my scars, has been silenced in this moment because of her. She's more than I could ever hope for in a woman. How did I get so lucky?

She's mine now.

Until she finds out you've been lying to her.

The thought torpedoes into my chest and I stumble backward.

"Love." I lay my hands on her shoulders to stop her. "If we're gonna do this, I need to tell you something about Cameron." She smacks my hands away and shakes her head, her tongue sliding along my waistband meeting my happy trail. "Stella," I groan. "It's important. I don't want—"

She halts the movement of her tongue and rises from the bed. "You don't want to do this? I'm sorry. I'm such an idiot. Of course, you don't."

Her pink cheeks and downcast eyes cause a stabbing sensation in my chest and my words jumble in my mouth. "There's nothing I want more than this. God, nothing I've dreamt about more since the moment you yelled at me months ago."

Her shoulders heave with a sigh and she looks at me with conviction in her eyes. "Then I don't want to talk about CJ. He doesn't deserve space in our minds right now."

A shudder ripples down my spine when she palms my erection, slowly stroking and gripping my length. Having her hands on me scrambles my mind like an eight ball and I immediately forget why I wanted to stop her.

My emotions run haywire when her fingers toy with my waistband, releasing my cock. Fear floods my veins when she pushes my pants down over my thighs, but I stand stoic and brace myself for what I know she's about to see, what she's already seen.

Tendrils of brown hair block my view of her expression. I swipe them behind her ear and glance down, terrified to see pity on her face. Her eyes are wide and focused as her fingers coast over the gnarled scars I've given myself. My erratic heartbeat stalls, and my lungs squeeze when she presses her soft lips to the jagged lines.

My skin burns from her touch, and I lean down and consume her with a kiss.

Taut as a tightrope, my cock bounces as we part. Her liquid brown eyes follow the motion, and she grips my hips as she leans forward.

Questions blast through my mind like a battering ram. What will it feel like? Is she comfortable? Is she doing this because she wants to or because she pities me? Will I last long enough?

My heart gallops in my chest awaiting the minute her warm mouth will close around my shaft. I exhale when her lips touch my thighs again, pressing soft kisses over the gauze as she makes her way back up to my cock, goosebumps erupting on my arms.

"Is this okay?"

"Mmhmm," I mumble, dazed by the silkiness of her lips. The wet heat of her mouth surrounds me, and her lips close over the ridge of my cock.

"Bloody hell," I groan.

I massage the tense muscles of her neck, urging her to relax so she can take all of me. A guttural noise rips from my throat when she swats my hand away and takes me in further, licking me from root to tip. Like waves in an ocean, her tongue coasts along the vein underneath my shaft knocking the air from my lungs.

Fuck. How is she so good at this?

Wait, I don't want to know.

Focus, Jameson.

"Stella." Her name is a whisper, my voice hoarse and gravelly.

"Hmm?" The vibration of her mouth sends me spiraling toward euphoria, and before I know it my hands are tangled in her hair, hips pumping in short bursts.

This feels better than I could've imagined.

The suction of her cheeks, the velvet touch of her tongue, it's all encompassing, a warmth drawing me closer to climax. My body has craved her since the moment we met, but with Stella, I'll never be satiated.

Her fingernails dig into my arse, and the tip of my cock hits the back of her throat. She lightly drags her teeth up my shaft and swirls her tongue around the head before diving down deep again.

I gather her hair in my hand and slow her pace, watching my cock disappear into her mouth. I wish I could capture the image, burn it into my brain so I'll never forget how amazing this woman is, how she makes me feel. My lungs expand and deflate as if I've run a marathon, but it's simply Stella's amazing mouth drawing every ounce of restraint I have from my body. Her whimpers and moans bring me as close to the edge as does her mouth.

Cool fingers wrap around the base of my cock, and she pumps her hand in time. I grunt, begging myself to not come yet. To relish this moment, this woman who has me enraptured.

I'm glad I never let anyone else do this to me, that I waited for the person who wouldn't shutter or blink an eye at the gnarled skin on my thighs, who'd make me feel desired instead of ashamed of my weakness.

This moment was meant for Stella.

For the woman I *can* be weak for.

Waves of heat rush over me as she touches me in another place I've never been touched. She moves her hand to cup my balls and tugs lightly as her finger presses against my perineum. "Fuck," I murmur, clenching my abs. "I'm close, Love."

I brace myself on the nightstand as her head bobs faster, greedy for my seed. Tension coils at the base of my spine as she deepthroats my shaft and all noises cease inside my brain like the calm before the sky opens up and all hell breaks loose.

I pump into her mouth, a carnal need taking over as my balls draw up and my vision wavers. Lightning courses through my veins rocketing toward my groin. Her pace slows as I spill into her mouth, her tongue lapping up every last drop.

She releases my cock with a pop, and air rushes from my lungs as my body descends from its high. Her breath stutters, and I draw her to me and kiss up the column of her neck before making it back to her lips. Our foreheads meet, bodies slick with sweat as our tongues fight for dominance. She consumes me, coaxing me to give her the reins.

"Thank you," I whisper into her mouth.

She pulls back, her eyes bright and warm. "Thank you for trusting me."

"Don't thank me yet." I nip at her lip and wrap my arm around her back.

Her brows scrunch, eyes searching. "What?"

I scoop her up and lower her back onto the bed. "It's my turn."

She scoots back toward the headboard, a blush rising to her cheeks. "You don't have to do that." Her teeth saw her bottom lip. "I didn't do it so you'd...you know. Reciprocate."

I crawl up her body, my lips caressing her soft torso, my tongue sweeping across the firm peaks of her breast, her purrs stirring a need deep inside me.

"Love, that's like putting a five-star meal in front of a man and telling him he can't eat it." She swipes the pad of her finger along my bottom lip, and I draw in her thumb, sucking and swirling my tongue around it. "And I'm starving."

Chapter Twenty-Nine
Stella

Jameson's deep voice brushes against my ear, sending a shiver down my spine and spiking heat through my core. "I need to taste you."

Fuck, that's hot. His words aren't inherently dirty, but his voice as he says them makes me feel like we're in a back alley and he has me pushed up against a brick wall ready to devour me. He leans back, a slow smile spreading across his face, his thumbs toying with the waistband of my panties. Energy crackles through the air between us, and my stomach somersaults at the way he completely consumes me.

What CJ saw as a chore, Jameson sees as a privilege.

The throbbing between my thighs hasn't subsided but grown, almost to the point of pain. My body begs for his mouth, for the relief I've needed since I met him. The kind that cleanses and rejuvenates your body. I rub my thighs together, biting my lip as I give him my consent.

He grins and sprawls out on the bed between my legs. Hooking his arms underneath my thighs, his fingertips move down my bikini line and his thumb brushes along my soaked underwear. My face heats, embarrassed by how desperate my body is for him.

He sneaks his fingers beneath the seam of my panties, a low growl rumbling at the back of his throat. "You're already so wet for me."

I swallow, his words sending a rush of arousal through me. His hooded eyes soak me up like a sponge, and my core aches for his dirty mouth to be all over me.

He runs his fingers along my folds and brings them to his mouth, tasting me. "Bloody hell," he says. "A Michelin star meal."

I swear I could orgasm from his words alone.

I've never had someone talk to me like this, worship my body the way he does. It makes me feel desired, yet respected.

I close my eyes and bask in being the center of his attention. He crooks his fingers around the material and peels my drenched panties down my legs. Heat curls in my stomach and he spreads me open, baring my swollen center to his darkened gaze. Gliding over my landing strip, he inches closer and closer to where I need him.

"So fucking perfect," he murmurs right before his tongue sweeps up my slit.

I cry out and grasp the sheets, grounding myself to Earth by digging my heels into the mattress. Pleasure floods me with each soft, slow lap he takes to my clit. A low noise of satisfaction sounds at the back of his throat, and he slips a finger inside, teasing me with the suction of his mouth.

"Oh, God," I moan, grasping for something, anything, as I rock my hips.

"Fuck," he whispers. "You feel amazing."

I rise on my elbows and watch him devour me, the way he uses his tongue as a weapon, the sensual way his mouth closes across the throbbing apex of my thighs. Jameson seems determined to break a Guinness world record of most licks to a clit before the brain short circuits.

A tremor shoots through me when he sucks my clit into his mouth and adds another digit, stretching me further as he curls his fingers inside of me, rubbing my g-spot.

Pressure builds in my core, and I arch, chasing the orgasm. Jameson edges me, slowing down and speeding up. The flame inside me grows hotter, pouring molten need into my veins.

"Please," I beg.

He chuckles and the vibration of his hearty laugh against my center has me pulling him back to me. I reach up, rolling my nipples between two fingers, pinching them into stiff peaks. My eyes flutter closed, letting the sensations wash over me.

"Look at me, Stella." Jameson's voice is deep and commanding. "Stop touching yourself."

It's in my nature to challenge him, but I don't want to this time. My eyes snap open and I look at him, his face covered with my arousal.

"Good girl," he says. "I want you to watch me. Your pleasure is mine tonight."

Why is that so hot?

His eyes hold mine as his tongue slices through me like a hot knife through butter, dipping in and out, circling and lapping, a sound of approval rumbling in his chest. A liquid, burning heat blossoms in my stomach when he swipes his tongue up the entirety of me with one broad stroke.

I split apart, pleasure crashing over me like a tidal wave.

My mind hovers somewhere above my body for what feels like minutes on end before I snap back into reality. Jameson continues to tongue fuck me lazily as I pulse around his fingers. I open my mouth to speak, but he hooks his finger back inside me. The deeper he goes, the higher my chest rises. "What are you do—"

"Shh," he mumbles. "I'm not finished yet."

Not finished yet? I push his head away, too sensitive. I've never been able to achieve more than one orgasm in a solo session, let alone with someone else. He shakes his head against me and turns his fingers down, knocking the air from my lungs. The sensation he creates takes control of my limbs, and I'm completely at his mercy as my body clenches around his fingers. Bright colors burst behind my eyelids, and I groan something incoherent as pressure builds again in my core.

"Do you want to come on my fingers or my tongue?"

My head is in the clouds, unable to form a coherent sentence.

"Stella?" His thumb is still circling, teasing. "Fingers or tongue."

"Tongue, please," I moan as he hits that spot. "Oh God, yes."

"Good girl."

How did I go from hating him to begging him to do these things to me? Needing his mouth and his hands all over me. When did our need to challenge each other change into this? Jameson's enthusiasm between my legs shows me he's not doing this for my pleasure, but for his.

He grins and lowers his lips back to my core.

My stomach soars and falls like a rollercoaster when Jameson pumps faster, muttering praises into my skin. Shivers roll down my spine and detonate, sending fire through my veins as another orgasm overtakes me.

I collapse onto the bed, spent yet filled with energy.

He brought me to two mind-blowing, earth-shattering orgasms, and I still don't feel like I've had enough of him. He climbs up my body, leaving wet kisses on my thighs, torso, breasts, and neck.

"Made for me," he murmurs against my lips.

I flush, tasting myself on his tongue and returning his kiss with vigor. His cock nudges against my entrance, easily sliding through my folds when he claims my mouth. Blood floods to my core and my hips move without permission, grinding against his erection.

Our breaths mix, sweat coating our bodies as he rocks forward, putting pressure on my clit. My head is dizzy with arousal, clouded by the need to have him deep inside me, claiming my body as his. I shift beneath him, and he dips inside me.

"Fuck." Jameson stills.

His gaze locks with mine and he inches in further, pulling a moan from me. I know we shouldn't be doing this without a condom, shouldn't be testing the fates, but God does it feel heavenly.

"I've gotta stop and get a condom, Stella. You feel too good, and I won't last much longer without embarrassing myself."

I chew on my lip, waiting for him to pull out and leave me empty. He stills, his focus now on where we're joined. He slowly draws himself back before his hips move slightly forward again. He groans and shudders before pulling out of me, dragging a hand down his face.

A protest forms on my lips but I tamp it down. Be smart, Stella.

"Damn, that's scary." He climbs off the bed.

I laugh. "What is?"

His enormous cock sways as he strolls to the closet. Pulling out a condom, he sheaths himself before climbing back onto the bed and stealing a kiss. "That felt much better than it did in my dreams, and now I'm scared I'll go to jail for kidnapping because I can't let you go."

My laugh is stifled when his mouth closes over mine, his erection nudging at my entrance. I bite down on his lip and his animalistic growl sends shivers down my spine.

He presses through my folds, moving so slow I want to scream.

"Jameson," I groan. "Take me."

"Slowly, love. You're not ready to take all of me yet."

All of him? The thought sends fireworks popping along my spine. He inches deeper, capturing my nipple in his mouth as white light blinds me. I rest my hands on his shoulders and rock my hips in time with his.

His hand finds my clit, rubbing it in a circular motion, feeding the hot buzz in my core until slowly my body accepts all of him.

"Fuck," he grits out, staring down at where we're connected. "You feel incredible."

My body trembles with the need for him to move. I grab the back of his neck, bringing him down to my level. His heartbeat races against mine, muscles jumping beneath my fingers.

"Take me," I plead.

His gaze catches fire, trailing from my lips to where he slides in and out of me, bottoming out each time. Arousal drips down my thighs, the sound of it between our bodies filling the room with erotic noise. I nip at his neck, and he thrusts into me, our bodies slick and my mind swirling in blissful numbness.

He slowly pumps his hips before breaking into a piston pace.

A tendril of pleasure unfurls through my middle, hanging just out of reach. I tilt my hips, chasing the right angle but unable to find it. I've never been able to achieve an orgasm during sex, but damn if I don't want to try with him.

"Tell me how you need it." Jameson leans forward, sucking my nipple into his mouth, letting it go with a loud pop. When I don't answer he leans down, his voice a threat against my neck. "I won't move from this bed until I've cataloged every inch of your skin, every taste your body has to offer, and learned what each of your moans means. Tell me how you want me to make you come."

He punctuates every sentence with a thrust, his words causing my core to flame. He talks about my pleasure as if he was made strictly for this purpose, and by the way his body moves with mine, I'm starting to believe that's true.

"Can I get on top?" I ask.

"Absolutely." His grin is infectious as he turns us.

Every worry that was hidden beneath the surface decides to bubble up once I'm on top. Do my breasts look saggy? Is my tummy flat enough? How do I even ride someone with a cock as big as his?

Jameson quiets my thoughts by running his hands all over my chest and pinching my nipple. He squeezes my hips, lifting me up so I can line up his cock with my entrance. Slick with desire, Jameson meets no resistance as he glides into my body, filling me. I take a moment to catch my breath, seeing as his enormous cock has shifted my entire organ system on its way to giving me pleasure.

"Are you okay?" he asks, noticing my wince.

I nod. "I'm fine."

I'm more worried about grazing his legs than the amazing pressure of him filling me. His hips slowly move, the sting now accompanying a deep throbbing in my sex as he stretches me. I place my hands on his chest and rise until his tip is nearly out of me before sliding back down his length. He groans and his grasp on my hips tightens as I begin to ride him, throwing my head back as pleasure streams through me.

Jameson sits up against the headboard and snakes his arm around my back. The change in position increases my pleasure ten-fold. His cock feels deeper, his pelvic bone rubs up against my swollen center, and his mouth, that perfect mouth is within kissing distance. I arch into his hand splayed on my back, begging him to drive into me. His thrusts are hard and quick, our tentative grasp on sanity stretching thin as he ruts into me over and over.

I cry out as the orgasm blasts through me, my inner walls fluttering rhythmically around him. Jameson covers my screams with his mouth, groaning as he finds his release too.

He falls back against the headboard, his body glistening with sweat.

I splay out like a starfish on the bed beside him, spent and fully sated, wondering how I ever thought I was satisfied.

He pulls me back on top of him, fingers swirling down my spine. "I can't believe I almost let this job keep me from you."

With the cloud of lust clearing, thoughts of work and the promotion creep back inside my mind.

Can whatever this is between us survive one of us losing?

Chapter Thirty
Jameson

"Name five things you love most in the world."

I tilt my head, watching as she draws circles on my abs. "Hmm...my job, my friends, my bike, Yorkshire tea...your cunt."

She frowns and a crease appears on her forehead.

"What's wrong?"

"You didn't name yourself."

I stare into her soft eyes, not understanding her train of thought. "And?"

"You should be at the top of that list, Jameson."

A tightness creeps into my chest at her words, and I can't bring myself to speak.

"You, more than anybody in the entire universe, deserve *your* love and affection." She resumes her exploration of my torso. "I want that for you. I want you to see what I see, what I feel when I look at you."

I press a kiss to her hair, breathing in the scent of shampoo and soap, allowing it to calm my racing heart. The words are stuck in my throat, itching to free themselves, but I can't open my mouth. I can't tell her how ashamed I feel when I look at my scars, that I wonder how even with an amazing life, I feel so out of control that I need to dig a blade into my skin.

She continues. "I used to think you were a self-centered asshole, but you're not. You're someone worthy of love and acceptance."

I hear her words, and as much as I want them to be true, I know I haven't earned that type of love yet.

Stella picks up on the tension coiling inside me and changes the subject without hesitation. "What made you want to go to school for finance?"

I run my fingers through her damp hair, contemplating how I want to answer that. "It was what my father wanted me to go to Uni for."

She looks up at me, her dark lashes blinking away a hint of sadness. "You didn't want to be an investment manager?"

"No."

Her fingers skim over my Adonis belt then back up to my chest. "What did you want to go for?"

I blow out a breath and brush my fingers along her arm. Growing up, saying the word art had the effect of summoning a demon in my house. But here with Stella, there's no fear of retribution. "Art."

"Oh yeah, the paintings." She props her head on my chest, her brown eyes boring into me. "Why didn't you tell your father you wanted to go for art instead?"

I shrug. "You know what he's like."

"What do you mean?" Her brows scrunch.

Fuck. Backtrack, backtrack, backtrack.

I wipe my clammy palms on the bedspread. "I mean, you know how parents are. If it doesn't fit with their idea of success, then it's a pointless endeavor."

My dad's words echo inside my head: *Real men work hard instead of coloring like children, expecting someone to put their lackluster picture up on the refrigerator.*

"I guess so." She snuggles closer. "Do you still paint?"

I shake my head. Even though I've started sketching again since I've met Stella, I'm still not at the point where I'm ready to delve back into art. "I haven't picked up a brush since that last art show as a kid. I doubt I'd be able to paint anything worthwhile anyway."

"I bet you can," she says. "I wish I had talent like yours."

"Oh, Love. That's not even my best talent." I skim my fingers down her abdomen and cup her cunt, nipping at the shell of her ear.

She laughs and stretches up to give me a kiss. "Seriously though, why didn't you keep up with it?"

"My father made sure I was only taking worthwhile classes at school, and those didn't include art classes. Most of the boys I went to school with were rich kids of business moguls who didn't have the same types of interests either. I had to adapt to make friends."

Stella shifts beside me, and I wrap my arm around her. "If you don't mind me asking, your mom wasn't supportive either?"

I close my eyes against the memories pushing forward. I know Stella won't judge me, but it's still scary to open up to someone after being closed off for so long. "My mum was an addict. Nothing meant more to her than money, drugs, and my father. I knew I had to be more like what they wanted me to be if I wanted their love, so the art went away, and I focused on business."

Stella caresses my face, her soft hands running through my beard. "It's not your fault you had shitty parents. It wasn't your responsibility to make them love you. Parents should love and protect their children's dreams, not crush them."

My fingers automatically drift to my scars. "My parents didn't get that memo."

Her eyes widen and fall to my hands on my thighs. "Did they...was it them that did this to you first?"

The image of my mum hitting me so hard the table sliced into my legs, seeps into my mind and makes my stomach curl. I try to force down the lump in my throat, but it doesn't work.

Warm fingers lace into mine and squeeze. "You don't have to talk about it. But I'm here if you want to."

God, I love this woman.

I don't know how or when it happened, but with every fiber of my soul, I do. I don't care if she was my brother's first, or what people will say if they find out about us. I would do anything to make her happy, to make her feel more loved and desired than she ever has in her life. To prevent her from ever feeling less than or unworthy of what she deserves.

And that means she deserves the truth from me, no matter if it costs me my chance with her.

"It was my mum." I stretch out my fingers, willing the tension away. "She got knocked up by my father on one of his business trips to London, and she used me as bait to keep him coming back. If I did well in school or sports, he came to visit often, but when I messed up and he chose not to visit, she beat me for it."

Electricity buzzes through my veins and I clench my hands into fists to prevent her from seeing me shake, the memories pushing me closer to the edge. I shiver and draw in a breath.

"I'm sorry, Jameson." I look down, scared to see pity on her face, but anger fills her narrowed eyes. "I understand now why you acted the way you did at the funeral home. She was a horrible person."

"She was." I shrug. "But she wasn't like that before the drugs got hold of her, and then it got worse when things went downhill with my father."

"And where is your father now?"

I suck in a sharp breath and stare at the ceiling. I know what I have to do, but I don't know if I can do it. All that we've shared, everything that's forming between us, could shatter the minute she finds out I've been lying to her. I don't want her to feel like I took advantage of her or regret what we did, but she deserves the truth.

My heart pounds in my ears and a weight drops in my stomach. "Stella," I croak. "We need to talk about something."

She props up on her elbow and her eyebrows knit together. "Okay...about what?"

Sitting back against the headboard, I suck in a deep breath and hold it, counting to ten and back. Stella shifts into a seated position, crossing her legs and clasping her hands together in front of her.

"Earlier, I told you we needed to talk about Cameron—"

"How do you even know him? I thought you moved here a few months ago."

Sweat slides down my neck, and the weight on my chest presses me into the mattress as dread pools in my stomach, making me want to hide. If she reacts poorly, I'll lose her. But the longer I let it go on, the less chance I have to win her back.

"We've known each other our whole lives."

Hurt pierces through her eyes, knocking me back. "How? In all the years I've known CJ, he's never mentioned you."

"Because he hates me."

"You're not making sense, Jameson. Why does he hate you? And why didn't you tell me earlier?"

I exhale into the pillows and close my eyes. I know the minute she finds out who my dad is, she'll get up and leave. There's still so much I haven't told her. I doubt she'll be able to see past the lies and know that what we have is real. "My father would have been upset with me."

"I don't get it." She runs a hand through her tangled tresses. "What does your father have to do with CJ?"

"Everything." I scoff. She makes to get off the bed, but I grab her hand. "Please, let me explain."

She snatches her hand back and paces the room. "You're talking in circles, Jameson. Be straight with me. What's the issue between you and CJ, and why would your father care about it?" When it takes me a moment to answer, she picks up her clothes and heads toward the bathroom. My heart tries to ram itself out of my chest when she says, "Tonight was fun, but—"

"Cameron's my brother." The words rush out of me, and my head falls into my hands, unable to even look in her direction.

She blows out a rush of air. "Your what?"

I sigh, forcing myself to look at her. Her hands are stuck to her hips, clearly not ready to accept any of my shit. In her mind, she's comparing my light brown skin to his ivory, the different shape of our mouths. I can tell the moment she realizes the features in my face are similar to the ones she's looked at for years. My tongue is gummy in my dry mouth, and I can't help digging my fingers into my leg. "He's my half-brother. We share a father."

Her hand moves to her stomach. "I'm gonna be sick." She takes a deep breath and rubs her eyes. "I don't understand. I've been with CJ for four years, and our dads were business partners for years before that. They never mentioned you."

Hearing that Dad never mentioned me shouldn't hurt, but a small pang of sadness rumbles in my chest. I push it down and drag a hand through my beard, tugging at the ends to distract myself.

"I'm the bastard no one wanted to claim." I sink into the bed. "It would've hurt my dad's businesses for a scandal like that to come out."

She paces the floor in a pair of my boxers and a long t-shirt, not speaking. Her expressions go from surprised to hurt to angry within a moment. "Everything makes more sense now. The reason Mr. Weston has been praising everything you do is because you're his son, and he can't tell anyone that. Did I even have a shot at the job? Were you guys laughing behind my back every time I thought I was ahead in the race?"

I grab her hands, and she slinks away from me. "Never, Stella. You're an amazing advisor, much better than me. I don't want the job if it means losing this."

The words slip from my mouth before I have a chance to stop them. But I realize they're true. Stella is more important to me than the promotion.

If my dad heard me, he'd be furious. He'd call me weak for wanting to give up this opportunity for a woman.

"You'd risk everything for me?" she asks, disbelief written in the crease of her forehead.

"Absolutely," I say without missing a beat. "You're more important than any job."

And it's true. I'm not daft. I know I'll never find another woman who'll accept me like she has, another woman who is as amazing, and smart, and beautiful.

She's the only one.

Minutes pass as she paces, flattening the carpet with her soft stride and increasing my heart rate.

"Where do we go from here, Jameson?" She stops in her tracks and turns toward me. "I don't want you to drop out of the running. I want the promotion because I deserve it, not because you fell on your sword for me."

Hope blooms in my chest, but the small voice in the back of my head reminds me I'm still keeping something monumental from her. Worried my thumping heart can be heard halfway across the room, I wrap my arms around myself.

Part of me wonders if she'd still want the promotion if she knew she didn't need it. The night I met her at the bar I took the documents from my dad's office and copied them, so I could examine them, but I still haven't figured out why he's keeping the trust a secret, and if I tell her before I know the full story, then her life, and my dad's could be irreparably damaged.

My stomach sinks.

If I betray my dad's orders and tell Stella about the money in the blind trust, she'll hate me for not telling her sooner, and I'll lose the relationship I have with my dad. If she brings litigation into the mix, his job at the firm could be in jeopardy, and the board would most likely fire him to save face, not to mention how the courts would deal with it.

"Jameson?" Stella asks. "Is everything okay?"

My head thumps. I press my fingers into my eyes to quell the sensation. None of it matters if I don't know why he's keeping it a secret. Deciding to stay quiet isn't easy, but causing unnecessary waves won't help either. I stifle the sickening feeling with a swallow and promise to sort it out tomorrow.

"We'll figure it out. We can find a way to work together regardless of what happens with the promotion. I just want you."

She sits beside me on the bed, pulling nervously at her lip. The opportunity to tell her about her trust is pushed to the back of my mind when she says, "Why do you and CJ hate each other so much if you're brothers?"

"Half," I correct.

She rolls her eyes, but the anger from earlier has dimmed a bit. "Half-brothers."

"I tried for the first couple years to be close with him, but he hated me from the moment we met." I shrug and tense my hand on my thighs, itching to dig into my skin. "He and Colleen didn't want to share my father, and everything became a competition for his attention."

Stella lays her hands on top of mine, redirecting my attention back to her. "What do you mean?"

I rub the raw skin on my wrists and flounder at gathering my words. Stella laces her fingers back into mine and squeezes.

I breathe a sigh of relief.

I know this doesn't mean she forgives me, but she's not running either.

"My father only came to see me when I did something good, something worthy of his time. Colleen wanted to keep dad's attention on Cameron, so she made sure he played every sport possible, was the best at everything he did, so Dad would be so proud of Cameron he'd forget about me. It wasn't like Dad could miss one of Cameron's awards ceremonies in favor of attending one of my art shows. All of his business partners' kids played on the same teams."

"That's awful." She rubs my knuckles with her thumb.

"It was, and it got worse when I was caught tagging bridges and got sent to boarding school to teach me discipline. But eventually, while Cameron was focused on sports, I was focusing on grades, networking, and planning for college so I could get away from my mum. Dad kept on top of me about my grades, urged me to follow in his footsteps in business, and got me the job at Thompson."

"So, you gave up on your dream to please your father?" Her lips pinch and I know she's disappointed.

"I don't look at it like that. He motivated me to become the best version of myself, and I'm good at what I do. That's why he brought me here because eventually he wants me to take over."

"But are you happy?"

Her words give me pause.

Up until I met Stella, I would've said yes to that question in a heartbeat. I have my dream car, a beautiful flat, and a phenomenal career, but I can't gloss over the fact that something's still missing.

Or someone.

I grab Stella's hand and pull it to my lips, planting a kiss on her knuckles. "I didn't realize how unhappy I was until I met you. I thought gaining my father's respect and approval would change that, but since I met you, I've realized life is about so much more. I want to give you everything you deserve."

"I don't need you to give me anything." She tilts her head. "And lying to me isn't treating me like I deserve."

I blow out a breath and run a hand through my hair. "I know it's not. And I admit I cocked that up, but we weren't friends then." Her nose wrinkles, but I continue before she has a chance to stop me. "I couldn't divulge we were related to anyone. My dad has a lot riding on me working for Thompson, so I needed to stay away from you."

"Why are you telling me all this now? Is it because we're *friends*?"

I exhale a harsh breath, a dark chuckle releasing from my chest. "Because...fuck, Stella. We're much more than that, and you know it. What we have is more important than pissing off my dad."

She throws her head back and closes her eyes. "Jameson...what do *you* really want?"

"I want you." I softly grab her face. "Every smart remark that leaves your perfect mouth, every eye roll you give me when I frustrate you. Every infuriating inch."

She nearly smiles, and I continue.

"I'm sorry. I should've told you sooner, but I was terrified to lose you, to lose my father and my job. No more secrets from here on out, I promise."

Except for the glaring lie that you're actually a millionaire and don't need this job. Resolve settles in my stomach. Once I find out why my dad is hiding the trust, I'll tell her. I could look like the villain, or the hero, but it's a risk I'm willing to make.

Her jaw tenses beneath my palms, and my heart is in my throat, ready to throw itself out of my body if she tells me we're done. It'll be another thing I've fucked up.

Another thing I wasn't worthy enough to keep.

"I forgive you but—"

"You forgive me?" A wave of relief swells inside me, crashing as the weight of her words settle.

"Let me finish." She holds up a finger and I mimic zipping my lips shut. "I forgive you, but I don't know if I can trust you."

Warring emotions battle in my stomach. How can I ask her to trust me when I'm not telling her the whole truth? And if this has already rocked her trust in me, will she be able to forgive me for the bigger secret?

"That's understandable, but I won't give up. I'll spend every day earning your trust back. I don't care if it takes me longer than it did to build the Great Wall of China, I won't give up. I'm asking for a chance to prove it to you."

She chuckles and rolls her eyes. "Ok."

My tongue is heavy in my mouth. "Ok, what?"

"I'll give you a chance to prove it to me."

My heart launches into my throat, and I wrap my arms around her and lift her onto my lap, burying my face in her neck. Relief washes over me, and I push all the 'what ifs' and 'buts' away. I'll deal with them another day. "I promise you won't regret it."

"Good, because I'm sure you won't want to take Pop-Pop's cane to the ankle."

Chapter Thirty-One
Stella

Soft kisses on my shoulder and the smell of soap rouse me from my sleep. I pop an eye open expecting to see light through the curtains but the room is still dark. I turn into Jameson's embrace and meet his lips, allowing the kiss to wake up more than just my mind.

"What time is it?" I whisper.

"Six o'clock." He kisses his way down my neck, fingers gliding over my bare hips.

I push his face away, his beard scratchy against my palm. "Too early. Go back to sleep."

We stayed up late last night chatting after his confession. I hate that he lied to me, but I can understand why he felt he had to. He barely knows me. Two months may be enough time to fall for someone, but I've known Mr. Weston a long time. He demands perfection, and I can only imagine the type of pressure Jameson was...*is* under.

"I've got some business to take care of and didn't want you to think I left you here."

Business? My shoulders tense, and a thought snakes its way into my mind. He said he'd give up the promotion for me, but what if this meeting is something to do with that? Was he just placating me so I'd stop pushing last night?

"Your thoughts are rather loud," Jameson says.

"What?"

"You tensed up the moment I said business."

Feeling exposed, I gnaw on my lip. I don't want him to think I've changed my mind about it being a fair fight for the promotion, but I also don't want to be taken for a fool.

His warm kisses on my neck redirect every thought that was running through my head. I turn over and wrap his arm around me, begging him to stay in bed. "Let's pretend we're actually in Australia where it's bedtime."

He laughs and snuggles into me. His erection presses against my ass, sending a pop of electricity to my core. I grind back against him.

"Love, are you trying to keep me in bed?" He nips at my neck, his hand snaking around to my waistband.

"Ten more minutes," I say, nearly panting with want.

"I don't need ten minutes." He slips his fingers beneath the elastic, growling when he finds me already wet. His muscular body moves over me, and I notice he's already dressed. He rolls up the sleeves of his white oxford, baring his tattooed arms.

He pulls down the boxers he let me borrow last night and throws them to the side before he buries his face between my legs, stroking me in one long, broad lick. The wet heat of his tongue sweeps through me, driving my body into a frenzy.

The noise of satisfaction that escapes Jameson has me vibrating and fighting off the building orgasm. The way this man can bring me to the edge so quickly has to be magic.

A drop of sweat runs between my breasts as I grip his hair, keeping his attention where I need it. He pushes a finger inside and swirls his tongue around my clit before drawing it back into his mouth.

Sparks burst in my core, lighting my bloodstream on fire as the orgasm blindsides me.

Jameson laps up my release and kisses my inner thighs. He grins from between my legs before slipping his fingers out of me and into his mouth to taste.

"Told you I didn't need ten minutes." He slides off the bed.

I laugh. "You're so cocky." He chuckles and pulls on his suit jacket. I turn onto my stomach, watching him slip into dress shoes and grab his wallet from the dresser. "Where are you going?"

"I have a meeting this morning with a client, but I'll pick up breakfast on my way back. Please don't leave."

"I need to send some emails and check on my grandfather."

"You can use my computer," he says, eyes pleading with me to stay.

"Are you sure? If you have things to do, I can go."

He slips on his watch and leans down to capture my lips. "No, I want you to relax and choose what you want for dinner tonight, and how you want me to ravish you for dessert."

A chill skitters across my skin, and my nipples perk up beneath the sheet. The way this man wields his words makes me ache for him.

Pale, yellow light bathes Jameson as he turns to me in the doorway. "Waffles or pancakes?"

I tap a finger on my chin, pretending to be deep in thought. "Pancakes."

He flashes me a grin and leaves.

I pad around his apartment and take in the views on the balcony. In downtown San Antonio, you can see buildings, restaurants, and highways for miles and miles, but facing the Hill Country, there's nothing but rolling green hills. Okay, well, brown, dry hills, but hills, nonetheless. The sun peaks over the horizon as I send emails, check on Pops, and wait for Jameson to return with breakfast.

My phone chirps on the nightstand where I left it to charge.

Rosay: It's been like...10 hours. Getting ready to send out a search party. Where are you?

Me: Umm...at Jameson's apartment.

Rosay: Say what?!?!?! I knew it! He's hung like a horse, isn't he?"

I send her a zipped lips emoji and she sends back a middle finger. I chuckle and swipe out of her message. I sit at the island, playing through last night.

The sex was amazing, more than I ever expected, but the conversation is what's weighing on me this morning. Hate bubbles up inside me for Jameson's parents as I filter through everything I learned about him. How his mom could hurt him so badly, how his dad made and still makes him feel less than.

Mr. Weston has been a constant in my life. He took me under his wing and helped me when my parents died, but that isn't the man Jameson described. I've seen little moments of tension between CJ and his father, and all the times I overheard him berating Jameson, I finally understand his persona with me has always been a façade.

I hate that Jameson still feels the need to prove himself, and that he gave something up he loved to appear worthy to a dad who won't even acknowledge his existence.

An idea pops into my head.

Christmas is a few weeks away, and I want to send Jameson something special. I spend the rest of the time perusing crafting sites before I land on what I'm looking for. The door lock disengages and swings open as I finish ordering my gift.

"Oh, you're up." Jameson arrives with bags hanging on his arms and a cup holder in his hands.

I jump up from the island and grab the holder, nearly spilling the contents of the cups.

"Please tell me one of these is for me?"

"They're both for you." He sets the bags on the counter before scooping me up for a kiss.

"Both for me?"

"I wasn't sure if you drank coffee or tea in the mornings, so I bought your usual Yorkshire with milk and honey, and a black coffee."

I used to say having fuzzy feelings was a stupid expression, but now I completely understand. I can find no other explanation for what's happening to my body right now. On tiptoes, I crush my lips to his. "Thank you." I grab the tea and sit at the island. "Did you go on a shopping spree?"

"Something like that." He pushes the bags toward me with a nod. "I figured you didn't want to go outside in my trousers and t-shirt."

The closest bag to me has the name of a store I've never even dared to step inside. My hackles rise as I reach inside and latch onto something soft. I lift the material out of the bag, eyes settling on a beautiful champagne-colored skirt that costs more than my car payment. "Jameson, this is too much. I could've driven home to get clothes."

He brushes his fingers along my jaw. "Nothing is too much when it comes to you."

I purse my lips. "Jameson..."

"Stella, for someone always talking about helping people, you sure have a problem being helped. It's a skirt, a blouse, and some trousers. I wanted you to be comfortable while you're here. That's all."

I bristle, struck by the truth in his words. My cheeks heat, embarrassed by how bratty I sound. "I'm sorry, you're right. Thank you for thinking of me."

His dark eyes settle on me. "I wasn't thinking about you when I picked out that skirt." A devious tone in his voice makes my heart flutter as he stalks toward me. "I was thinking about me, bending you—" Jameson's phone rings in his suit pocket, cutting off the prowling lion. He sighs, leaning his forehead against mine. "Sorry, Love. I've gotta take this."

I give him one last kiss before he answers the phone and retreats to the balcony. I sigh and sit back on the stool, looking through the bags for a top to pair with the skirt. Did he have one of the associates help pick out the outfit or did he traverse the store himself? My heart swells imagining him handpicking this outfit, regardless of his intentions to take it off me later. After finding the cream blouse he chose, I also find a pair of denim jeans and a t-shirt.

In my size.

I grab the clothes and head into the bathroom, picking up my phone on the way. Jameson couldn't know my exact size unless he had help, and I doubt that help came in the form of a cranky, old man.

Me: Did Jameson ask you for my size?

I set my phone on the bathroom sink and pull on the skirt. It fits like a glove. Three little dots appear on the screen as I wait for a response.

Rosay: Error: 61414. We're sorry. The person you're contacting is currently evading your messages and pleading the fifth. Please try again later or go to youdeservetheworld.com

I laugh so loud I flinch and peek out at the balcony to make sure I didn't interrupt Jameson's conversation. Rosay is the best type of friend. She's honest to a fault, but I know without a shadow of a doubt that she loves me and would do anything for me. I shoot her a quick message thanking her before I leave the bathroom, hoping Jameson's off his phone call.

Sunlight filters in from the balcony, blinding me as I step into the room. Jameson paces outside the sliding door, one hand on his phone, the other in his pocket. I can tell he's tense by the way his jaw ticks. Whatever information he's on the receiving end of must not be good.

A flash of blue catches my attention as Jameson brings his hand out of his pocket.

No.

My feet take me to the door quicker than I thought humanly possible. Quietly, so I don't interrupt his call, I step onto the balcony and grab his wrist. His thumb hovers over the tip of the blade and his dark eyes settle on me, filled with shame as a loud, berating voice booms from the small speaker.

I swipe my thumb across his wrists and step behind him, snaking an arm around his core, hoping to help calm him down. Our heartbeats thump in time and Jameson slowly begins to relax. He closes the knife and laces our fingers, squeezing gently as he hums in agreement to whoever is on the line.

"Yes, sir."

He spins around to face me, pressing me against the sliding door, his erection heavy on my center as he brushes his lips against my neck and inhales deep. I shiver, my body getting on board with his change in mood as he hangs up the phone and kisses me. He may not want to talk about it right now, but if he wants to move forward together he can't use sex to distract himself from the feelings he doesn't want to deal with.

He lifts me up and wraps my legs around his waist, not breaking our kiss for one second as he steps into the room. No words pass between us as he takes me to the bed and gently lays me down. I know what's coming next, and dear Lord am I ready.

Chapter Thirty-Two
Jameson

I could spend every minute of the rest of my life enjoying Stella's body. Her scent, her taste, the sounds she makes when I do something she likes. They're all mine now. She's burrowed herself so far into me that I'll never be able to get rid of her, even if I wanted to.

The soft orange hues of the sky have turned purple. Our entire day has been spent between the sheets learning all the best ways to bring each other to the edge. After the conversation with my father earlier, I didn't think I would make it the rest of the day without relieving my tension, but the feel of Stella's fingers wrapped around my wrist immediately quelled the rise of emotions.

She's my own form of Xanax, an immediate-release tablet to fight the crippling anxiety. All I need is her melting on my tongue, her taste mainlining through my bloodstream, and I'm refocused.

Stella's stomach grumbles, and I reach for my phone to see what time it is, noticing a missed call from Red McComb's secretary. I was so wrapped up in Stella I must've forgotten to take my phone off silent. Excitement has me tapping my fingers on my leg as I call her back, but I groan when it goes to voicemail.

I turn to Stella. "Do you want to go out for dinner or stay in?"

She cuddles up next to me, one leg over my thighs, her head on my chest. "Let's stay in and order takeout or something."

"What counts as 'or something?'"

Stella chuckles and slaps my chest. "Feed me and find out."

I bite down on my lip and shake my head. She is so unexpected. How did my brother ever end up snagging a woman as amazing as this? And thank God he royally mucked it up.

I throw on some clothes and head to the lift, leaving Stella flipping through channels on the telly.

Across the street is a restaurant that serves food from local farmers and artisans, and according to their website, they sell an heirloom beet salad to die for. Thoughts of what Mr. McComb's secretary will say when she calls back spin around my head as I wait for the waiter to bring my roasted poblano relleno. He returns a few minutes later and I'm on my way back up to my flat.

The silence of the lift has me running back through the conversation with my dad. I thought I was past letting his disappointment of me affect my life, but I still bear the weight of his expectations. This is what I've been working for the past few years. I'm supposed to lead the company into the next decade, and getting this promotion is the way to do that. Since Dad knows about me and Stella now, the fight for the promotion is on equal grounding. It has to be a fair fight.

He's disappointed I let a woman deter me from what I came here for, but Stella isn't just *some* woman. She's everything. Everything I don't deserve, and everything I desire.

And if I was a better man, I'd let her go.

But I'm not a better man.

She didn't even have to hear the conversation to know I needed her. At first, I was embarrassed to look weak, for her to see how hard it is to fight the urge to cut. Like I'm a child without any impulse control. But that small act of support meant more than any words. Her affection doesn't hinge on how successful or strong I am, and I'm slowly realizing I'm worth that type of love.

The lift dings and the doors open. I insert the key into the lock and push into the foyer, juggling the bags and a bottle of wine. A soft clicking from the kitchen heralds Stella dressed in the skirt and blouse I bought her. I knew the champagne color would go beautifully with her warm, brown skin. And I was right. The sleeveless, cream-colored shirt displays her toned arms and the ample bosom she tries so hard to hide.

"You are absolutely stunning." I spin her into my arms, grabbing a handful of her arse. We share a passionate kiss before she breaks away, her attention stolen by the food. Her eyes widen, pupils so large I'm worried she's fallen harder for the goat cheese mousse and pecan-balsamic drizzle than she has for me.

I pour two glasses of cabernet and settle in next to her while she turns on a movie. An hour into the film we've finished one bottle. My phone vibrates in my pocket, and Stella shifts so I can grab it. I frown at the loss of her heat, and unease lodges in my throat when I see it's Mr. Lewis.

I get up from the couch and lean down to plant a kiss on Stella's soft lips. "I've gotta take this."

She nods and refills her wine glass. I head out to the balcony and sit down, seeking a fresh breath of air before answering.

"Hello, Mr. Lewis."

"Evening, Jameson. Great work on getting those accounts set up. I know it was a quick turn around."

I blow out a breath, not expecting any type of praise. "Thank you, sir."

"I have some meetings with potential landowners coming up, so I'll need you to be on call for that. I can't lose out on opportunities because you're not answering your phone."

His reprimand is reminiscent of my dad's when I do something he doesn't like. Tension rises up my spine, and the thread of control I've been gaining starts to unspool. I'm not required to be at a client's beck and call, but he's an important client to my father. Even if I don't get the promotion, having him on my portfolio will make me more money.

The sliding door opens and Stella steps out, her cheeks rosy from the wine. Our bodies have been entwined enough in the past two days I'm sure she felt the string between us pull taut when I answered the phone. I hold my finger up, asking her to wait a minute. She catches my hand and wraps her warm mouth around my finger. I pull my hand back and swat her ass, urging her back inside.

"Take a deep breath," she says, nudging my legs wider.

"Yes, sir." I struggle to focus on Mr. Lewis's distant voice. My hand travels up the slit in Stella's skirt, her soft thighs tempting me. Lewis mumbles something about emailing me an Excel sheet with names and dates, but my focus is being pulled back to my hand lifting the champagne skirt in front of me.

The professional side of me is struggling with the new person I feel like in her presence.

Someone who values something more than work.

What has she done to me that I can't even focus on a simple business call? The minute the thought torpedoes into my mind, I wonder if she's purposely distracting me. I told her I didn't want the promotion, and I was being truthful, but she told me she wanted to win fair and square.

I'm not sure this is in line with a fair battle, but when I see her lace panties my cock jolts awake in my trousers, and I can't find it in me to care.

"Pay attention," she whispers, her tongue flicking against my ear in a challenge as she palms my erection.

I curse beneath my breath, angry Mr. Lewis called me this late. Grinding my teeth, I swipe my thumb across the seam of her panties and smother a groan when I find them damp.

You've always been a great multitasker.

I prop the phone between my ear and shoulder, pull off her panties, grab her leg and set it on the wicker table beside me. Fireworks explode in my stomach when I see her glistening cunt.

You are so bad, I mouth to her right before I lean forward to taste her.

She moans and I scramble to cover the speaker, pressing a finger in front of my lips to quiet her. "Can you have that to me by Monday afternoon?" Lewis asks, pulling me back to the call.

"No." My voice cracks, and my restraint over my emotions waver.

"What do you mean 'no'?" he asks.

"Sorry, I meant yes." I curse under my breath and Stella moves away. By the look on her face, I can tell she's worried her distraction is hindering my ability to form coherent sentences, but I pull her back and nip at the inside of her leg. "I'll have it sent to you by lunchtime."

I swipe a long, broad stroke up Stella's core and her fingers tangle in my hair, keeping me close as she grinds into my face. The fact that she came out here and is letting me taste her while I'm on a phone call stirs the beast inside me, making my trousers too tight.

Lewis continues to drone on, and I bury my face between her legs, nipping, tasting, lapping up every drop of her like a man lost in a desert. I coat my fingers in her arousal and groan when I plunge them inside her.

She throws her head back and loudly moans. I scramble to cover the speaker and whisper, "Quiet, Love."

"Jameson? Are you even listening?" Lewis asks.

"Mmhmm...yes." I clear my throat. "Yes, sir."

The sound of my fingers moving inside Stella fills the air, drowning out everything he's saying.

"Take yourself out," she whispers. "I need you."

"Sir, I've got to call you back." My voice is gravelly and winded as I stand.

"But—"

I hit the end button and the phone drops to the floor.

The voice in the back of my head chastises me for hanging up on my client, but it's stifled by my heart telling me this woman's pleasure is more important. "I've got to get a rubber."

She firmly pushes me back onto the seat, then reaches into her blouse and pulls out a foil packet. I swear if I had a ring in my pocket, I'd drop down to one knee right now and beg her to be mine forever. Her lips quirk up into a wide smile and she slowly rips open the condom and holds it between her fingers.

Making quick work of dropping my trousers, my cock springs up the minute it's released. I grab the condom from her and sheath myself so fast I'm sure I've set a record. She lowers herself onto me slowly, her body stretching to accommodate my size. I grasp at the hem of her blouse, lifting it up and over her head before bunching the skirt around her waist.

"What did I ever do to deserve you?" I whisper into her ear. She doesn't answer with her words. Her body draws me into her warm center, and she grinds against me, stealing the pleasure she needs.

I unsnap her bra and her breasts bounce, begging for me to cover the pebbled flesh with my mouth. Moonlight reflects off her beautiful brown skin like she's an angel sent from heaven to bless me. I take shallow breaths and fight off my climax as the crisp December air wraps around us.

"Turn around." I slow her movements.

Her mouth parts like she wants to say something, but she doesn't speak. She hesitates a moment before she lifts her leg and turns, my cock riding the carousel of slickness between her thighs.

"Fuck, that feels good." She leans forward and places her hands on the railing, giving me the best view of her pretty, round arse. My eyes settle on where we've connected and my cock twitches inside of her, my release threatening to break the dam.

She curses when I steal her essence and rub the pearl at her center while she rides me. My other hand reaches to her chest, pinching the raised buds. She comes apart, her orgasm blasting through her, making her clench around my engorged head.

The slapping noise of our flesh drives me to the edge. I wrap my fist around her ponytail and turn her head to me, claiming her moans. Losing myself to the high of being inside her, I pick up the pace, my hips thrusting, bouncing her and her plump arse up and down until my climax spills out of me. Our tongues wrestle, the urge to bite, coax, and devour each other so immense we're lost in a daze.

"There's nothing like the view out here away from all the city lights," she says, leaning back into my embrace, spent.

My phone screen lights up on the table, and I silence it before it can break the moment, focusing back on the beauty in my lap. I should be worried about losing a client or my job, but I'd sacrifice it all for her. She's always there to pull me back from the edge, to show me I have control when I feel it slipping through my hands. Even though she's been in my bed all weekend, she's been working her way into my heart with our long conversations.

"I don't know about that." I run my hands along her sides. "The view from where I'm sitting is a thousand percent more beautiful than those stars in the sky."

She peeks over her shoulder, her wine-glazed eyes sleepy and hooded.

I lean forward, capturing her lips in one last kiss, begging the stars to let me keep her for one more day.

***

The ceramic coffee cup warms my hands as I sit at the kitchen island staring at the missed phone calls and messages from my father. On a normal day, I'd be midway through swimming laps, but I've spent the last two days in the arms of an angel, biding my time until the Devil drags me back to hell.

My mind won't quiet long enough for me to figure out where we go from here. I brace for what happens tomorrow when the weekend is over and the real world crashes back in, shattering everything we've built here in my flat.

Will she come to her senses and see I'm not worth all the effort? Not worth the dirty looks or whispers she'll have to endure if Cameron's jealousy gets the best of him, and he divulges our connection to spite me? What happens when the project manager is announced and one of us is the other's boss?

I know how toxic work environments can get when relationships are involved.

That's if you still have a job.

I reach for my pocket, itching to feel the cool press of the blade against my skin. I flex my fingers, filling my lungs with a deep breath and think about Stella. How disappointed she'd be if she knew I couldn't fight the urge without her.

It's not that I don't want to stop.

I hate myself each time I do it.

But nothing but pain and a rush of adrenaline replaces the impending doom I feel when I let someone down. I use an app to set up an in-person meeting with the next available therapist and slide my phone into my pocket.

"Good morning." Stella's scratchy voice steals my attention, her unruly curls covering dark honey eyes as she ambles into the kitchen.

"Good morning." I grab her and wrap my arms around her waist. "How'd you sleep?"

"With my eyes closed." She chuckles and yelps when I swat her arse. "I slept well. You?"

"Peacefully." I grab a take-out menu and put it in her hands, brushing her hair over her shoulder so I can explore the column of her neck with my lips. I know things will be different at work, but I'm soaking up the last moments of bliss before that happens. "Pick something for breakfast and I'll order while you get in the shower."

"Hmm…" Her hands slowly move to my trousers, a devilish look on her face. "None of these restaurants have the type of breakfast I want."

My cock wakes up instantly. I could survive feasting on her body as my only source of sustenance, but we've barely made it out of the bedroom the last two days, and I'm worried she'll wither away if I don't get some actual nourishment into her system.

"That…is on the menu twenty-four seven. However, you haven't eaten since six last night. I'm sure you're famished."

She purses her lips. "French toast sounds perfect."

I swipe a loose curl behind her ear and dust my lips across hers, savoring the soft, feather-like kisses she returns. I close my eyes and pray today never ends.

I call in the order, busying myself by gathering the remnants of Stella's strewn clothes and dishes. Once I'm done, I grab my phone and sit at the island responding to emails and text messages I've missed. My dad's messages are a string of curses about ignoring his calls and how massive of a disappointment I am, and Cameron's are a never-ending spew of hatred because Dad made him call me to see if I was avoiding him.

I swipe away the messages, promising to focus on the last few peaceful hours I have before reality begins again. Knocking on the bathroom door, I let Stella know I'm leaving to grab breakfast.

I wander through dank alleyways searching for the small mom-and-pop shop Mike told me about and stumble upon tents filled with worn, weary faces surrounding an oil drum. My eyes land on a familiar face.

"Ernest," I say. "What are you doing here?"

He's dressed in clean dark jeans, a brown polo, and New Balance shoes, not the typical vagabond attire. "It's nice to see you, Mr. Jameson." He says something to the woman he was speaking with and then heads my way. "I'm giving back, what are you doing here?"

"Giving back?"

He nods to the meal truck handing out food across the street. "Now that I've got that cushy job you set me up with, I want to give back to those who helped me when I was down and out."

Warmth spreads through my chest at his generosity. Before Stella, I never would've thought about helping out these people here on the street, but now I find myself pulling out some cash and handing it to him. "Make sure they've got dinner too."

"Wow, Mr. Jameson." His brows pinch and he gives me a wide smile. "Stelly did a number on you, didn't she?"

I chuckle and put away my wallet. "I guess she did change me."

He claps me on the shoulder. "A good woman doesn't change you; she shows you potential and makes you want to change for yourself."

His words fill my chest with hope.

Since meeting Stella, I've tried to fight the urge to cut so I could be the man she deserves, but what Ernest says sets off a ripple inside my brain. If I want to truly change, I have to want the change for myself.

Stella showed me the potential I had to truly love someone, but she also reminded me that I must love myself first.

I make a silent promise to get the help I need to break the cycle.

"Thank you, Ernest." I return his shoulder squeeze. "I actually came here looking for YaYa's Café."

He points me in the right direction. "Take care of my Stelly, or you'll have me to answer to."

Chapter Thirty-Three
Stella

Driving away from Jameson's apartment leaves me feeling giddy. We spent ten minutes making out in the hallway before I had to pull myself away and get to the funeral home. The rational part of me wants to dissect what all this means for us, but I push it to the back of my mind. The conference is tomorrow, and we'll figure out what happens between us after.

"I was just about to call in the National Guard." Pop-Pop peers down at me through his glasses with a smile on his face.

"For little ol' me?" My eyes fall to the papers spread out over the desk. "What's all this Pops?"

He busies himself, fiddling with items strewn all over his desk. "It's Mr. Garcia's offer to buy."

I collapse into the seat and press my fingers into my eyes. "Pops, I can still save this place."

He takes off his glasses and clasps his hands on the desk. "I'm ready to retire, Punkin. It's too stressful on both of us to run this place, and I've seen some nice senior communities I can move into so you can have the house."

My tongue sticks to the top of my mouth. "Pops."

The failure clogs my throat. I can't let his dream go down the drain. All the money they spent on me throughout the years could've been used for their savings. My braces, my college, my first car. Pop-Pop and Nunny sacrificed so I could have the things I needed to be successful, and I can't even help him keep his dream alive.

"It's fine, Stella." Pop-Pop gathers the documents into a folder and puts it into his desk. "I'll pray on it. If this is where the good Lord is leading me, then I want to listen."

"Okay," I huff and grab a bottle of water to drink. "They announce the new project manager tomorrow at the conference mixer."

With the McCombs account, it might be the boost I need to stave off selling the funeral home. I don't bother telling him what I learned about Jameson over the weekend. He'll tell me if I'm meant to get the promotion, then I will.

"Either way we'll be fine, sweetheart. Maybe you were only supposed to be trying for the promotion so you could meet Jameson."

Water shoots up my throat and I cough as I gather my bearings. Pop-Pop doesn't know I spent the weekend with Jameson, and it's not something I'm ready to talk about yet. But the idea I was meant to meet him doesn't feel too far off the mark. What would've happened to him had I not found him in the locker room? Would we have ever progressed to where we are now, or would he have continued to push me away?

"Maybe." I shrug and wipe the spittle away from my mouth. "I guess we'll find out tomorrow. I'll be setting up the family room if you need me."

I leave him to putter around the office while I move chairs and hang pictures on tripods for the next viewing. Plans form in my mind on how to save the place I grew up in, the place that shaped me into the woman I am today. A commitment from Charlotte McCombs is the first step I need to take.

I slip my phone out of my pocket and send her an email to check in on the progress with her father.

"Are we ready?" Pop-Pop asks.

"Yup. We're ready." I set boxes of tissues at the end of each row for the family and sneak out of the room to give them privacy. My phone rings as I close the viewing room door.

"Hello?" I answer quickly, stifling the loud noise so it doesn't disturb the bereaved.

"Ms. Daniels?" the woman says.

I pull the phone away from my ear and look at the name, cursing myself for not checking before I answered. "Good morning, Ms. McCombs."

"Now what did I tell you about calling me that?" she says. "It's Charlotte. I got your email, and I'm sending over the paperwork from my father now. Would you be able to meet today so we can set up our portfolio?"

"Absolutely." I mime screaming and dance giddily on my feet in the waiting area. All my hard work has given me a potential last minute save for the funeral home. My spirits lift, and I stand a little straighter. "What time would you like to meet?"

***

My meeting with Charlotte McCombs went better than I could've imagined. We swapped her real estate accounts over to Thompson, and she also wanted to get started on the ventures we spoke about during our lunch meeting. All this added revenue should finally help put me in the black.

I've typed and retyped a message to Jameson but can't bring myself to send it. I know he wanted to get Red, and now that we've crossed into uncharted territory, I don't want it to look like I'm rubbing it in his face.

Sliding past his office, I find it empty. I heard his voice outside the meeting room earlier, so I know he made it into work.

"Have you seen Jameson?" I ask a passing coworker.

They shrug and continue down the hallway.

I shoot him a text to say I'm thinking about him.

Figuring he may be in his own meeting, I head to let Mr. Weston know about my success with the account. After seeing the anxiety Jameson has about disappointing his father, I understand why he didn't tell me. I don't blame him. Mr. Weston has always been a proud man, in charge of everything and everyone. Part of me hates him for that, but the other part is thankful for how he swooped in to help me through my parent's mess of finances.

Thankfully, it's not just him that makes the final decision on the project manager spot. The board will also be happy with my success, and they'll decide who is better for the job.

Raised voices halt me outside the door.

"Don't worry about the trust," Mr. Weston says to whoever is in his office. "...screwed over! It should be mine!" his voice booms.

When I'm sure no one is approaching, I lean closer to eavesdrop.

"It's not your business to worry about. You've already fucked up enough." I check my phone and see Jameson still hasn't messaged back. "Is she why you missed phone calls all weekend?"

The hairs on the back of my neck raise and my stomach coils. Jameson spent all weekend with me, and I'm sure a few phone calls were missed during our tryst. If it's him in the office, then he's getting reamed out because of me and his lack of focus.

No part of me delights listening to Jameson get beaten down by his father, especially knowing the impact it'll have on his mental health.

I knock on the door, hoping to break the tension.

Hopefully hearing I've acquired the McCombs account for Thompson will put his father back into a better mood and relieve some weight from Jameson's shoulders. Keeping the accounts increasing is the most important part to running a successful investment company, so Mr. Weston should be ecstatic.

"Come in." Mr. Weston opens the door, and his mouth parts in shock.

I put on a happy face, so he doesn't realize I was out here listening to him chew an employee out. "Sorry, am I interrupting something?" Feigning confusion, I step into the room. Even though I had a feeling it was Jameson getting yelled at, I'm still surprised to find him here. "Oh, hi, Jameson."

His throat visibly bobs with a swallow and his eyes are wide like he's terrified I'll say something I shouldn't. I don't know if he told his father I know, or if we're playing like I'm still in the dark. We probably should've spoken about this before today, but our mouths were too busy doing something else.

"Hello, Stella."

Mr. Weston's gaze shifts between us like he's waiting for one of us to break and fess up to the truth. I figure it's best to pretend like nothing has happened, so naturally, I stare at Jameson a moment too long before I bring my attention back to the reason I'm here. "We've got the McCombs account."

Jameson's face lifts into a smile. "Great job."

His genuine praise makes butterflies take off inside my stomach.

Mr. Weston grimaces but recovers quickly. "That's great news, Stella. I'm sure that'll make the board extremely happy. Kudos to you."

"Thanks." My heart pounds in my throat as we stand in the office with fake celebration for my accomplishment hanging in the air. The stifling awkwardness is apparent. My attempt to decrease the tension didn't work, and somehow I know I've just made it worse for Jameson.

In his father's mind, that account should be his.

And he lost it *because* of me.

Unease settles in my stomach right beside the elation I felt walking in. "Just wanted to make you aware before the conference."

He gives me a curt nod before turning his attention to his computer. My gaze sweeps past Jameson, and an emotion I can't quite place crosses his face. Is it apprehension? Regret? Fear?

I close the door, taking a deep breath as I move away from the office. I don't want to hear how upset Mr. Weston is with his son, and I'm not sure I can hold my tongue any longer without lashing out at him. Jameson deserves to be treated like the amazing man he is, all his talents included. If his father can't see the incredible son he has, then it's his issue.

I spend the rest of the day in my office, waiting for Jameson to stop by. At five, my phone chirps, and my face cracks into a smile when I see the message.

Jameson: Dinner at my place tonight? 8pm.

I type back a flirty emoji and get ready for my last two meetings of the day.

Time passes slowly. When I finally slide into my car, I'm jittery as I drive to Jameson's for dinner, hoping he isn't about to break it off before we've even gotten started.

The aroma of garlic and rosemary hits me as I knock on the door.

My hands are clammy as Jameson stands in front of me in jeans and a tight black t-shirt that molds to his abs and biceps. Less than twenty-four hours ago, this man was exploring my body like he was searching for the eighth wonder of the world. Now I stand in front of him, sheepish like a schoolgirl going on her first date.

"Hi."

He chuckles. "Hi, Love." He takes my coat and lays it on the back of the couch before pouring me a glass of wine. He shuts the notebook he was working in and places it on the desk. "How did your meetings go?"

"They went well." I take the red wine from him, and he leans forward and kisses me breathless. "How was the rest of your day?"

He shrugs. "It was fine." I can tell he doesn't want to talk about it more, so I don't push. He opens the oven and pulls out a baking pan. "I made some focaccia and vegetarian eggplant parmesan."

My mouth waters. "It smells amazing. Where'd you learn to cook so well?"

"I spent a summer in Tuscany with one of my friends from boarding school." He fixes our plates and takes them to the table.

It should feel weird doing something so…domestic with him, but it feels natural. He kisses me before he takes his seat, and we chat about everything except work. I find out Patty knows about his father, he has so many tattoos because he finds it therapeutic, and that if he could, he'd want to head up his own art investment department for Thompson.

"I don't see why you couldn't do something like that," I say, topping off my glass of wine. "Depending on who gets the promotion tomorrow, one of us will be free to pursue other endeavors."

His shoulders tense, and it's on the tip of my tongue to ask him what happened after I left. His weary expression keeps me quiet. I don't want to sully our otherwise great evening with talk of his father.

He scrubs his beard, his focus solely on me. "I don't care what happens tomorrow as long as I still have you."

The remnants of our meal are left on the table, forgotten as we head back to his room.

"Bloody hell," he inhales my hair. "I love the way you smell."

I wiggle and turn around. "And what exactly do I smell like?"

He nuzzles into my neck and kisses my collarbone. "Like home."

I didn't think it was possible for my heart to melt anymore, but Jameson's words do just that. His hand traces the curve of my hip, and he grips my side with a groan. "I want you so bad right now."

We lock lips, and he lifts my legs and wraps them around his waist. Steam rises to my skin, spurred on by the need to be devoured by him. "What are you waiting for?"

Chapter Thirty-Four
Stella

My mind is now crammed with information about estate planning, economic and market updates, new tax laws, and addressing shifting risk tolerances of clients. With the finance industry continuously changing, it's more important than ever to differentiate our company.

At least the all-day conference is finally over, and I don't have to listen to Alex hitting on Rosay during the breaks. I can focus on what I'll do if I don't get the promotion.

Having the McCombs account has eased the main burden of the loan off my shoulders, but the project manager's pay increase would help even more.

"Did you see how Alex was following me around the entire time?" Rosay asks as we lounge in her apartment.

"I swear he's in love with you and doesn't know how to tell you without sounding like a douche canoe."

"You're delusional," she says, applying more blush to her high cheekbones. "He's not used to being rejected. Anyway, what are you wearing tonight?"

I reach into the dry-cleaning bag I brought with me and pull out my strapless, dark green bodycon dress. The velvet is tight and hugs my curves in all the right places. The neckline is modest, and the hem falls right above my knee. Paired with my black ankle-strapped stilettos, it's the perfect dress for a business event.

"Hot damn, girlfriend." She fans herself and falls back onto the bed. "Jameson is gonna die when he sees you in this getting congratulated for the promotion."

I swallow down the nausea pushing against my throat. Jameson's parentage isn't my story to tell, so Rosay has no clue how badly tonight can take a turn for the worse if those two get into it again.

"Let's see your outfit." I move the conversation away from my predicament.

She spins around, and sunlight bounces off her rose sequins turning her into a disco ball. The dress is a shade lighter than her pink hair, and surprisingly it doesn't clash. Applying my makeup only takes a few minutes. A little eyeliner and mascara, a hint of Petal Poppin' blush, and a light coat of the new Fenty Fu$$y lip gloss are all I need to feel ready to take on the world.

"Ready to go?" I ask.

She nods, and we get onto the road. I'm hoping I'll be celebrating with Jameson later, but if not, I'll need some girl time to get over the loss.

Most of the people I invited RSVP'd to let me know they are coming, so now it's up to me to woo them. I have talking points on a notecard in my clutch I can review if I forget any details about what is important to each potential client.

Rosay pulls up to valet parking at the Hyatt Regency and my mouth falls slightly open. I stare at the massive tree filled with red, orange, and yellow bulbs in the center of the roundabout. The walkway is paved and lit with pale yellow light from the streetlamps, and each banister is wrapped with multicolored Christmas lights. The interior holds the same luscious decorations. Poinsettias on every available surface, employees decked out in Christmas hats and ties, Christmas trees in every corner.

They've essentially brought the North Pole to South Texas.

I pass a few coworkers dressed in elegant gowns and tuxedos as a hotel employee takes us to the Independence Ballroom. The line for the bar is long, but most people are chatting while waiters pass out canapes. I take a moment to absorb the scene.

Our company's logo is on the massive projector screen at the front of the room. Each table is draped in red and green tablecloths and placed in such a way as to invite conversation. The drinks are flowing, and laughter and dancing fill the center of the room beneath the massive chandelier.

I'll give it to Mr. Weston. He knows how to throw a party.

My eyes flit around the room, seeking out Jameson but coming up empty.

"Let's get this over with." Rosay tugs on my arm, heading to the bar.

I slip out of her grasp. "Go ahead. I need to find some of my clients before the announcement."

I'm searching for one client in particular. I scan the room and find her sandwiched between a bunch of men in suits. I straighten and lift my head high as I stroll toward her. My ankles slightly wobble when I see she was able to get her father, Red, and her other siblings to attend with her.

I instantly regret not getting a drink and turn back to the bar, running into a solid wall.

"Oops," I say, looking up and into stormy eyes.

"You are stunning." Jameson raises his glass to his lips, staring me down over the rim.

Watching his Adam's apple bob as the dark liquor moves down his throat sends my stomach into a tailspin. Gah, what this man does to me.

I told myself having no eye contact with him was the only way to make it through this event without jumping his bones. No staring at the lips that were all over my body, the hair I want to run my fingers through and tug on as he explores every inch of my skin, and definitely not at the muscles straining in the navy tux he's wearing that fits his body as if Giorgio Armani made it personally for him.

Right now, I'm royally failing.

The heat between us expands then shrivels the minute CJ slides his hand around my shoulder. I grit my teeth and push him away.

"Nice party, spare." CJ raises his glass like he's toasting Jameson, a hint of snideness lacing his words.

I assume Jameson hasn't told his father or CJ that I know about their relation, so I shrug off CJ's arm and leave the men to their cock-measuring contest. Though I know who'd win in that particular fight, I'm here to woo clients, not to play referee for two grown men.

I find Charlotte and her father at a table with Mr. Weston. She perks up the minute I approach, and all eyes fall to me, including my boss. A frown pulls at the corners of his mouth, but he quickly fixes on a stale smile.

"I've been looking for you, Stella. This," Charlotte gestures to an older gentleman to her right, "is my father, Red."

"It's good to finally meet you." He shakes my hand. "My daughter has been gabbing on about how you've got a plan to usher McCombs Enterprises into the next generation."

My cheeks blush and I give Charlotte a thankful smile. "I have ideas on how you can expand your communications group as well as boost the revenue for your automotive and energy endeavors."

His lips purse and he slowly nods, contemplative. I shift on my feet wishing I had a drink in my hands instead of leaving them empty and useless at my sides.

He reaches into his suit jacket and pulls out a white business card, handing it to me with a smile. "I'm glad to hear we've signed on with such an eager advisor. I'd love to meet with you and see how we can expand on Charlotte's ideas."

Meeting with the head of the company feels significantly more nerve-wracking than it did meeting with his daughter who's poised to take over. I'm sure my gulp is audible, but I somehow shake the nerves away and offer a confident smile.

This is exactly the boost I needed.

"Can't wait."

Charlotte gives me a thumbs up and I excuse myself to chat with the other guests. After an hour of schmoozing, my future with Thompson is brighter. Along with the McCombs account, three other guests have committed to opening new accounts at the beginning of the year.

My body buzzes with excitement, anticipating Jameson's reaction—but as my gaze sweeps the ballroom floor, he's nowhere in sight. Alex passes me and I stop him to ask if he's seen Jameson. His eyes are glazed over, and he's a little unsteady on his feet. "I think I saw him walk into a conference room?"

"Which one?"

He shrugs, his attention now on Rosay. Curiosity nudges me toward the hallway with conference rooms. My heart thumps, pounding like a tribal drum.

Why am I so nervous?

I press my hand to my chest, willing myself to calm down. I have nothing to be worried about, yet I can't shake the feeling something is wrong.

Cool wood touches my ear as I lean against the door, peering through a crack.

"I told you to stay focused on the job I brought you here for," Mr. Weston sneers," and now you're fucking it up over her?"

"You need to tell her," Jameson says.

"No. Her dad was nothing but a cheat. The money he put in her trust was money from an investment he swindled me out of. It should be mine, not hers."

I have a trust? No, he can't be talking about me...right? Mr. Weston took me under his wing to help me in the wake of their deaths. He may not be the nicest guy, but he's never shown me to be calculating or dishonest.

What about him bringing Jameson here?

Dread washes over me, and within a few seconds tears fill my eyes.

"The money is rightfully Stella's," Jameson brings himself to his full height, "as well as the house."

"If you're so worried about her, why didn't you tell her when you found out? It's been...what three weeks? Where's *your* loyalty at, son?"

My sluggish heart aches inside my chest, and my lungs refuse to fill. Ropes of anguish wrap around my throat, suffocating me as I realize Mr. Weston has been keeping this from me the whole time, watching me struggle, and Jameson knew about it. Did CJ know too? Was he with me for the same reason?

Anger flashes through my mind at how stupid I've been all these years.

I push the door open with the force of a hurricane, and their heads snap toward me, eyes wide with surprise. My fingers curl into a fist and my pulse thrums in my ears, but I steel my spine.

"Why?" It's all I can manage to say past the tight knot in my throat.

"Stella," Jameson starts to speak but I cut him off.

"I don't wanna hear anything you have to say." I force myself to turn away from the man I thought I was falling for and I lock eyes on the man I thought I could trust.

Mr. Weston scoffs. "Why what?"

The gall of this man has no bounds. How could I be so stupid? So pathetic I didn't know I was being used. All the overheard conversations splice together, and disgust swells up inside me.

"How could you do this? You knew I was struggling, and you've been sitting on my trust fund? You pretended to help me after they died. You became like a father figure to me, but it was all for show."

"Cut the dramatics, Stella." Mr. Weston picks at a piece of lint on his suit as if giving me eye contact is beneath him, the façade fully shed. "I'm a businessman. If you were in my situation, you would've done the same."

I struggle to keep my composure as my world crumbles. I splay my hand across my stomach. "What's in the trust?" Mr. Weston doesn't speak and a muscle in his jaw ticks as he looks to his son with disgust. My voice raises as I ask again. "What was so important to you?"

Jameson tries to speak again, and the pain in his voice makes my stomach twist. Tears burn a line down my cheek, and I swipe them away as I realize he's not upset for me but because he was caught. "Were you in on it with him?"

"No," he says. "When I saw the paperwork, I—"

"How long ago did you find the paperwork?" I ask. "Was it before the pool?"

His throat rolls, and he wets his lips like they're dry. The muscles of his jaw move, and in that instant, I know the answer. My head is screaming at me as the realization makes me lightheaded. "You've known all this time."

He moves forward, but I step back. "Love, please. I didn't—"

"Don't call me that," I say, cursing the tears still sliding down my cheeks. "How can I ever believe you after you've done nothing but lie to me?"

"Because I lo—"

I raise my hand to cut off his declaration. "You don't know the meaning of the word. I can't believe I trusted you."

My eyes flit to Mr. Weston. He's standing off to the side, the lines of his face relaxed as if my world isn't on fire. Anger clogs my throat and seeps into my chest. He won't get away with what he's done, but there are no repercussions for Jameson's betrayal. I turn back to him, to the man I was falling for.

"I feel sorry for you though. You don't care enough about yourself to know that nothing you do will ever make him love you. Even if you got my trust, you'd never be good enough or reach his standards. And that matters more to you than being a good person, someone actually worthy of the love you so desperately seek from the wrong people."

Jameson's mouth parts, stunned by my words. Angry tears pour down my face, and my chest heaves as I compose myself. I can't bear to let them see me unravel.

"Stella. Wait!" Jameson tries to stop me, but I'm already headed out the door. My lungs cramp as a tidal wave of emotion crashes down on me and a heaviness settles on my chest. I've got to get out of here without causing a bigger scene.

I speed back into the cocktail party and grab my purse. I'm headed to the door when I realize Rosay drove, not me.

Fuck.

I drag a hand down my face and grab my phone to call an Uber.

The screen is blank.

I must've forgotten to charge it when I got home from the conference. Patty enters the room and stops short when she sees me. "What's wrong, Stella?" she asks, her hand halting at her mouth with a canape.

I shake my head, my throat too tight to form a coherent sentence. "I'm too heavy," is all I can choke out before I push past her and find a place to hide. I swipe at the tears on my cheeks and my feet start moving with one place in mind.

Chapter Thirty-Five
Jameson

Fuck. Fuck. Fuck. Tonight couldn't have gone worse than what just happened. Confronting my dad at the conference was a bad idea, but I couldn't bear knowing Stella would lose out on the promotion because of me, and potentially also lose her family's business because my dad was cheating her out of her trust fund.

"Well, I guess that takes care of the promotion issue," my dad says, scrolling through his phone like nothing happened.

My blood boils.

All the years I've spent striving to attain his respect and admiration sit heavy in my stomach. If my mum was still alive, she'd laugh at me. She sought his love for years and I didn't learn a damn thing from her. I thought he'd love me because I was *his*. Part of his family, even though I was on the outskirts. But it was all a lie. I've never meant anything to him, and I gave up the one person I meant something to because I held onto hope he'd love me back.

"Piss off, Dad." I move toward the door, preparing what I'll say to Stella when I find her. I doubt she'll ever forgive me, but I have to try.

He grabs my arm and stops me in my tracks. "This promotion will solidify you in the family business."

My fists tense at my sides when he mentions the family business. How did I not see that my dad was never worthy of the control I gave him?

How could I let him ruin the one good thing I've ever had in my life, all in favor of being part of a family that never wanted me?

"What family?" I demand. "I've never been part of your family. You made sure of that by hiding me away, and having the job won't change the fact that you know nothing about what it means to be family."

I hoist the door open, and his voice bellows. "If you leave and embarrass me, you're done. I don't want anything to do with you anymore."

"Go right off and fuck yourself, Dad."

Adrenaline floods my system as I head into the mixer and search for Stella. She's nowhere to be found, and she's not answering her phone. Cameron pushes past me, and I almost stop to ask him if he's seen her, but he's too wrapped up in the woman he's with to notice my frantic searching.

"I saw her a few minutes ago." Patty bumps into me, shoving food into her mouth. "She was upset and crying."

"Where'd she go?"

She shrugs, a small frown on her face. "I don't know. She said something about being too heavy and ran off down the hallway."

I scratch my beard, wondering what she means. Bloody hell, why didn't I tell her sooner? I should've told her everything the other night. We could've worked through it and found a way to fix it together, but once again I put my father's needs over my own.

Where could she have gone? If she didn't leave the building, she must still be here somewhere. Patty and I check the stairwells and the hotel bar but can't find her. Standing in front of the hotel directory, the memory crashes into me.

"I know where she went." I grab Patty's hand and give it a kiss. "Thank you, Patty."

I take off down the hallway, scanning the signs for which direction I need to go. I'm well aware people are staring at me as I run through the hotel, but I need to get to her.

I turn the corner and my chest heaves as I find the door I'm looking for.

My eyes fall to the body inside the pool.

Air leaves my lungs in a whoosh and a weight settles on my chest. The ache in my throat expands when I push through the door.

"Stella."

"Jameson?" Her voice is shaky. "Help me."

My stomach bottoms out.

She's in the middle of the pool, nowhere close to the edge.

Running to the deep end, I get down to my knees and reach out for her. Her eyes are wide and filled with fear as she stretches out to meet my hand. Water ripples around her, causing her focus to waver and her legs to fall beneath the water again. "Grab my hand."

"Jameson," she yells. "I can't. I'm too scared."

"It's okay. Breathe. I'll get you out." I lean back on my heels and scan the room for something to help. I'm a fine swimmer, but if I jump into the pool to grab her, she'll freak out more and make it harder to rescue her. My eyes lock onto an adjustable pool skimmer. "I'll be right back."

"Don't leave me," she cries and my heart plummets to my feet.

"I'll never leave you. I promise."

"Okay." She exhales and inhales another breath.

"You're doing great." I scramble to the other side of the pool. "Keep filling your lungs." With the skimmer in hand, I run back to the edge and adjust it to the height I need. "I'm gonna reach this out to you. I need you to grab onto it so I can bring you to me."

She doesn't answer, but I know she heard me because her hand slowly moves out to her side.

I lean over the edge and extend the skimmer, pushing it into her opened palm. "Grab on tight, and don't freak out when I pull you. Just keep breathing."

She nods and closes her eyes. I pull slowly, stopping every few seconds to make sure she's okay. When she's within reach, I grab onto her arm and hoist her out of the water. She throws her arms over my shoulders and wraps her legs tightly around me.

I drop the skimmer and embrace her shivering body, squeezing her tighter to me. I murmur into her hair as she cries into my shoulder. "It's okay, you're safe now. I've got you, Love."

"I'm so stupid." Her breath warms my cheek. "How could I be so stupid?"

"I'm the stupid one." I capture her lips, begging her to open and let me in. Her heart is pounding against my chest, but her resolve softens. Tears mix into our kisses, and I'm not sure whether they're mine or hers.

I pull her close and steal as much as she's willing to give. I know I have moments before she comes to her senses and pushes me away, but I'm too far gone to care. I love her, and I know I'm losing her because of my own actions.

"I can't." She pulls away. "I can't do this."

"Please, let me explain."

She gets up off the ground and wipes her hands across her face, clearing away the remnant of makeup from her cheeks. "The time for explaining was weeks ago. Nothing you say could make this right. You lied, again. You knew I was struggling, and you chose to keep quiet about what your father was doing. You let your fear of losing his approval make you lose me."

My heart shrivels as she trudges towards the door.

"The bottom line is, deal with your shit." She pauses, face turned halfway to me. "Or you're gonna keep hurting yourself and everyone around you."

"Stella," I beg.

She holds up a hand, brown eyes red-rimmed. "I need time to process before I can communicate with you."

Without turning around, she leaves me at the pool on my knees, stomach cramping as if even my body is disgusted with my actions and wants to get rid of me. Where there was once warmth, there's nothing but a hollow ache creeping inside and filling my chest.

Punching the tile floor does nothing to abate the anger swelling inside me. How could I do this? I'm such a fuckin' arsehole to have lost the most amazing woman in the world because I was too scared to upset my dad.

I get up and squeeze out my drenched trousers before heading back inside. I'm done with trying to impress my dad. I'd rather move back to the U.K. and beg for my job back than to stay here and be surrounded by everything I've lost, everything I gave up for the chance to be loved by someone who didn't deserve it.

"What the hell did you do?" Cameron steps into my way as I reach for my keys on the table. His chest bumps mine, and a fire ignites in my core.

"I suggest backing the hell up if you'd like to keep that pretty face of yours," I grit out, reaching around him.

"Or what?" He pushes against my chest.

My fist connects with his face and the loud crack sends adrenaline knifing down my spine. He stumbles into a stool, half-collapsing over it, then rights himself and pivots. His body hunches into a linebacker position and he clenches his fists at his side.

A sick sort of glee twists his face as he charges me.

We crash into a table like a pair of bulls, taking it down. Glass crashes around us as we pummel each other, decades of pent-up rage powering the fists we rain onto each other.

Until we're jerked apart and handcuffs snap onto my wrists.

Before I'm even aware of what's happening, my head is pushed into the back seat of a cop car.

Chapter Thirty-Six
Jameson

The infuriating drip of the cell's tap rouses me before I catch the whiff of vomit being scrubbed from the cement floor. Coughing on the noxious mixture of bleach and mildew, I sit up and wince at the crick in my neck from sleeping on a steel bed. It's safe to say, this is not how I imagined waking up. I should be warm and tangled up in the sheets with Stella, not sitting on a cold bench staring at my pathetic excuse for a brother through iron bars.

"This is your fault." Cameron peers through the cage separating us. "All of this is your fault. You have everything. Money, brains, looks, why take what's mine? You couldn't stay in London, could you? You had to come all the way here to ruin my life."

I scoff. He doesn't know a thing about me. He assumes all people with British accents must be from London as if it's the entirety of the U.K. I don't bother correcting him. He hasn't tried to get to know me for the last thirty-five years, and I don't imagine he actually wants to now.

"I didn't ruin your life, Cameron. I came here because Dad asked me to."

"I'm sure he did. You're the prized child." He shakes his head and sneers. "It's always *Jim this, Jim that. Why can't you be more ambitious like him?* You've always had to overshadow me. You didn't have to take Stella too."

I rear back, thrown off by his statement. "The prized child?" Heat flares through me and I fist my hands on my legs. My chest rises with a calming breath, staving off my rapid heartbeat. "I've never been the prized child. I got to see him four, maybe five times a year. You got him every single day of your pathetic existence while I had to beg to be noticed."

He angrily rubs his chin. "Just because I saw him every day doesn't mean he noticed me."

His small, childlike voice surprises me.

"What's that supposed to mean?"

"Nothing, forget it." He turns away and stares out at the passing guards.

I lean forward, nearly touching the germ-ridden bars before I realize what I'm doing and place my hands on my trousers. "Cameron, what do you mean he didn't notice you?"

How could he not? Dad was there every day. He got to wake up and have breakfast, eat dinner, and be tucked in by him.

All the things I didn't get to have.

Most days it was me making dinner and tucking both me and my mum in bed.

"The only thing that matters to him...that's always mattered to him, is business." He runs a hand through his hair, tugging on the strands as if to rip them out. "He worked from sunup to sundown every day. He was never home for dinner and only came to my games to save face. I didn't matter to him until I was old enough to learn about the business."

I recall the few summers I came to visit, failing to find the lie in what he's saying. Summer was a busy time for my dad. Between the real estate and vacation homes people wanted to buy, he was always attending some benefit or gala to support local businesses. I guess I didn't realize he was gone because I was used to not having him around. "I didn't know."

He scoffs. "Of course, you didn't know. You got to spend your life in Europe, surrounded by everything you ever wanted, all on my dad's dime."

My fists tense on my thighs and my jaw clenches so hard pain radiates down my neck. I wish they would've let me keep my rubber band at intake.

"Don't presume to know anything about what my life was like in Europe. You know nothing about me."

"Oh, I know enough." He leans forward. "I know Dad paid for your nanny while my mom took care of the house and raised me. I know he paid for your mom to keep vacationing at some fancy resort while my mom was so stressed out and in need of a break she broke down and had to be admitted to the hospital and now takes antidepressants every day. So don't whine to me about how bad your life was when you know nothing about mine either."

A tightness creeps up my neck, constricting my vocal cords.

I swallow past the stiffness and clear my throat.

"I didn't have a nanny. I had a caretaker. Someone who made sure my mum didn't spend the money dad sent on drugs instead of groceries. And they weren't resorts, they were rehabs to get her clean."

Cameron's face falls and his eyes turn somber. I guess both of us never really knew or cared what life was like for the other. We couldn't see past our own situations, our own feelings about our father, to find any common ground.

Stella's voice echoes inside my head, reminding me we shouldn't have to work to be worthy of our parent's love. The thought of her sends a sharp pain into my chest, but a weight lifts off my shoulders when it finally clicks for me.

I've spent so much time wanting my dad to notice me, begging him to love me and treat me as his son, but the problem isn't with me.

It's with him.

He's incapable of giving the type of love a parent should, and that's not my fault.

Or Cameron's.

"We both got shorted in the dad department."

He sniffs and I swear I see him clear away a tear. I never thought I'd feel anything but contempt for Cameron, but a small part of me feels sorry for him. I finally understand why he hated me.

"I'm sorry about what happened with Stella." Cameron runs his hands down his trousers.

"I cocked that up myself. I should've been honest with her." My shoulders sag. "I was too worried about how Dad would react."

"What are you gonna do?"

I shrug. "I'm not sure. I came because Dad wanted me to, but I think it's best I move back to the U.K. I can't be here, so close to her, yet not be able to have her."

I swallow, forcing the sadness back into a tiny box. I need space from everyone and everything. I need to get help and heal from the mental wounds my parents created so I don't keep hurting myself and those around me.

Cutting ties with my father is the first step.

"Brooks," a guard calls. "You've made bail."

"Finally." I hop up from the warped bench and stand at the iron bars, waiting for release. I used my one phone call to ring Patty, hoping she'd help me, and it looks like she has.

"Jim?" Cameron's voice is hoarse, and he clears his throat before speaking again. "I'm sorry I never took the chance to get to know you."

I chew on my lip, unsure of what to say. If we didn't end up in that fight and in jail together, we never would've realized we weren't each other's enemies.

"You'll keep in touch, right?" Cameron asks.

Surprised by his question, something flutters in my chest. "Yeah, mate. Now that we don't hate each other as much, I'd actually like to get to know you." A smile tugs at the corner of my lips and I turn back to him. "Can you help me with something when you get out?"

He nods, twisting his hands in his lap.

I follow the guard to out-processing and grab my belongings: my cell phone, wallet, rubber band, and my knife.

I stare down at it.

This is the first time I've been without the knife in my possession, and I felt…lighter. Like its dark presence didn't have a hold on me anymore. I go to throw it away, but the guard calls for me, so I slip it back into my pocket. He takes me to where Patty waits, a scowl permanently fixed on her face.

I briefly look at my phone, hoping Stella messaged me, but it's dead.

"You owe me, big time." Patty turns to the door.

All I can focus on is finding Stella and begging her to listen to me. I know I have virtually no chance of convincing her I had nothing to do with whatever plan my father hatched, but I need her to know I'm sorry for what he did, for what she thinks I was a part of.

I need her to know that I love her.

I don't know how I let it happen. I was supposed to be focused on nabbing the promotion, but she wiggled her way inside my brain and took over my thoughts. Showed me I was worthy of love and kindness and taught me that needing help isn't a weakness, but a strength.

She changed me, and all I've done is bring her strife and sadness.

"Patty, can I borrow your phone?"

She takes a minute to finish a text and hands it to me. I quickly bring up the search engine and find a florist, hoping they can deliver today. I know Stella hates them, but if watching Hallmark movies and reading romance books has taught me anything, it's that flowers can brighten anyone's day, and sometimes they can also speak words to someone who isn't ready to hear them from your own mouth.

After ordering, I hand Patty back her phone. "Have you heard from my father?"

She shakes her head and an uncomfortable feeling knots inside my chest. Cameron will probably spend much longer in that cell than he should, but something about that doesn't sit right with me.

Patty drops me off at my car and I head to a bail bondsman to pay for Cameron's release.

I can't abandon him.

Not after we finally made some headway in our relationship.

I hope it acts as an olive branch, one we can continue to build around and grow.

***

Parked in front of Stella's house, I chew on my fingernails, unsure if I should even attempt to fix things with her. I could grovel, beg, and plead for forgiveness, but why would she even want to give me another chance? I lied to her about my brother, let her continue to struggle knowing I could help her, and now she assumes I'm involved in whatever my dad planned.

The door opens and Stella's grandfather makes his way to the rocking chair on the porch. I slouch in my seat, hoping he didn't see me. He lifts his cane, points it at me then the chair beside him. I look out the window to make sure he isn't waving at a neighbor, but when I turn back around to face him, he repeats the action.

I swallow, open the door, and head up the stairs. "Hello, Mr. Daniels."

"Jameson." He nods to the seat beside him. "What brings you here today?"

Sweat drips down my back as I sit. "I cocked things up with Stella."

He chuckles. "I gathered that. Why else would you be sitting in your car for an hour outside of my house?"

I smirk, not surprised the old man called me out. "She won't answer her phone. Is she here?"

"No," he says.

"Do you know where she is?" I ask. "I need to fix things with her."

He turns and levels me with a hard stare. "Do you deserve forgiveness for whatever you did?"

My mouth dries and my shoulders slump. Do I deserve it? Am I worthy of it? Normally, I'd tell myself no. But after spending the last few months with Stella encouraging me, showing me I *am* worth the type of love I've craved, I have to believe the answer to that question is yes. Even Ernest noticed the differences in me, the ones she helped me make.

"I hope so." I wipe my slick palms on my trousers. "She deserves to know how sorry I am and how special she is to me."

"Son," Pop-Pop says. "Stella isn't special. She's one-of-a-kind. You won't find another woman like her."

I blow out a breath. "I know. She's perfect."

Another chuckle. "No one is perfect. We all have hang-ups, things we wish we did or didn't do, mistakes we'd take back. It's not about being perfect. It's about being willing to grow. To forgive, to encourage, and to help one another."

"I want all that with her."

"Then ask for her forgiveness and give her time. If she's meant to be yours, she'll return."

"Thanks, Mr. Daniels." I extend my hand. "I appreciate your advice."

"Good luck, son," he laughs, picking up his cane and standing to shake my hand. "You're gonna need it."

Chapter Thirty-Seven
Stella

"How long are you gonna stay here? I already covered two of your meetings." Rosay steps through the hotel door with a take-out container and an overnight bag in her hand. Her eyes widen, no doubt surprised by the state of my appearance. My hair is an elegant rat's nest piled on top of my head, and I haven't showered or washed the mascara from beneath my eyes.

If my heart wasn't already shattered into a million tiny pieces, maybe I'd be embarrassed by how I look or ashamed about how easily I was taken advantage of.

Manipulated.

Deceived.

But I don't.

What Mr. Weston and Jameson did sent me down such a dark path that I almost pressed a key to my leg and began digging into my skin.

I couldn't do it.

I couldn't understand how it makes him feel more in control when all I felt was fear and pain.

I hate how even though I'm so angry at Jameson, I'm also worried this probably made him want to cut. I hate how I wish I could be there to stop him, to help him through losing me.

But right now, all I feel is empty.

Helpless.

I shrug and climb back into bed, pulling the covers over my head and knocking the container of ice cream to the ground. I've been here two days and still don't know what to do.

"Stella." The bed dips and the covers are ripped away from my face. "You can't stay here forever."

I harumph. "I know that."

She squeezes my hand tightly between hers, pity written all over her face. "Are you ever gonna tell me what happened? I thought everything was going well, and then Jameson got arrested and you —"

"Jameson got arrested?" I squeak.

"Yeah, him and CJ both. They got into a fight at the conference and damaged a few tables. Ruined the whole event."

A brick of lead drops in my stomach.

They got into a fight because of me.

No, Stella. They manipulated you and got what they deserved.

I fight back the wave of emotions and focus on the Chinese food in her hands. "Is that for me?"

"Yup. Got you extra spring rolls too."

"You're the best." My stomach grumbles in agreement.

"Are you coming back to work tomorrow?"

I stare out the window. "I can't."

"Can't come back tomorrow or...?"

My throat tightens with each passing moment. "At all."

She shoots up from the bed. "No, not happening. I'm not letting you quit because things didn't work out with him."

Tears prick the backs of my eyes. "That's not what happened."

Suddenly, the food has no taste and my head swims, dizzy with the chaos of this weekend.

"Please, Stella. Tell me what happened. I can't help if I don't know the details. If you need to go to HR, I'll be right there with you. If you need me to keep a lookout while you slash some tires, I've got you. Don't shut me out when you need me most."

I cave and tell her from beginning to end what transpired, culminating with the atomic bomb of truth that Mr. Weston has been keeping my trust fund secret all these years.

"So, did CJ know about the fund?" Her brows furrow. "Is that why Mr. Weston brought Jameson here?"

"I honestly don't know." I sigh, wishing I still had tears that would fall but finding my eyes drier than the desert.

I'm all cried out.

She wraps her arms around me. "I'm sorry, girl. I thought Jameson had genuine feelings for you."

The lump in my throat swells, stifling my words and nearly choking me. "Me, too."

We sit in silence for a few minutes, watching reruns on the ID channel before she pops up. "What's the plan from here?"

I keep my eyes closed, inhaling a deep breath. "I don't know. I can't go back to work and face him every day. Maybe it's time to go back to school and finish my master's."

Rosay gets up and clears away the takeout containers. She paces, wearing down the already frayed carpet in the hotel. "What about the funeral home and Pop-Pop?"

I knew she'd pinpoint the gaping hole in my plan. Not that I haven't thought about every option I have for fixing what I've ruined, but I've spent years taking care of everyone else.

It's time I focus on me.

"Pops wants to sell the funeral home and move into a senior community. I've tried everything, but it didn't work. I have to let go of the reins."

"I hate this. It should be them leaving and losing their livelihoods, not you."

I shrug. "Life isn't fair, and the longer I sit here wallowing, the longer I let them win."

Chapter Thirty-Eight
Stella

After spending two days holed up in the soft sheets and room service, I'm ready to get back home. I've been dodging everyone's calls so I didn't have to explain what happened with Jameson, but real life will always be waiting.

A knot forms in my stomach as the Uber driver heads toward the Thompson building.

Facing Mr. Weston and Jameson won't be easy, but I'll show them they didn't break me.

Rosay meets me at my desk with a cardboard box and a frown on her face. "You sure you want to do this? I have my knife ready, and enough bail money saved for both of us if you want to give your notice on his car."

I laugh. "You're the best, but we're too pretty for jail."

She flips her pink hair over her shoulder. "You're damn right we are."

I roll my eyes and pack away the little knick-knacks on my desk and clear out my files.

"It's time," I say.

Rosay bangs her head against the wall. "This is bullshit."

I embrace her and plant a kiss on her cheek. "I know."

With clammy hands, I head toward Mr. Weston's office. Thankfully, Patty isn't at her desk when I arrive. I can't deal with her blubbering if she knows what I'm about to do. His office door is cracked, so I take a deep, calming breath and push inside.

"I wondered when you'd finally show your face here," a deep voice from behind the desk startles me. "You've been a bigger disappointment than I could've imagined."

His voice drips with disdain, and the hairs on the back of my neck raise. My stomach hollows out and immediately refills with gasoline, ready to be ignited. The chair spins around when I close the door and step forward.

Mr. Weston's face falls into a frown when he sees me. "Oh, it's you." He stands, bringing himself to his full height like he always does, hoping to intimidate me like he does his business partners. "I'm surprised you're alone."

"I don't know why that would surprise you." I make my way over to the desk and paste a smile on my face. "Oh, wait. I forgot both of your sons were arrested."

He sucks in a quick breath and his nostrils flare. "Which one told you?"

I ignore his question and lay my notice on the desk.

"They're both pathetic anyway," he snarls.

I scoff. "The pathetic one is you."

"Excuse me?"

"How do you live with yourself? You made me believe you were helping, that you genuinely cared about what happened to me after my parents died."

He shrugs as if everything about this situation is par for the course.

"I can't help it you didn't investigate further. You could've found it if you kept looking or asked the right people."

Blood fills my mouth, the taste of copper seeping out of the punctures my teeth have made in my lip. How could I have ever looked up to this man, and trusted him to do right by me knowing my father and his business relationship ended poorly? The fact that he brought his sons into the mix makes my stomach harden.

I could call him out on his blatant disregard for his fiduciary responsibility as the trustee, but he'd find some way to spin it around on me.

"You're disgusting," I say, fighting back the lightheadedness my racing heart has caused. "And what piece of shit father brings their son halfway across the world to con someone out of a trust they don't even know about?"

He scoffs. "I didn't bring Jim here for that. Though, I should've. Apparently, you like the bleeding-heart type."

My fists tense at my sides. I breathe deeply, calming myself down. He doesn't deserve a reaction. With my anger boiling underneath the surface, it takes a moment to register the first half of his statement.

He didn't bring Jameson here for that.

Air rushes out of me and a wave of nausea thrashes against my insides. "You didn't bring him here to con me?"

Another scoff. "No. I wouldn't waste two sons' potential on you. You've never fit in with the Weston name. But for some reason, neither of them got that memo. That money should be mine."

"Why is my trust so important to you?" My voice raises. "You're already rich!"

"Not anymore." Anger contorts his face. "Your dad made some bad investments with our businesses that are causing issues for me now. Why wouldn't I want what I'm owed?"

"You're delusional." I walk to the door. "Money isn't worth what you're losing. No one cares if you have millions of dollars if you're a shitty person. The people standing around your casket won't be talking about how much money you have, but what type of person you are. From where I'm standing—" I pause with my hand on the doorknob"—you're a pretty poor excuse for a person."

My cheeks are warm, and tears prick the backs of my eyes, begging to be let out. I won't let him see me cry though.

I blow past Patty's desk and go to Rosay's office to grab my belongings. She's in a meeting, so I shoot her a text and call for an Uber to take me to the funeral home. I should've gone back to Rosay's house to pick up my car after I left the hotel, but doing this was more important.

After the short car ride, I pay and get out, grabbing my small overnight bag, and the cardboard box filled with eight years of my life at Thompson. Pop-Pop knows what happened, but he hasn't said anything other than we'd talk about it when I came back.

Inside, I nearly stumble over an abundance of yellow roses covering the foyer area. I turn around and take in the empty parking lot. I hadn't realized Pop-Pop had a funeral while I was away, but maybe he didn't want to disturb my wallowing and handled it on his own.

"Pop-Pop?" I lay my belongings on the front desk and search each room until I find him. "Was there a funeral?"

He looks up and smiles. "No."

"Then what are the six dozen roses out in the foyer for?" I ask. "A donation from a hospital or something?"

He rises from the desk, grabs his cane, and walks over to me. "Or something."

"What's that supposed to mean?" I follow him to the front. Stopping at a bouquet, he picks up the white card and holds it out to me. "Who is this from?"

He shrugs and leans on the desk. My lips are dry, fingers trembling as I turn the card over.

I'll never be able to tell you how sorry I am for hurting you.

My breath catches in my throat and my stomach spins when I see it's Jameson's handwriting.

I shouldn't care.

I *don't* care.

And if he thinks flowers that wilt and die are the way to seek my forgiveness, then he'd be very wrong.

I look to Pop-Pop, hoping to find…I don't know. Moral support? A look of disappointment on his face? Something to tell me what he thinks about all this, but his face is blank.

Curiosity nips at me, urging me to pick up the next card.

It took twenty years for the Great Wall of China to be built.

I suck in my cheeks and fight back the prickling behind my eyes. Why am I letting these words affect me? He knows I hate when people apologize with flowers.

I swallow and move forward, picking up another card.

I don't care if it takes me that long to prove I'm worthy of your love and forgiveness.

A tear drips onto the card, spreading out like a blot of ink. I clench my teeth, trying to keep the rest from dropping.

Jameson.

The world's most frustrating man.

The man I hated at first, who I put my trust in to teach me, who saved me when I needed it most, who I…fell in love with. He made a fool of me and lied to me. Even if he wasn't lying about the trust stuff, he still omitted things he knew would hurt me. His words, as beautiful as they are, mean nothing anymore.

I take a deep breath and wipe the tears from my eyes. He doesn't deserve them.

"Read the rest of them."

I turn and look at Pop-Pop. "I don't want to."

Sharp pain spreads down my calf after Pop-Pop swats me with his cane. "Read them."

"You didn't have to hit me," I grumble, rubbing the back of my leg. He rolls his eyes, and I grab the next card.

If I had one regret, it would be not telling you how amazing, how smart, how beautiful and kind, how funny and frustrating you are every day since I met you.

My stomach winds like a pit of snakes. Why is he saying these things? He was the one who wasn't genuine in his interactions with me. He was the one with the ulterior motives, the lies that kept piling on top of each other.

I exhale hard, wishing I could blow away the memories of the time we spent together, all the moments and soft touches we've shared since he came into my life.

I guess it's only fitting to tell you where we first met, where you yelled and scolded me while my poor mum laid in the other room.

A laugh rips out of me as the memory resurfaces. Now that I know how shitty of a person his mom was, I kind of feel bad for yelling at him, even if he was being a total asshole.

I pick up the final card, my lungs squeezing and holding me hostage. I don't want to read the words I know will be on this card. He couldn't love me, could he?

You don't lie and humiliate the person you love.

All the things he did: teaching me how to swim, buying my favorite food or my favorite tea, asking what I liked in bed, he didn't do those because he loved me...right?

With shaky hands, I stare at the card, gnawing on my bottom lip.

The truth is. I am an arsehole. But I'm an arsehole who loves you with all his heart. I've spent my whole life trying to be worthy of love from someone who didn't deserve it, and it made me careless with your love. I can't take back what I did, and I'll live with the heaviness crowding my chest, but I want you to know I'll work every day to be worthy of your love.

Sobs build in my throat, strangling me on my way to the bathroom. I want to forgive him. To forget everything that happened so I can keep him in my life, but I'm not ready yet, and neither is he.

I clear my face, patting the wetness on my cheeks with a paper towel before I head back out to the front. Even though I want to throw them away, I'll place the roses in the viewing rooms...to liven up the place.

I snort at my humorous thoughts and end up choking when I see CJ and Rosay at the door talking to Pop-Pop.

"What are you doing here?" I ask, my voice harsh.

"Stella," Rosay starts, and I cut her off.

"No. Don't." I turn to CJ and my fists ball up at my sides ready to punch him. "Haven't you done enough? Was it not enough to lie to me for four years and then humiliate me at the event?"

His mouth drops and his eyes flit back and forth from me to Rosay like he's waiting for her to answer for him. "Well? Go on, say something."

He swallows, twisting his fingers together in front of him like a child. "I'm sorry, Stella. I didn't know anything about what my father was doing." He steps forward, reaching his hand out before pulling it back to himself. His face turns a shade of red I've never seen on him.

"Don't penalize Jim for my dad's actions. He didn't lie to you. He honestly didn't know what my dad had planned. He loves you, Stella."

The inside of my mouth is sticky and dry, and my eye twitches as I listen to him. Rosay stands off to the side with Pop-Pop and I chew on my lip, not allowing tears to fall again. I want to believe what he's saying. That what Jameson and I had was real. But why is CJ suddenly defending Jameson when they've never gotten along?

Unless they were putting on a front to fool me.

My head is dizzy and filled with too many emotions. I can't shake the feeling he's being honest now, but I also don't want to allow myself to believe it and be hurt again.

Pop-Pop canes over to me. "Stella, he came to the house looking for you, to apologize."

"Okay, but I'm not ready to forgive him."

Pop-Pop scrubs a hand down his dark, weathered skin, and his misty eyes settle on me. "That's your choice, sweetheart. But I think you're making a mistake, and I can't hold my tongue anymore. I didn't speak up when it came to your mother staying with your father, but maybe if I would've, she'd still be around." I swallow against the lump in my throat as he continues. "Jameson is a good man. I can tell that from how much he's taken care of you, and how broken he was when he sat with me. You've taken care of everyone but yourself, and it's time for someone to take care of you."

CJ pulls an envelope from his pocket and hands me it. "He asked me to give you this before he left."

"Before he left?" I ask. "Where did he go?"

"Just read it."

They each hug me and leave.

My lips are dry as I walk into one of the viewing rooms and sit down. My hands tremble as I open the envelope and pull out the papers.

A key drops onto my lap.

I inspect it and find the name of a small bank down the street from Thompson's offices. Confused, I start to read the letters.

Love,

Here is the key to a security deposit box that contains copies of your trust paperwork. Mike knows a lawyer that will help you petition for access to it, and further assist with any legal action you'd like to take. I'm moving back to the U.K to get the help I need to heal. I've spent too much time letting the wounds my parents inflicted control me. There's nothing more I want than to be with you, but I can't risk hurting you anymore than I already have. I hope we'll eventually find our way back to each other, but if not, I hope you find the happiness you deserve.

I love you.

Jameson.

Saliva sticks to my mouth, and my throat aches as I fight back the tears. I look at the other page, and my heart squeezes so tightly I'm sure it'll explode. A beautiful drawing of a brown-skinned girl, who looks suspiciously like me, is throwing a lifesaver to a man floating in the middle of the pool, rescuing him. Beneath the picture he's written.

"Thank you for showing me there is strength in weakness. You saved me."

The unshed tears burst from my eyes, and sobs rack my body. I want to run after him and beg him to stay, but I know he's right. We both need to heal before we can find our way back to each other.

When the tears clear, and the sobs subside, I know exactly what I need to do.

Chapter Thirty-Nine
Jameson

6 months later...

The uncomfortable chair squeaks as I shift, counting the ticks of the clock at the front of the waiting room. Each painting on the wall is generic, abstracts using pale tones with splashes of neutral whites to give them contrast, all secured to the wall with overly ornate golden frames. Waiting for Dr. Marin, I've stared at these paintings for the last six months, my hand mimicking the brush strokes like a conductor in a symphony.

"Mr. Brooks." The doctor pushes her tortoiseshell glasses up the bridge of her nose, ushering me into her office.

I rub the pads of my fingers together and follow her inside, taking a seat in one of the overpriced but comfortable wingback chairs.

She settles into her seat. "How's your week been?"

When I first got back into therapy, this was the part I had the most trouble answering. Her question was clear, but my mind always floated back to the judgment I still expected. I was convinced what she really wanted to ask was, 'how many times this week did you think about cutting?' but now, after breaking through some of my trauma, I know she's just curious about my week.

"It was great." I wipe my sweaty palms on my trousers. "I got offered a chance to start an art investment firm back in the States."

"That's amazing news. How are you feeling about that? I know you left rather quickly after the incident with your father."

Talking openly to a therapist about what happened when I was in the States wasn't easy. I thought if I was away from everything that made me want to cut, I'd be able to stop.

I'd be whole again.

Strong.

But my scars weren't only physical.

While I have the now faint pink lines along my thighs, the internal scars were etched into my brain. I couldn't get healthy. Couldn't thrive. And each time I walked into the therapist's door, my dad's voice echoed in my mind.

Men are supposed to be strong. If you need a shrink, you're weak.

I flex my fingers, my knee bouncing with nervous tension. "I'm not sure how to feel, or if I'm ready to go back."

"That's okay," she says, scribbling onto her notepad. "Have you made a pros and cons list about the situation yet?"

I nod. "Yes, but it didn't help."

She stays silent.

I've realized when this happens, she's waiting on me to elaborate more.

"The pros are, the opportunity to be the official art investment company for a gallery in Texas, being able to see my mates again, spending more time with Cameron, and potentially fixing things with Stella."

"Those are all great pros, Jameson." She lays her pen down. "Now, what's holding you back?"

This is the part I've been dreading.

Where I must remind myself that it's okay that I don't have a relationship with my father.

After the fallout, I had to cut all ties with him. I couldn't be healthy and have him in my life. Cameron and I kept in touch, and he's even flown out here to spend time with me, but he's the only person other than Mike I consider family. Add in the fact I'll be so close to Stella, and it's a stress bomb waiting to happen.

"My contract with the Whitworth is ending soon, and I've been offered another position at the Manchester Art Gallery."

She clasps her hands on her lap and removes her glasses. "You have two great opportunities in front of you, and you have to choose which one will bring you closest to your goals, not only for your career, but for your overall happiness. If staying here and working at the gallery is what will make you happy, then go for it. But if it won't, then maybe the other opportunity is better. You must make that decision. Maybe it's time you wrote that email we've been talking about."

The rest of the hour passes in a blur. My shoulders are lighter as I walk down Oxford Road, past the gallery I've worked at since I came back, arriving at my flat. My old job had filled my position as Art Investment advisor, and The Whitworth, one of the UK's best art and design sites, welcomed me with open arms when I had nowhere else to go.

Their curator helped me realize that the art world is where I belong, where I'm happiest and strongest as an investor. With my love of art, and my investment background, he urged me to start my own investment firm that caters to galleries and artists.

"Afternoon, Mr. Brooks." The security guard tips his cap as I step into the lift.

Drenched in the familiar scent of acrylic paint, my flat greets me. Easels and canvases litter every available surface outside of the kitchen, and my brushes are piled in the basin, waiting to be washed and reused.

After I flew back, I had all my mail forwarded to my new address. When I received Stella's Christmas gift of art supplies, it helped me dive back into the love I had for creating. I couldn't bring myself to reach out and say thank you, but all the artwork I've made with those materials has a distinctive feel to it.

Yearning, resignation, and desire.

At my laptop, I answer emails and check on the gallery's social media page. I busy myself with showering and get into my sweats as I wait for the alarm on my phone to chirp.

I'm sure it could be considered stalking how much I look at a certain firecracker's social media page, but stalkers have no impulse control.

I'm disciplined.

I've learned not to give into the urges, even if I know it'll give me relief. Much like the knife that no longer sits in my pocket, taunting me.

Like clockwork, the minute my alarm goes off my fingers type Stella's name into the search box. I patiently wait for the page to load, and my stomach swirls when my eyes finally land on a picture of the woman I love. She's laughing, spending time at the Texas fair with Rosay, Mike, and Christine.

I should be with them, but I'm a coward. I know I'm ready to try again, but I'm worried too much time has passed for her. Has she forgotten about me? Have the wounds I opened closed, and therefore the love we had ceased to exist?

I'm too scared to find out, so I've only allowed myself to check on her this way. My therapist has urged me to make contact, to stop living in this suspended moment of 'what if,' and with the potential job opportunity in Texas, I know it's finally time.

I draw up a blank email.

My fingers tingle, and I blow out a breath as I figure out what to type.

Even a subject name eludes me.

To: Stella Daniels
From: Jameson Brooks
Date: June 1st, 2019, 8:30pm.
Subject: I'm a stupid arsehole.

Hello Stella,

It's been a while since we last spoke, but I wanted to reach out and let you know I'll be coming to Texas for a visit in a few weeks. If you're available on June 14th, I'll be at the Witte Summer Gala from 5-8pm. Blimey, why is this so hard? I've spent the last six months trying to figure out what I would say when it finally came time for me to contact you, and now that it's here, I have no words to convey everything I'm feeling inside. Dsgnaogrgnaeuograeuoge. You're a stupid prat Jameson. She doesn't want to hear from you. She would've reached out already. lllllllesifvj

I miss you. I miss you so fuckin' much sometimes just breathing makes me angry. I miss your scent, the berries and vanilla that always let me know when you've been in a room. The bright laughter that somehow made me feel lighter. Bloody hell, I even miss that smart mouth of yours that constantly put me in my place. Everything feels heavier without you.

I wish I could send this email to you. To show you that I'm a poor bellend who is still desperately in love with you. You've probably moved on, as you should've. You deserve more than a wanker like me could ever hope to give you, but if you'd give me a chance, I promise I wouldn't cock it up again. I'd appreciate you. I'd support you in whatever you wanted to do. I'm lost without you. Why did I not see what I had in front of me? I came all the way to Manchester to heal my heart, but the biggest portion I left with you. Shite, Jameson piss off you stupid plonker.

A knock at the door startles me.

I quickly hit delete on the email and close my laptop in case it's one of my mates. They'd surely riot if they saw the pathetic email of me begging Stella to forgive me.

Not that it'd matter.

If she was here, I'd be on my knees begging her in front of them. I've spent enough time in therapy to understand I don't need everyone's acceptance, and that includes the wankers banging at my door for poker night.

Chapter Forty
Stella

The jury's faces blur as Judge Knefel takes her seat.

It's been an arduous few months fighting it out in court to have Mr. Weston removed as the trustee to the account my father set up, and he's fought it at every corner. At one point, I almost gave up and let him have it, but when I realized how much he's taken from me already, I couldn't let him have more. I left the job I loved, the clients I worked so hard for the past eight years, and I pushed away my potential happy-ever-after because of him.

Time slows as the judge asks the jury to state their decision.

Mike squeezes my hand, but the numbness spreading through my body doesn't let me feel it. My lips and fingertips tingle, and my heart seems to only beat with my intake of breath. Cotton lines my ears, and it's only when Mike looks at me with a wide smile and an offered hand that I realize I've won.

"You did it." He thanks my lawyer and embraces Christine who's in the gallery with Rosay. "The house and the trust. It's all yours plus damages and suffering."

My throat closes and tears well up in my eyes.

It's finally over.

All the years I've spent struggling, keeping everything and everyone else afloat. I no longer have to worry about how to get by. I'll sell off the house and invest the money. I have no desire to live in something tainted by greed and deceit.

With my chest lighter, I turn and hug Rosay. She's been my rock since I left Thompson, and even though she wanted to quit, I urged her not to. It wouldn't be fair to her or her clients to allow one bad apple to spoil the entire company.

With this litigation looming, Mr. Weston was forced to resign. But I don't have it in me to spend any more time worrying about what happens to him. It's time to concentrate on me.

"Are you ready to celebrate?" Rosay asks.

"I'm not sure I'm up for a celebration." We walk down the courthouse steps, and she grabs my hand before I get to my car.

"We're celebrating, Stella." She rustles my shoulder. "You not only won the trial but got into the master's program you wanted. If there was cause for celebration, this is it."

Her excitement makes me smile, but it doesn't feel like I've won something.

I've lost so much getting to this point.

"Congrats, Stella," Christine says. "I know it's been a rough few months, but it's over and you can move on."

Mike pulls me to the side as the girls chat. "How are you feeling?"

I shrug. "I'm okay."

"You did a great job keeping your composure," he says, twiddling with the ring on his finger. "He reached out this week and asked about you."

My breathing becomes labored hearing Jameson's still checking in with Mike about me. He hasn't reached out since he vanished, and I've been too busy dealing with the fallout. My attention's been filled with finding Pop-Pop a good senior community, filling out applications for grad school, and deciding what to do about the funeral home. I haven't had time to think about how much I miss Jameson, or how my heart breaks each time I imagine what could've been.

If he wanted to fix things between us, he could reach out directly to me.

"What do you want me to tell him?" Mike asks, pulling me from the sadness.

I give him another shrug. "Whatever you want. I'm sure he'll hear from his father."

He nods and doesn't speak about Jameson anymore as we move back to the group. "You're still going to the Witte's gala with Rosay next week, right?" He asks.

"Hell yes she is," Rosay chimes in. "Free drinks and billionaire investors? Who would pass that up?"

I laugh, but it's wooden. Even though I left Thompson, Rosay kept her word about taking me with her if I got a big client. I'm still in contact with Charlotte, and hopefully, once I've finished my grad program and get set up at a good firm, maybe I'll be able to acquire her accounts again.

They fall into a conversation about the event, but I barely hear, too distracted by everything flitting through my mind. I watch the passing cars, beating back the emotions threatening to break the dam I've kept them behind. A heaviness soaks into my limbs, and my eyelids are heavy with exhaustion.

"I'm heading home to rest," I say. "Maybe we can celebrate tomorrow."

They frown but each embrace me and offer encouragement for the future. I hop in the car and turn up the radio, stifling the loud thoughts inside my head.

I clomp up the steps to the house and steel my shoulders. Pop-Pop would've been with me for support, but it's his move-in date at the senior community.

"Pops?" I yell.

Empty cardboard boxes stare me down as I traverse the living room, passing two of the muscled men from the community's moving team. They greet me with a head nod and a smile as they lift the last boxes from the kitchen.

"I'm out here," Pops says from the back patio.

He's hunched over a crossword puzzle, glasses nearly falling off the tip of his nose. Looking up, he raises his brows in question.

"It's all mine now." I collapse into the seat.

His weathered hands cover mine and he squeezes. "It was all yours to begin with. How are you feeling?"

"I'm not really sure." I shrug. "I want to be happy about it, but..."

"The house and the money are nothing if you can't share it with the person you want to," he chimes in, setting down his pen.

I nod as his candor lodges a knot the size of a golf ball in my throat. He hit the nail on the head.

I miss Jameson and what we were starting.

I've tried to concentrate on Pops moving and me starting school, but like clockwork, my mind always finds a way to veer to him.

He pats my hand and picks up his sweet tea. "You'll find your way back to each other."

His conviction swells my heart. He's always looking on the bright side, and he doesn't pull any punches when he's set on something.

"Thanks, Pops." I rise from the chair and stop outside the door. "I need to rest for a while, and then we can go out to dinner before I drop you off at your apartment."

Inside my room, I shed my clothes and step into the shower, letting the hot water beat out the knots in my back from the stress of the trial.

Beneath the stream, I contemplate reaching out to Jameson. It's been months of radio silence, and even though I know he's checking in on me through Mike, it's not the same.

I want more, but I won't be the one to take that first step.

After toweling dry, I grab clothes for dinner. It'll be weird eating alone once Pops is gone, but it's something I'll get used to.

My laptop dings with a new email.

I lean over the chair to ensure it's not school-related. Goosebumps rise on my skin, and even though my body tells me I'm cold, warmth permeates me as I look at the sender.

I pace the room and argue about whether or not to open Jameson's email. I was just telling myself I wanted him to reach out, but now that he has, I'm terrified to know what he has to say.

Mouth dry, I return to the bathroom and splash water onto my face. I stare into the mirror and encourage myself to meet it head-on. Whatever he has to say, I can take it.

I'm strong.

I've healed.

I'm ready.

At the desk, I move my mouse over the bold writing and double click the email, waiting for the words to load. My stomach tenses as I take a deep breath, holding in the air as I begin to read.

"It's been a while since we last spoke...coming to Texas...I'll be at the Witte.. from 5-8pm...I miss you...Everything feels heavier without you."

Fat tears drop onto the keyboard as Jameson's words fill me. Sprinkled between loving words and funny jabs at himself, I find the words I've needed to hear.

"*I came all the way to Manchester to heal my heart, but the biggest portion I left with you.*"

Biting on my lips does nothing to stop the sobs wracking my body. After months of wondering where we stand, I now know he still feels the same way I do. Realizing he probably didn't mean to send this, I start to text him.

Something stops me.

I had already planned to attend the gala, but now I have a reason to be excited.

I devise a plan and reach out to my friends to help me enact it. Jameson may not have been ready to tell me everything in his heart, but I've waited months for this moment.

Chapter Forty-One
Jameson

Aesthetes peruse 5,000 years' worth of art, culture, and people as I chat with the curator and various artists about their displays. Worried about impressing them, I spent the entire flight from Heathrow to DFW, and the five-hour drive down to San Antonio, learning everything I could about the exhibits they're featuring this month.

I'm in my element as donors visit my table, inquiring about the new art investment firm I've created. It's my job to help them buy, store, and sell paintings for the maximum profit. Had I not met Stella, I never would've gotten back to my roots as an artist. I would've let that part of me shrivel and die, like my father wanted me to.

"Hey, Jim." Mike stops at the table, Christine hot on his heels. He's dressed in a tuxedo, and the knee-length red dress Christine wears fits in well with the event. "I didn't realize this many people actually came to these things."

"Well, I certainly hope so because if not, my business will go up in flames." I chuckle and embrace him. He claps me on the back, and as I'm speaking with Christine, he leans over to take a canape from a passing server.

"You're gonna do great things, my friend." He shoves a bacon-wrapped scallop into his mouth and reaches for another before Christine smacks his hand away.

His praise fills me with warmth.

I'm finally proud of what I'm doing.

There's no voice in the back of my head telling me I'll disappoint someone, or that I'm unworthy of my success. Instead, excitement fills me at the prospect of how far I can propel my new company. If I'm able to gain some new clients tonight, it'll open the door to creating a program with the American Association of Museums.

"Your brother's here," Mike says, his cheeks puffed with food.

Cameron looks dapper in a three-piece gray suit. His light brown hair is shorter than the last time I saw him, and he's slimmed down. I was able to convince him to go to therapy for a month after the first time he came to visit, and he's kept up with it ever since. His relationship with our dad is rocky, but he's managing as best as he can.

"Hey bro." I stick out my hand, but he pulls me in for a hug. I never imagined I'd willingly touch him, but our relationship has grown so much it feels natural. "Glad you could make it out to support me."

His face cracks into a grin. "She'd have killed me if I didn't show."

My forehead scrunches. "Who? I thought you and Mindy broke up?"

He steps aside, and the light from the chandelier reflects as a beautiful goddess in a champagne-gold dress steps into the room.

All the air is sucked from my lungs as my gaze lands on Stella. My eyes take on cartoon hearts, and my chest beats so furiously against my ribcage I'm worried it'll rip through my skin and fall at her feet. A chorus of angels takes up residence in my head as she walks towards me.

"Are you okay?" Mike waves his hand in front of my face, but I can't focus on anything but the woman in front of me. Questions bounce around my head the closer she gets. Did Mike or Cameron tell her? Is she here because they begged her? Or are she and Cameron back together, and they chose tonight to tell me?

"Hi." Her voice shatters the chorus, and I'm pulled back down to earth.

"You're here."

I clear my throat of the dryness, and everyone moves away to give us some privacy. My stomach rolls, waiting for the bad news. I can't say I'd be happy for her and Cameron, but it wouldn't be right for me to be angry. She was with him first, and I told her I wanted her to find happiness even if it wasn't with me.

"Yeah, well, you invited me," she laughs but stifles it as she bites down on her lip. "...So here I am."

My spine straightens and sweat gathers at the back of my neck. "I invited you?"

A smile tugs at the corner of her mouth. "Umm...yeah. The email you sent me? You asked me to meet you here."

Oh, bollocks! I smack my forehead as shame envelops me. I must've hit send instead of discard when my mates came over. My cheeks heat as I cover my face. "I'm so sorry. I didn't mean to send that to you."

"I gathered that." She chuckles, and soft hands pull mine away from my face. "Did you not want me to come?"

"Of course, I want you here, Love." The endearment slips through my lips, and when she doesn't draw away and instead smiles, my posture relaxes a bit.

"Good, because I wouldn't miss it for the world." She wraps her arm around mine, and I breathe a tiny sigh of relief as the spark reignites in my core. I don't know if she can feel the electricity humming between us, but the fact that she's here, supporting me, means there's hope. "Now, show me your favorite exhibits."

We walk around as I show her my favorite statues and paintings. Her fingers tense on my bicep each time she gets excited about a new piece

I'm showing her. The giddy feeling of watching her happiness bubbling over, makes me feel light again.

"Would you—"

"How have—" Stella stops and laughs. "You first."

"No, no." I wave a hand in the air. "Ladies, first."

"How have you been?" Her whiskey eyes land on me, and I swear she's seeing into my soul. "I've missed you."

Hearing those words makes my chest combust. I reach up, brushing my thumb across her cheek. "I've missed you more than words can convey. I'm doing well. Been back in therapy for a while and started this company."

"Congratulations." Her smile is the most amazing, heartstopping thing in the world.

"I have you to thank for that."

"Me?" Her eyebrows hit her hairline. "What did I do?"

"You reminded me what it meant to love something, and how I needed to live my life for me and not worry about others' expectations. Your Christmas gift arrived at the perfect time."

A tendril of hair falls into her face. "I'm glad to hear it."

My cheeks ache, but I can't stop smiling at her. "Could I maybe...take you to dinner after the event?"

She nods. "I'd love that."

We spend the rest of the time chatting with our group of friends. Rosay is fashionably late, but as she catches up with everyone, I step aside and speak with clients. The night has been a success for me, and I can't wait to see if that success will continue after the dinner with Stella.

"Are you ready to go, Love?" Now that I've called her it, I can't stop.

She doesn't seem to mind and places her hand in mine as we step out into the night. Our hands stay entwined the entire ride to the restaurant and I only let go when I pull out the chair for her to sit.

"Congratulations on a successful night," she says, laying the napkin across her dress.

The sommelier takes our wine order, and we fill the time with chit-chat about what's going on in her life. I find out she's taking night classes to finish her master's degree in finance, that her grandfather is selling the funeral home, and she informs me on the trial with my father concerning her trust fund. Mike gave me the rundown, and I got a nasty message from my father blaming me for him losing the money and the house, but I'm glad to hear she got what she deserved.

"You look radiant." Unable to help myself from touching her, I reach across the table for her hand. Her delicate fingers lace with mine.

"You clean up well yourself."

I squeeze her hand and inhale deeply. "I need you in my life, Stella. I know it'll take you a long time to forgive me, and I'll wait, but I can't go back to not speaking with you."

"Jameson—"

"I've loved you since the moment you yelled at me across the parking lot, and I know that's hard to believe, but it's true. Each moment with you made me feel more alive than I have in years, and I'll spend the rest of my life showing you how special you are, how much I cherish you and want to make you happy."

"Jameson." Her voice raises and she halts my words with a hand in the air. "I forgive you."

"You do?" My voice breaks like I'm a lad who's just hit puberty. I clear my throat and try again, my voice taking on a deeper bravado. "You do?"

She laughs. "I do."

I never thought I deserved her forgiveness, but I wanted it all the same.

Learning to forgive yourself, and the people who have hurt you, was a roadblock I had to overcome in therapy. Some people won't offer apologies for their actions, but forgiveness helps release the pressure you've allowed their indiscretion to put on your chest.

In my case, I put the pressure on myself because I allowed my father's actions to change how I viewed myself and how I thought others viewed me. In all reality, I was strong even though I felt weak. I was worthy even though I felt useless. And I was deserving of love, but I needed to learn to love myself and the person I was becoming before I could accept anyone else's love.

Even standing in front of Stella knowing she may not return those same feelings, I know I'm worthy of them now.

"And I love you too," she says after a moment.

Relief washes over me, cleansing the emotional grime I've lived with for the past six months, and the tension in my spine finally eases. Air puffs out of my chest when I reach for her hand and the warmth of her palm meets mine.

"I've had enough time and space to realize how much pressure we were both under and were putting on each other," she continues. "I've grown since then, and it seems like you have too. The feelings never left, regardless of how long or how far you were away." She pats the area over her heart. "You've never left here. You clawed your way in and never left."

Bollocks.

Tears leak from my eyes, and like the strong man that I am, I let them fall, baring my heart to the woman I'm desperately in love with.

I lean across the table, my gaze locked on the woman who's stolen my heart, and our lips make a promise of forever.

Chapter Forty-Two
Stella

I used to think nothing was sexier than his cocky, British accent, but watching Jameson wield a tape gun as he helps pack up the funeral home is like porn. His tattooed forearms flex, straining against a tight black shirt as he carries a box of cremation pans to where Pop-Pop's cataloguing the materials for sale. Their laughter floats into my ear, rousing me enough to get up and see what they're getting into.

"Y'all are supposed to be working, not laughing." Jameson wraps an arm around me and pulls me to his side. His soft lips dust over my cheek, and I shiver at the warmth of his hand on my lower back. "What's going on?"

Something passes between them, and a moment later, Pop-Pop finally speaks. "Geraldine left a surprise on my bed."

Geraldine is one of the elderly ladies at Pop's senior community. She's a feisty Bridge player, and she's been after him since he moved there.

When he sat me down and told me he was ready to retire, everything warred inside me. I thought it was my fault, that I failed him by not being able to save the funeral home, but he assured me it had been on his mind for some time, and that he was worried about letting me down.

We both thought we had to hold on for each other, but letting go and removing the weight off our shoulders has strengthened our bond. I look forward to when he swings by the house to visit me and Jameson, and I know Jameson appreciates the fatherly role Pop-Pop has taken on in his life too.

"A pair of knickers," Jameson whispers into my ear.

Pop-Pop's cheeks blush, and my mouth parts. "She didn't. That woman has no couth."

Mr. Garcia enters, pulling Pop-Pop into a conversation about the move. He's been a huge help to us with the transition, and he and my grandfather have become fast friends.

I thought saying goodbye to this place would be more difficult for both of us, but all I find is excitement for the future.

"Love." A block of heat encompasses my back. "I need you to do something for me."

I turn in his arms and link my hands around his neck. Since moving back, we've spent time actually dating and getting to know one another. Our relationship was built on the physical when we first met, but with time has deepened into so much more. We're each other's rock and support when life gets heavy, the compass that guides us when we veer off course.

"What do you need?"

He reaches into his pocket, and my breath catches when he palms the knife. It's been laying on our dresser since Jameson moved in. It wasn't easy for him to shake off the thoughts ingrained in him by his parents, but since attending weekly therapy sessions, he's been progressing each day.

Healing isn't linear. He's had a few setbacks, but each time he bounces back stronger and ready to start again. Art has been his solace when life gets too out of control, and the at-home gym system helps him to de-stress daily.

Learning to remove stress triggers was a part of his mental health journey, but this one he's kept.

My chest inflates as he places the knife into my hand.

"Can you cremate this?" He cracks a smile, and laughter bubbles up inside me.

"Are you serious?" My heart sprints in my chest.

He nods and plants a kiss on my forehead. "I don't need it anymore."

I wrap my arms around him and breathe in his scent. "Unfortunately, Mr. Garcia wouldn't be happy if we exploded his cremator."

"It's not going to explode," he scoffs.

I laugh. "I didn't know you took up a career as a mortician while you were away. Forgive me for being a novice in this area you're *so* experienced with."

His chest deflates beneath my cheek. "It would explode?"

I laugh at the lip he has poked out like a sad child. "Sadly, it could. But I have an idea."

He lifts a brow then narrows his eyes at me. "What kind of idea?"

"Follow me."

Jameson links our hands as he walks beside me to the back room housing our embalming fluids. I swipe my thumb across his wrist, and his heart rate hammers in the same rhythm as mine.

"You're going to embalm it?" he asks.

I snort. "No, but we can put it in an alkaline bath."

Jameson hums and takes one last glance at the knife before placing it in the glass cylinder. He watches me mix the solution and pour it over the thing that's kept him shackled for years.

With a large exhale, he gathers me into his arms.

He likes to say I saved him, but I believe we saved each other.

We were both drowning in our own silent battles and needed each other. To support and encourage, to challenge, to break out of the comfortable lives we made for ourselves and look to the future, chasing after what we deserve.

This life wasn't what I expected, but it's more than I could ever possibly hope for. It's been filled with a ton of heartache but also with a lot of love, a lot of growth, and a lot of forgiveness. But each day we work to better our lives and the lives of those around us. And there's no better investment than that.

"I want you," he whispers, wrapping my hair around his hand and turning my head to capture a kiss. I press my butt against him and wiggle, and his soft hiss in my ear sends goosebumps down my arms.

"I know someplace private." Darting past Mr. Garcia and Pop-Pop, I pull Jameson into a darkened room. Our tongues fight for purchase as we stumble through the maze of wooden boxes until we reach my secret hiding spot. Nipping at his lip, I coax Jameson onto the luscious, cream-colored satin of my favorite place to nap—only today I have no intention of napping.

Bonus Scene

Want to know what Jameson has in store for Stella on Halloween? Sign up for my newsletter for a bonus scene!

Get my bonus scene

Thank You

Thank you readers!

With so many books out there, it means a ton to me that you've chosen to spend your time reading my book.

Reviews help books find their readers, so I'd love it if you could leave one for *The Bottom Line* on [Amazon,](#) [Goodreads,](#) and/or anywhere else you tend to buy books!

If you want to stay updated on new books and giveaways, you can sign up for my [Substack.](#)

Acknowledgements

There are no words meaningful enough to thank everyone who helped bring this book to fruition.

I have the best writing army in the world, and y'all should prepare for a lovefest below.

First, to God for blessing me with a never-ending well of stories to write.

Second, to my wonderful husband who has been my cheerleader from the beginning. I can never thank you enough for all the encouragement you're ready to give when I'm getting down on myself, for reminding me that God blessed me with this gift of story weaving, and for making sure I get the time I need to hone my craft.

You're my best friend, and I love you a billion million.

To my Yaya, who spent many walks hashing out the story with me. These characters wouldn't be who they are without you, and nor would I. Thank you for believing in me and encouraging me, for always being ready with an off-the-wall thought that brings me to exactly what I need to do, and for always being down to get Dutch Bros. I love you, Citag.

Nonna. Mama Knef. Thank you for always being willing to read my crazy stories, for listening to me ramble on about my characters, and for always being encouraging when I got down on myself. Luh you, bye!

Ingrid. Ingrid. Ingrid.

Have I said how blessed I am that you chose me as your mentee during the KissPitch program? How the hell did I luck out with such an amazing mentor? This is as much your baby as it is mine. I can't thank you enough for seeing the broken man in Jameson, not blanching at his struggles, and for being a champion for mental health representation when so many others turned away. I'm blessed to call you a friend and sister.

Michelle. Mich. My sister. Have I told you how thankful I am to have met you? I'm forever grateful that you never let me get away with bullshit writing. This book would be filled with nothing but the words eyes, chest, walk, and need, if it wasn't for you. You make me better. Thank you for always being down to get drinks and chips and salsa and for being my sister! I love you!

Kelly. My co-host for the #ThrillsandChills chat and one of my very best friends. I cannot thank you enough for carrying the load this past year for me while I worked on this book and grew a human. You are my hero, and I look up to you in more ways than I can count.

My Twisted Sisters, thank you for inviting me into your suspense group and not kicking me out when I decided to tackle romance writing. You ladies have been the bright spot during dark days and I'm so thankful to know you! Thank you for always believing in me and never letting me give up.

#ThrillsandChills group. Thank you for always being supportive, even though I took a little detour and started writing romance. I appreciate your support and encouragement, and I promise I'll get back to suspense writing soon!

KISSPITCH '22- You are all badass writers that I am so happy to know. I love our little Discord group. Thank you for always being supportive and encouraging. I can't wait to have each and every one of y'alls books on my shelf.

Mo. You might bring the pie, but I bring the meat. Love you bestie.

Chrissy. How has it been 7 years? You've been with me since the beginning and you'll be with me until the end. Thank you for our zoom bagel dates and for all the encouragement. I promise I'll make it to Canada one of these days.

Marysa. You are my spirit animal. I'm so glad we met at the WLT conference. You have become a sister to me. Your positivity and tenacity inspire me to never give up.

Josh. Yao. Asuh bro? Thanks for your help with my cover! I know it was a labor of love, and this book cover wouldn't be as amazing as it is if you didn't spend hours with me on Zoom and Photoshop. I appreciate you!

I was blessed to have a ton of friends who read multiple versions of this book, and even though I'm sure I'll forget to name a few, I'm at least going to try- Kamista, Trista, Maritza, Allie from Cali, Scarlette, Dallas, Dyan, Samantha, Elizabeth, Deana, Maggie, TT Lex, Allison A., and so many more. Thank you.

To the entirety of SF 2.0 Discord, thank you for always being a wealth of knowledge, for keeping me entertained when I should be writing, and for sprinting with me! I'm so appreciative of being invited into the fold!

Special thanks to Laya and Jess for always being willing to impart wisdom and answer any questions I had about self-publishing this book. And to Vienna for copy-editing for me!

And to my three reasons for never giving up, my babies. You kiddos show me that life is worth living, that every day brings something new, and that no matter how dirty I think something is, you can make it dirtier. Thank you for always being ready with a hug and a kiss for Mommy. I love you.

About the Author

Tobie Carter is a fiction writer of contemporary romance stories that speak to the heart of the reader and leave them with a story that lingers in their mind long after finishing. Her stories are fast-paced, angsty, high heat, and feature relatable characters who refuse to settle for less than they deserve. She lives in Central Texas with her husband and three young children.

Made in the USA
Coppell, TX
03 February 2026

70264568R00204